CCC Collaborative Literacy

Making Meaning®
THIRD EDITION

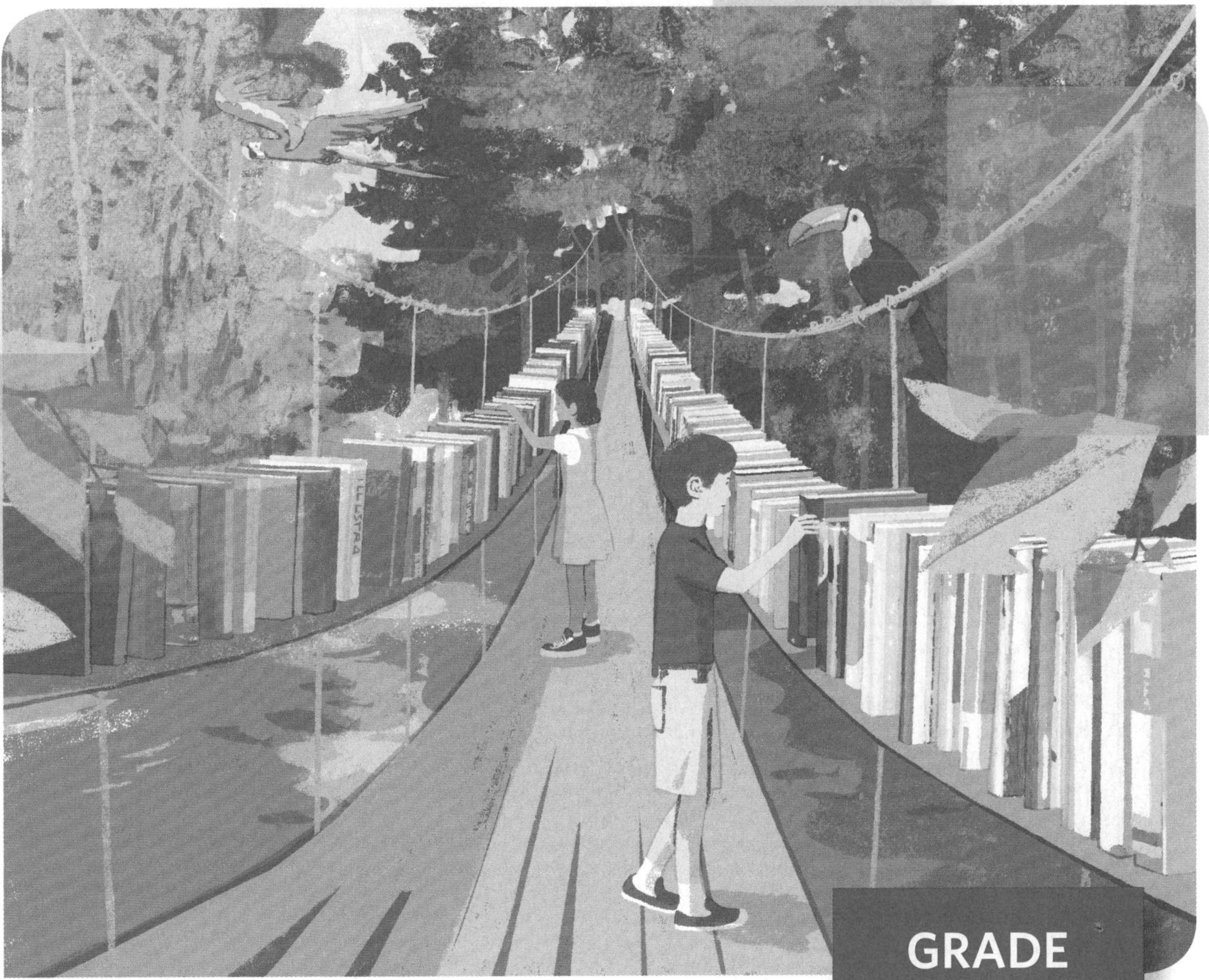

GRADE
3

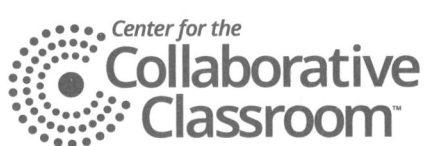

Center for the Collaborative Classroom
1001 Marina Village Parkway, Suite 110
Alameda, CA 94501
(800) 666-7270, fax: (510) 464-3670
collaborativeclassroom.org

ISBN 978-1-61003-585-9

Printed in the United States of America
  3 4 5 6 7 8 9 10 WCR 23 22 21 20 19 18

CONTENTS

VOLUME 2

Lessons

Appendices

RESOURCES

Read-aloud

- *Sonia Sotomayor: A Judge Grows in the Bronx* by Jonah Winter, illustrated by Edel Rodriguez

More Strategy Practice

- "Play 'Antonym Match'"

Extensions

- "Explore Related Words: *Comfy*, *Comfortable*, and *Comfort*"
- "Explore Similes in *Sonia Sotomayor: A Judge Grows in the Bronx*"

 ## Online Resources

Visit the CCC Learning Hub (ccclearninghub.org) to find your online resources for this week.

Whiteboard Activities

- WA1–WA11

Reproducibles

- Week 17 family letter (BLM1)
- (Optional) "Week 17 Word Cards" (BLM2)

OVERVIEW

Words Taught	Words Reviewed
unexpected	advise
abandon	blow your top
industrious	shuffle
comfy	snug
successful	strain
unsuccessful	

Word-learning Strategies

- Using the prefix *un-* to determine word meanings (review)
- Recognizing synonyms (review)
- Using the suffix *-ful* to determine word meanings (review)
- Recognizing antonyms (review)

Vocabulary Focus

- Students learn and use six words from or about the story.
- Students review using the prefix *un-* and the suffix *-ful* to determine word meanings.
- Students review synonyms and antonyms.
- Students review words learned earlier.
- Students build their speaking and listening skills.

Social Development Focus

- Students work in a responsible way.
- Students develop the skill of contributing ideas that are different from their partners' ideas.

⏱ DO AHEAD

✓ (Optional) Prior to Day 3, review the more strategy practice activity "Play 'Antonym Match'" on page 358.

✓ Prior to Day 4, visit the CCC Learning Hub (ccclearninghub.org) to access and print this week's family letter (BLM1). Make enough copies to send one letter home with each student.

✓ (Optional) Visit the CCC Learning Hub (ccclearninghub.org) to access and print "Week 17 Word Cards" (BLM2). These cards can be used to provide your students with more opportunities to review the words.

Introduce *Unexpected, Abandon, and Industrious*

In this lesson, the students:

- Learn and use the words *unexpected, abandon,* and *industrious*
- Review the prefix *un-*
- Review synonyms
- Build their speaking and listening skills
- Work in a responsible way

Words Taught

unexpected (p. 3)
Unexpected means "not expected." If something is unexpected it is surprising. You did not expect, or think, that it would happen.

abandon (p. 3)
Abandon means "leave and not return."

industrious
Industrious means "hardworking."

INTRODUCE AND USE *UNEXPECTED*

1 Introduce and Define *Unexpected* and Review the Prefix *un-*

Briefly review *Sonia Sotomayor*.

Show pages 2–3 and read the first paragraph aloud, emphasizing the word *unexpected*.

Explain that the first word the students will learn today is *unexpected*. Explain that if something is unexpected, you did not expect, or think, that it would happen. It is surprising. Show the illustration on pages 2–3 and point to the flowers. Explain that it is unexpected, or surprising, to see flowers blooming on a chain-link fence. Most flowers bloom near the ground in gardens and parks.

Display word card 97 (WA1) and have the students say the word *unexpected*. Point to the prefix *un-* in *unexpected* and review that *un-* is a prefix that means "not." Explain that *unexpected* means "not expected."

Materials

- *Sonia Sotomayor*
- Word card 97 (WA1)
- "Tell Me a Story" chart (WA2)
- Word card 98 (WA3)
- Word card 99 (WA4)

Ask:

Q *When have you seen something unexpected? Why was it unexpected?*

Click ❶ on word card 97 (WA1) to reveal the prompt and have one or two volunteers use the prompt to share their thinking with the class.

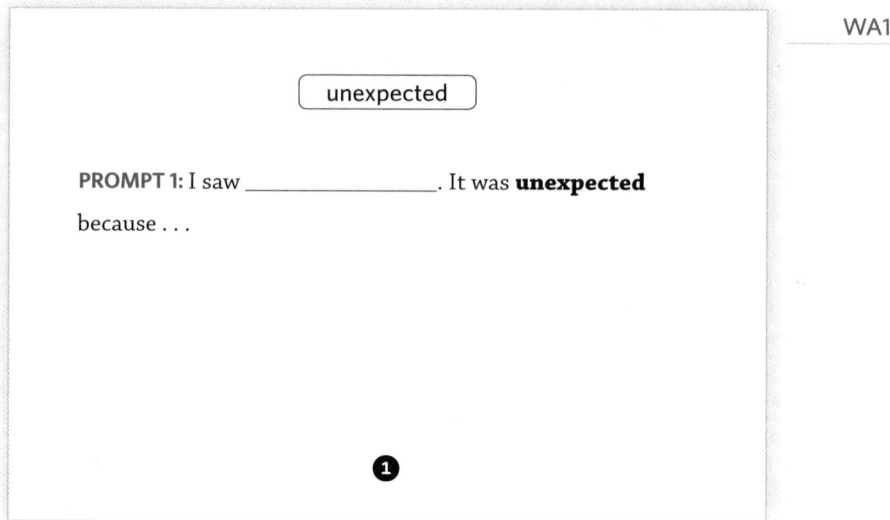

WA1

PROMPT 1: "I saw [a mouse in my shoe]. It was unexpected because . . ."

❷ Do the Activity "Tell Me a Story"

Tell the students that partners will do an activity called "Tell Me a Story." Review that you will tell them the beginning of a story that includes the word *unexpected*. Then they will use their imaginations and what they know about the word to make up an unexpected ending for the story.

Display the "Tell Me a Story" chart (WA2) and show story 1 and its accompanying prompts. Read the story aloud, slowly and clearly:

- Story 1: *Today my family and I went to the grocery store. One unexpected thing that happened was . . .*

Use "Think, Pair, Share" to discuss:

Q *How might you finish the story? What unexpected thing might happen at the grocery store?* [Pause; point to prompt 1.] *Turn to your partner.*

WA2

Tell Me a Story

Today my family and I went to the grocery store. One unexpected thing that happened was . . .

_____

PROMPT 1: One **unexpected** thing that happened was . . .

PROMPT 2: _____ is **unexpected** because . . .

Teacher Note

If you are not using an interactive whiteboard, write each story where everyone can see it.

Teacher Note

If the students have difficulty thinking of an ending, review the definition of *unexpected* and think aloud about an ending. For example, say "I saw a kitten on the checkout counter." Then reread the beginning of the story aloud and repeat the questions. If the students continue to struggle, ask questions such as "What is something that might happen at the grocery store that would surprise you?" or "What is something that might happen that would cause you to say 'Wow! I didn't expect that!'"

PROMPT 1: "One unexpected thing that happened was . . ."

After partners have talked, have a few volunteers use the prompt to share their thinking with the class.

Follow up by asking:

Q *Why is [a monkey walking down the milk aisle] unexpected?*

Point to prompt 2 and have one or two volunteers use the prompt to share their thinking.

PROMPT 2: "[A monkey walking down the milk aisle] is unexpected because . . ."

Show story 2 on the chart (WA2) and use the same procedure to discuss the following story:

- Story 2: *On Julio's walk to school, he notices something squirming in the bushes. The unexpected thing Julio sees is . . .*

 Q *How might you finish the story? What unexpected thing might Julio see squirming in the bushes?* [Pause; point to prompt 3.] *Turn to your partner.*

PROMPT 3: "The unexpected thing Julio sees is . . ."

After partners have talked, have a few volunteers use the prompt to share their thinking with the class.

Follow up by asking:

Q *Why would [a purple starfish in a bush] be unexpected?*

PROMPT 4: "[A purple starfish in a bush] would be unexpected because . . ."

Point to the word *unexpected* and review the pronunciation and meaning of the word.

Discuss as a class:

Q *When has something unexpected happened to you?*

INTRODUCE AND USE *ABANDON*

3 Introduce and Define *Abandon*

Show pages 2–3 of *Sonia Sotomayor* and read the first paragraph on page 3 again, emphasizing the word *abandoned*.

Explain that *abandon* means "leave and not return." Explain that an abandoned building is empty because people have moved out and never returned.

Display word card 98 ( WA3) and have the students say the word *abandon*.

Teacher Note
You might point out that students learned the word *squirm* earlier and that *squirm* means "wiggle, or twist your body from side to side, usually because you are bored or uncomfortable."

🌐 ELL Note
The Spanish cognate of *abandon* is *abandonar*.

4 Discuss Things That Have Been Abandoned

Imagine that you are at the park and you come across an abandoned bicycle—a bicycle that someone left behind and did not return for.

Use "Think, Pair, Share" to discuss:

 Q *Why might someone have abandoned the bicycle?* [Pause; click ❶ on WA3 to reveal the first prompt.] *Turn to your partner.*

PROMPT 1: "Someone might have abandoned the bicycle because . . ."

After partners have talked, have a few volunteers use the prompt to share their thinking with the class.

Follow up by discussing as a class:

Q *What would you do if you came across an abandoned bicycle?*

Ask the students to imagine that at the same park they come across an abandoned puppy. Discuss as a class:

Q *Why might someone have abandoned the puppy?*

Follow up and use "Think, Pair, Share" to discuss:

 Q *What would you do if you came across an abandoned puppy?* [Pause; click ❷ on WA3 to reveal the next prompt.] *Turn to your partner.*

PROMPT 2: "If I came across an abandoned puppy, I would . . . "

Point to the word *abandon* and review the pronunciation and meaning of the word.

INTRODUCE AND USE *INDUSTRIOUS*

5 Introduce and Define *Industrious* and Review Synonyms

Show pages 10–11 of *Sonia Sotomayor* and read the first paragraph on page 10 aloud.

Tell the students that the last word they will learn today is *industrious*. Explain that *industrious* means "hardworking" and that *industrious* and *hardworking* are synonyms. Explain that Sonia's mother was industrious. She worked hard during the day to support her children and studied hard at night to become a nurse. Explain that Sonia grew up to be industrious, or hardworking, like her mother.

Display word card 99 (◖ WA4) and have the students say the word *industrious*.

Teacher Note

If you started a synonym chart, add *industrious* and *hardworking* to it.

Discuss as a class:

Q *Who is an industrious person you know? Why do you think the person is industrious?*

Click ❶ on word card 99 (WA4) to reveal the first prompt. Have a few volunteers use the prompt to share their thinking with the class.

PROMPT 1: "[My sister] is industrious because . . ."

6 Play "Is Olive Industrious?"

Tell the students that partners will play a game called "Is Olive Industrious?" Review that Olive is the name of an imaginary girl in third grade. Tell the students that you will describe how Olive is acting. Partners will then discuss whether Olive is industrious and why.

Begin by saying:

- *Olive is learning to play the tuba. She practices for an hour after school each day.*

Ask:

 Q *Is Olive industrious? Why?* [Click ❷ on WA4 to reveal the prompt.] *Turn to your partner.*

PROMPT 2: "Olive [is/is not] industrious because . . ."

After partners have talked, have a few volunteers use the prompt to share their thinking with the class.

Using the same procedure, discuss one or both of the following scenarios:

- *Olive knows she should be doing her homework, but she keeps putting it off. She has a snack, calls her friend Tommy, and takes a nap.*
- *Olive's mom isn't feeling well. To help her, Olive washes the dishes, vacuums the floor, and folds the laundry.*

Point to the word *industrious* and review the pronunciation and meaning of the word.

Materials

- Daily review cards (WA5)
- Daily review activity (WA6)

In this lesson, the students:

- Review and practice using the words *unexpected, abandon,* and *industrious* from Day 1
- Build their speaking and listening skills
- Contribute ideas that are different from their partners' ideas

Words Reviewed

unexpected
Unexpected means "not expected." If something is unexpected it is surprising. You did not expect, or think, that it would happen.

abandon
Abandon means "leave and not return."

industrious
Industrious means "hardworking."

REVIEW THE WORDS

1 Briefly Review the Words

Display the daily review cards (WA5). Review the pronunciation and meaning of each word.

Ask:

Q *Which of the words you learned yesterday was the most fun to talk about? Why?* [Click ❶ on WA5 to reveal the prompt.] *Turn to your partner.*

WA5

| unexpected | abandon | industrious |

PROMPT 1: I think _____ was the most fun to talk about because . . .

PROMPT 1: "I think [*industrious*] was the most fun to talk about because . . ."

After partners have talked, have a few volunteers use the prompt to share their thinking with the class.

PRACTICE USING THE WORDS

2 Review the Game "Find Another Word"

Tell the students that partners will play the game "Find Another Word." Review that you will show a sentence with one or more words underlined. You will read each sentence aloud, and partners will decide which vocabulary word can replace the underlined part of the sentence.

Display the daily review activity (WA6) and begin playing the game:

1. Click **1** to reveal the first sentence. Point to the sentence and read it aloud, emphasizing the underlined words.

   - Sentence 1: *During lunch, the fire alarm in the cafeteria sounded and the sprinklers went off. It was <u>very surprising</u>!*

2. Give the students a few moments to think about the sentence and the underlined word. Then point to the three word choices and ask:

   Q *Which vocabulary word could replace the underlined words? Why?* [Click **1** again and point to the prompt.] *Turn to your partner.*

PROMPT 1: "I think the word [*unexpected*] could replace *very surprising* because . . ."

   After partners have talked, have one or two volunteers use the prompt to share their thinking with the class.

3. Conclude the discussion by clicking **1** a third time to highlight the correct vocabulary word and reveal the sentence with the correct word in place.

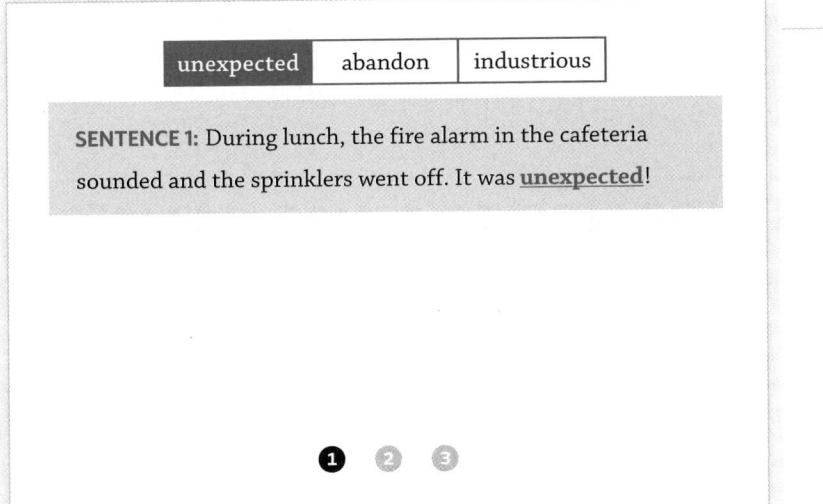

WA6

| unexpected | abandon | industrious |

SENTENCE 1: During lunch, the fire alarm in the cafeteria sounded and the sprinklers went off. It was <u>unexpected</u>!

1 **2** **3**

4. Click **1** to clear the screen.

Teacher Note

For a fully written-out example of this activity, see Week 3, Day 5, Step 2.

Teacher Note

You might explain that the students may need to change the form of the word to complete the sentence by adding an ending such as -*s*, -*ing*, or -*ed*.

Teacher Note

Each sentence on the daily review activity (WA6) has a corresponding number: the first sentence is **1**; the second sentence is **2**; and the third sentence is **3**. To play the game, click the corresponding number four times:

- The first click reveals the sentence.
- The second click reveals the prompt.
- The third click highlights the correct answer and reveals the sentence with the answer in place.
- The fourth click clears the screen.

Use the same procedure to discuss the following sentences:

- Sentence 2: *Today, Paula cleaned her room, read a book, and finished her art project. She is <u>hardworking</u>.* (industrious)
- Sentence 3: *On their road trip, the Juarez family drove by a town where the buildings were empty and all the gardens were overgrown. The town was <u>without people</u>.* (abandoned)

Day 3 | Introduce *Comfy, Successful,* and *Unsuccessful*

Materials

- *Sonia Sotomayor*
- Word card 100 (WA7)
- Word cards 101–102 (WA8)

In this lesson, the students:

- Learn and use the words *comfy, successful,* and *unsuccessful*
- Review the suffix *-ful*
- Review antonyms
- Build their speaking and listening skills
- Contribute ideas that are different from their partners' ideas

Words Taught

comfy (p. 22)
Comfy means "comfortable."

successful
If you are successful, you do what you set out to do or do something well.

unsuccessful
Unsuccessful means "not successful." If you are unsuccessful, you do not accomplish what you set out to do.

INTRODUCE AND USE *COMFY*

1 Introduce and Define *Comfy*

Show pages 22–23 of *Sonia Sotomayor* and remind the students that in this part of the book Sonia has just moved from the Bronx and is studying at college. Read the last three sentences of the first paragraph aloud, emphasizing the word *comfy*.

Explain that *comfy* means "comfortable." Explain that Sonia's family is like a warm and comfy, or comfortable, blanket that makes her feel safe and loved. Explain that college is not the comfy, loving place her home was. She feels uncomfortable at college because she is different from a lot of her classmates.

Display word card 100 (WA7) and have the students say the word *comfy*.

2 Talk About Comfy Places

Give an example of some comfy places.

> **You might say:**
> "My bed is very comfy. There are lots of pillows and a warm comforter. The hammock in my backyard is also comfy. I love lying in it and reading a book on a warm summer day. The reading chair in our library is very comfy. It is big and soft—the perfect place to curl up and read a book."

Use "Think, Pair, Share" to discuss:

Q *Where are you most comfy? Why?* [Pause; click ❶ on WA7 to reveal the first prompt.] *Turn to your partner.*

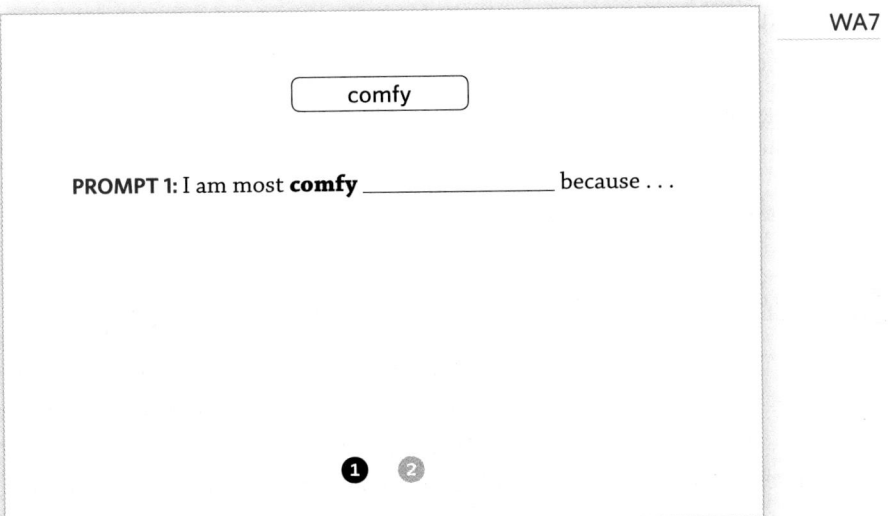

PROMPT 1: "I am most comfy [on my couch] because . . ."

After partners have talked, have a few volunteers use the prompt to share their thinking with the class.

Ask and discuss as a class:

Q *What are your most comfy clothes?*

Click ❷ on word card 100 (WA7) to reveal the next prompt. Have a few volunteers use the prompt to share their thinking with the class.

PROMPT 2: "My most comfy clothes are . . ."

Point to the word *comfy* and review the pronunciation and meaning of the word.

INTRODUCE AND USE *SUCCESSFUL* AND *UNSUCCESSFUL*

3 Introduce *Successful* and Review the Suffix *-ful*

Show pages 24–25 of *Sonia Sotomayor* and review that Sonia's hard work paid off and she became a judge. Read the first three sentences of the first paragraph on page 25 aloud, emphasizing the word *success*.

Explain that Sonia worked hard to become a judge, and that she was successful. Tell the students that *successful* is the next word they will learn today. Explain that if you are successful, you do what you set out to do or do something well. Explain that Sonia was successful because she did well in school and worked hard as a judge. Display word cards 101–102 (WA8) and reveal word card 101. Have the students say the word *successful*.

Point to the suffix *-ful* in *successful* and review that *-ful* is a suffix that means "full of." Explain that Sonia's life has been "full of success"—she has become a good judge.

Ask and discuss as a class:

Q *When have you been successful? When have you done something you set out to do or done something well?*

Click ❶ to reveal the first prompt. Have a few volunteers use the prompt to share their thinking with the class.

PROMPT 1: "I was successful when . . ."

4 Introduce *Unsuccessful* and Review Antonyms

Tell the students that the next word they will learn today is *unsuccessful*. Click to reveal word card 102 on word cards 101–102 (WA8) and have the students say the word *unsuccessful*. Explain that *unsuccessful* and *successful* are antonyms, and review that *antonyms* are "words with opposite meanings." Ask:

Q *If* successful *means "full of success," what do you think* unsuccessful *means?*

Click ❷ to reveal the next prompt. Have one or two volunteers use the prompt to share their thinking with the class.

PROMPT 2: "I think *unsuccessful* means . . ."

Teacher Note

You might point out the prefix *un-* in *unsuccessful* and review that *un-* is a prefix that means "not." Remind the students that they reviewed *un-* earlier when they discussed the word *unexpected*.

Teacher Note

If you started an antonym chart, add the words *successful* and *unsuccessful* to it.

If necessary, explain that *unsuccessful* means "not successful." If you are unsuccessful, you do not accomplish what you set out to do.

5 Discuss Whether Olive Is Successful or Unsuccessful

Explain that you are going to describe something that the imaginary third-grader Olive does. Partners will decide whether she is successful or unsuccessful, and explain why they think so.

Begin by reading the following scenario aloud twice, slowly and clearly:

- *Olive throws herself into writing a book about sharks. She goes to the library every day and learns as much as she can about them. She spends the summer working on her book and finally finishes it.*

Ask:

 Q *Is Olive successful or unsuccessful? Why?* [Click ❸ on WA8 to reveal the prompt.] *Turn to your partner.*

PROMPT 3: "Olive is [successful/unsuccessful] because . . ."

After partners have talked, have a few volunteers use the prompt to share their thinking with the class.

Using the same procedure, have the students discuss:

- *Olive wants to be better at basketball, but she doesn't want to practice. When her coach offers her suggestions for becoming a better player, she doesn't pay attention. Olive doesn't get better and finally quits the team.*

- *Olive wants to learn how to play the cello. She goes to her lessons and practices nearly every day for an entire year. At the end of the school year, she is invited to join her school's band.*

Point to the words *successful* and *unsuccessful* and review the pronunciation and meaning of each word.

Teacher Note

You might remind the students that they learned the idiom "throw yourself into something" earlier and that it means "do something with a lot of energy and enthusiasm."

Teacher Note

Invite the students to make up their own "Is Olive Successful or Unsuccessful?" scenarios. You might stimulate their thinking by providing them with a goal (for example, "Olive wants to learn how to swim" or "Olive wants to become a doctor").

Teacher Note

Alternatively, you may wish to write the antonym match where everyone can see it.

MORE STRATEGY PRACTICE
Play "Antonym Match"

Display the "Antonym Match" chart (❨ WA9).

WA9

Antonym Match

1	2
comfy	loud
fortunate	neat
gruff	uncomfortable
faint	unlucky
cluttered	nice

PROMPT: _____ is the antonym of _____.

Tell the students that partners will play a game called "Antonym Match." Point to the words in column 1, and explain that these are vocabulary words the students have learned. Point to the words in column 2, and explain that these are antonyms, or words with opposite meanings, of the vocabulary words in column 1. Explain that partners will match each vocabulary word to its antonym.

Point to the word *comfy*, pronounce it, and have the students pronounce it.

Then point to the words in column 2 and ask:

Q *Which word in column 2 is the antonym of* comfy?

PROMPT: "[*Uncomfortable*] is the antonym of [*comfy*]."

Have a few volunteers use the prompt to share their thinking. Then have a volunteer draw a line from the word *comfy* to the word *uncomfortable*.

Repeat the procedure to have the students match the remaining words. When you get to the final two words, have the students discuss them together by asking:

Q *Which word in column 2 is the antonym of* faint *and which word is the antonym of* cluttered?

EXTENSION

Explore Related Words: *Comfy, Comfortable,* and *Comfort*

Write the word *comfy* where everyone can see it, and review that *comfy* means "comfortable." Tell the students that knowing the meanings of the words *comfy* and *comfortable* can help them figure out the meaning of another related word—*comfort*. Write these sentences where everyone can see them:

> Nick didn't feel well so he went to the nurse's office. The school nurse helped Nick into bed and wrapped a blanket around him to comfort him.

Ask:

Q *Based on what you know about the words* comfy *and* comfortable *and clues in the sentences, what do you think the word* comfort *means? What does it mean to comfort someone?*

If necessary, explain that *comfort* means "make someone feel better or more comfortable." Point out that the nurse helped Nick into bed and wrapped a blanket around him to comfort him or make him feel better or more comfortable.

Discuss as a class:

Q *When has someone comforted you? How did they make you feel?*

Day 4

Review *Comfy, Successful, and Unsuccessful*

Materials

- Daily review cards (WA10)
- Copy of this week's family letter (BLM1) for each student

In this lesson, the students:

- Review and practice using the words *comfy, successful,* and *unsuccessful* from Day 3
- Build their speaking and listening skills
- Work in a responsible way

Words Reviewed

comfy
Comfy means "comfortable."

successful
If you are successful, you do what you set out to do or do something well.

unsuccessful
Unsuccessful means "not successful." If you are unsuccessful, you do not accomplish what you set out to do.

REVIEW THE WORDS

1 Briefly Review the Words

Display the daily review cards (WA10). Review the pronunciation and meaning of each word.

Ask:

 Q *Which of the words you learned yesterday do you find particularly interesting? Why?* [Click ❶ on WA10 to reveal the first prompt.] *Turn to your partner.*

WA10

> comfy   successful   unsuccessful
>
> **PROMPT 1:** I think _____ is particularly
> interesting because . . .
>
> ❶ ❷

PROMPT 1: "I think [*comfy*] is particularly interesting because . . ."

After partners have talked, have a few volunteers use the prompt to share their thinking with the class.

PRACTICE USING THE WORDS

2 Play "Which Word Am I?"

Explain that you will give a clue about one of the words and partners will figure out the word.

Begin by saying:

- *I'm how you might describe your favorite pair of pajamas.*

 Q *Which word am I? Why?* [Click **2** on WA10 to reveal the prompt.] *Turn to your partner.*

PROMPT 2: "I think the word is [*comfy*] because . . ."

After a few moments, signal for the students' attention and ask a few volunteers to use the prompt to share their thinking with the class.

Using the same procedure, discuss:

- *I'm how you might describe a person who tried doing something she'd never done before—and she did it.* (successful)

- *I'm how you might feel when you are snuggled up on the couch watching a movie.* (comfy)

- *I mean "doing what you set out to do."* (successful)

- *I'm how you might describe someone who sets out to make a loaf of bread and burns the loaf in the oven.* (unsuccessful)

EXTENSION

Explore Similes in *Sonia Sotomayor: A Judge Grows in the Bronx*

Show the illustrations on pages 12–13 of *Sonia Sotomayor* and review that they show Sonia and her family spending time together. Explain that the author of the book, Jonah Winter, describes Sonia's life at home by saying "Sonia's family surrounded her like a warm blanket." Explain that by describing her family in this way, the author is helping us imagine how comfortable and safe Sonia felt at home surrounded like a warm blanket by the people she loved.

Explain that "surrounded her like a warm blanket" is a simile and that a *simile* is a "comparison of one thing to another using the words *like*, *as*, or *than*." Tell the students that good writers like Jonah Winter use similes to help readers picture in their minds what is being described.

Show pages 22–23 and explain that on these pages the author describes how uncomfortable and lonely Sonia felt at Princeton. Tell the students that, as you read from this part of the book, you want them to listen for how Sonia decided to handle her unhappy situation and what the author compares Sonia to. Then read the first three sentences of the first paragraph on page 23 aloud. Ask:

Q *How did Sonia handle her unhappy situation at Princeton?*

Q *What is Sonia compared to in the sentences you just heard?*

Q *How does comparing Sonia to "a flowering vine that would not stop growing" help you imagine how strong and determined Sonia was?*

Teacher Note

Send home with each student a copy of this week's family letter (BLM1). Encourage the students to talk about this week's words with their families.

Day 5 | Ongoing Review

Materials

- Ongoing review cards (WA11)

In this lesson, the students:

- Review words learned earlier
- Build their speaking and listening skills
- Work in a responsible way
- Contribute ideas that are different from their partners' ideas

Words Reviewed

advise
Advise means "tell someone what you think he or she should do."

blow your top
"Blow your top" means "get very angry."

shuffle
Shuffle means "slide the feet along the ground or floor while walking." When people shuffle, they barely lift their feet. *Shuffle* also means "mix playing cards to change their order."

snug
Snug means "comfortable, warm, and cozy."

strain
Strain means "pull or push hard."

REVIEW THE WORDS

1 Briefly Review the Words

Display the ongoing review cards (WA11). Review the pronunciation and meaning of each word.

PRACTICE USING THE WORDS

2 Discuss "Would You?" Questions

Tell the students that you will ask them questions about the words.
Point to the word *snug* and ask:

 Q *If you were wearing a warm jacket with a hat and gloves on a cold winter day, would you be snug? Why?* [Pause; click ❶ on WA11 to reveal the prompt.] *Turn to your partner.*

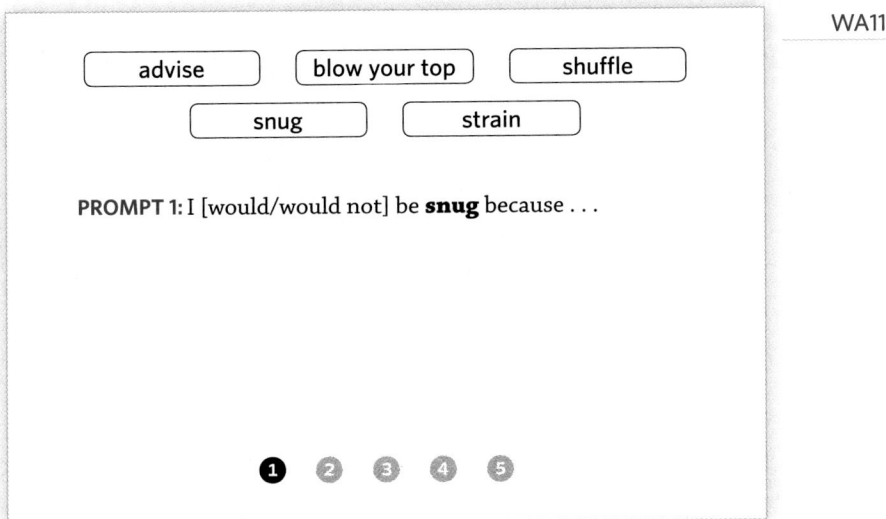

WA11

After partners have talked, have one or two volunteers use the prompt to share their thinking with the class.

Discuss the following questions using the same procedure:

[advise]

 Q *If a new student were roaming around our school lost, would you advise the student where to go? Why?* [Pause; click ❷ on WA11 to reveal the prompt.] *Turn to your partner.*

PROMPT 2: "I [would/would not] advise the new student because . . ."

[shuffle]

Q *Would you shuffle your feet quietly if you were dancing to your favorite song? Why?* [Pause; click ❸ on WA11 to reveal the prompt.] *Turn to your partner.*

PROMPT 3: "I [would/would not] shuffle my feet quietly because . . ."

Teacher Note

Support struggling students by reviewing that if you are snug, you are comfortable, warm, and cozy. Then ask questions such as "Would wearing a warm jacket on a cold day make you feel snug?" and "What would you wear to be snug on a cold winter day?" Then reread the sentence starter and repeat the questions.

Teacher Note

You might remind the students that they learned the word *roam* earlier and that *roam* means "wander or move about without any particular purpose or place to go."

[blow your top]

 Q *Would you blow your top if your best friend couldn't come to your birthday party? Why?* [Pause; click ❹ on WA11 to reveal the prompt.] *Turn to your partner.*

PROMPT 4: "I [would/would not] blow my top because . . ."

[strain]

Q *Would you strain to lift a feather? Why?* [Pause; click ❺ on WA11 to reveal the prompt.] *Turn to your partner.*

PROMPT 5: "I [would/would not] strain to lift a feather because . . ."

RESOURCES

Read-aloud

- *Morning Meals Around the World* by Maryellen Gregoire, illustrated by Jeff Yesh

More Strategy Practice

- "Review the Prefix *re-* and Discuss the Word *Reenergize*"

Extension

- "Discuss *Plain* and *Plane* and Other Homophones"

 More ELL Support

- "Draw a Picture of a Plain Object and Not Plain Object"

Assessment Resource Book

- Week 18 vocabulary assessment

 Online Resources

Visit the CCC Learning Hub (ccclearninghub.org) to find your online resources for this week.

Whiteboard Activities

- WA1–WA10

Assessment Form

- "Class Vocabulary Assessment Record" sheet (CA1)

Reproducibles

- Week 18 family letter (BLM1)
- (Optional) "Week 18 Word Cards" (BLM2)
- (Optional) "Week 18 Crossword Puzzle" (BLM3)

OVERVIEW

Words Taught	Words Reviewed
customary	cherish
energize	industrious
appetizing	lively
plain	persist
differ	sorrowful
refreshing	

Word-learning Strategies

- Recognizing synonyms (review)
- Using the prefix *un-* to determine word meanings (review)
- Recognizing antonyms (review)
- Using the prefix *re-* to determine word meanings (review)
- Recognizing words with multiple meanings (review)

Vocabulary Focus

- Students learn and use six words from or about the book.
- Students review synonyms and antonyms.
- Students review shades of meaning.
- Students review words learned earlier.
- Students build their speaking and listening skills.

Social Development Focus

- Students work in a responsible way.
- Students develop the skill of contributing ideas that are different from their partners' ideas.

Ⓙ DO AHEAD

✓ Prior to Day 3, identify two areas of the classroom that are different and easy for the students to see, to discuss the word *differ*. (See the Teacher Note on page 375, and Step 5.)

✓ (Optional) Prior to Day 3, review the more strategy practice activity "Review the Prefix *re-* and Discuss the Word *Reenergize*" on page 380.

✓ Prior to Day 4, visit the CCC Learning Hub (ccclearninghub.org) to access and print this week's family letter (BLM1). Make enough copies to send one letter home with each student.

✓ Prior to Day 5, make a copy of the "Class Vocabulary Assessment Record" sheet (CA1); see page 187 of the *Assessment Resource Book*.

✓ (Optional) Visit the CCC Learning Hub (ccclearninghub.org) to access and print the following materials: "Week 18 Word Cards" (BLM2) and "Week 18 Crossword Puzzle" (BLM3). These materials can be used to provide your students with more opportunities to review the words.

In this lesson, the students:

- Learn and use the words *customary, energize,* and *appetizing*
- Review synonyms
- Review the prefix *un-*
- Build their speaking and listening skills
- Contribute ideas that are different from their partners' ideas

Words Taught

customary
Customary means "usual or normal or happening regularly."

energize
Energize means "give energy or strength."

appetizing
Appetizing means "tasty or good to eat."

INTRODUCE AND USE *CUSTOMARY*

1 Introduce and Define *Customary* and Review Synonyms

Briefly review *Morning Meals Around the World*.

Show page 3 and read this sentence aloud: "All around the world, people start the day with delicious food and drinks."

Tell the students that the first word they will learn today is *customary* and explain that *customary* means "usual or normal or happening regularly." Explain that *customary*, *usual*, and *normal* are synonyms.

Display word card 103 (WA1) and have the students say the word *customary*.

Explain that around the world it is customary, or normal, for people to have a morning meal. People usually, or regularly, eat a meal in the morning.

Point out that morning is not the only time of day when it is customary to eat. Ask:

Q *When else during the day is it customary to eat?* [Click ❶ on WA1 to reveal the first prompt.] *Turn to your partner.*

Materials

- *Morning Meals Around the World*
- Word card 103 (WA1)
- Word card 104 (WA2)
- Word card 105 (WA3)

Teacher Note

You may want to explain that the word *customary* is related to the word *custom* and point out that you can see the word *custom* in *customary*. A *custom* is a "tradition or something that people do regularly."

> customary
>
> **PROMPT 1:** It is **customary** to eat . . .
>
>

PROMPT 1: "It is customary to eat . . ."

After partners have talked, have a few volunteers use the prompt to share their thinking with the class.

2 Discuss Customary Ways People Celebrate a Birthday

Explain that in many cultures it is customary, or normal, for people to celebrate a special event, such as a birthday, with food.

Ask:

 Q *What is customary for you to eat when you celebrate your birthday? What do you usually eat?* [Click **2** on WA1 to reveal the prompt.] *Turn to your partner.*

PROMPT 2: "On my birthday, it is customary for me to eat . . ."

After partners have talked, have a few volunteers use the prompt to share their thinking with the class.

Explain that in addition to eating, it is customary in many cultures for people to do fun things to celebrate a birthday.

Ask:

 Q *What is customary for you to do to celebrate your birthday? What do you usually do?* [Click **3** on WA1 to reveal the prompt.] *Turn to your partner.*

PROMPT 3: "To celebrate my birthday, it is customary for me to . . ."

After partners have talked, have a few volunteers use the prompt to share their thinking with the class.

Point to the word *customary* and review the pronunciation and meaning of the word.

INTRODUCE AND USE *ENERGIZE*

3 Introduce and Define *Energize*

Read this sentence on page 3 aloud: "Your morning meal is important because it gives you energy to start your day."

Explain that the second word the students will learn is *energize* and that *energize* means "give energy or strength." Explain that a nutritious breakfast energizes you, or gives you energy and strength to do things during the day. Explain that getting a good night's sleep and exercising can also energize you.

Display word card 104 (WA2) and have the students say the word *energize*.

Point to the word *energize* and explain that it comes from the word *energy*. Point out how you can see part of the word *energy* in *energize*.

4 Act Out Being Energized and Not Energized

Explain that when you are energized, you feel strong and healthy and ready to work and play.

Ask:

Q *What do you like to do when you feel energized? Why?* [Click **1** on WA2 to reveal the first prompt.] *Turn to your partner.*

PROMPT 1: "When I feel energized, I like to [play basketball with my friends] because . . ."

After partners have talked, have a few volunteers use the prompt to share their thinking with the class.

Explain that you would like a volunteer to act out how she looks and moves when she is energized. Then have a volunteer act out being energized as the class watches.

Ask and discuss as a class:

Q *What did you see [Natasha] do to show she is energized?*

Click **2** on word card 104 (WA2) to reveal the next prompt.

PROMPT 2: "I saw [Natasha] [move fast] to show she is energized."

After partners have talked, have a few volunteers use the prompt to share their thinking with the class.

Using the same procedure, have a volunteer act out how he looks and moves when he is *not* energized, and have the class discuss what they saw the volunteer do.

Point to the word *energize* and review the pronunciation and meaning of the word.

INTRODUCE AND USE *APPETIZING*

Teacher Note

You may want to explain that the word *appetizing* is related to the word *appetite*, which means "the desire or wish for food."

 **ELL Note**

The Spanish cognate of *appetizing* is *apetitoso/a*.

Teacher Note

If you have started a synonym chart, add *customary*, *usual*, and *normal* and *appetizing* and *tasty* to it.

5 Introduce and Define *Appetizing*

Explain that the last word the students will learn today is *appetizing* and that *appetizing* means "tasty or good to eat." Explain that *appetizing* and *tasty* are synonyms.

Display word card 105 (WA3) and have the students say the word *appetizing*.

Show pages 14–15 of *Morning Meals Around the World* and explain that Mexican children enjoy these appetizing, or tasty, foods for their morning meal. Point to and name each food: quesadillas, poached eggs and salsa, refried beans, mangoes and bananas, and hot chocolate.

Ask:

 Q *What is a food or drink that you think is appetizing?* [Click **1** on WA3 to reveal the first prompt.] *Turn to your partner.*

PROMPT 1: "I think [rice] is appetizing."

After partners have talked, have a few volunteers use the prompt to share their thinking with the class.

6 Review the Prefix *un-*, Discuss the Word *Unappetizing*, and Review Antonyms

Write the words *unappetizing* and *appetizing* where everyone can see them. Point to the prefix *un-* in *unappetizing* and remind the students that the prefix *un-* means "not."

Ask and discuss as a class:

Q *If* appetizing *means "tasty or good to eat," what do you think* unappetizing *means?*

Click **2** on word card 105 (WA3) to reveal the next prompt. Have a few volunteers use the prompt to share their thinking with the class.

PROMPT 2: "I think *unappetizing* means . . ."

If necessary, explain that *unappetizing* means "not tasty or good to eat." Point out that *appetizing* and *unappetizing* are antonyms, or words with opposite meanings.

Teacher Note

If you started an antonym chart, add the words *appetizing* and *unappetizing* to it.

7 Play "Appetizing or Unappetizing?"

Explain that partners will play "Appetizing or Unappetizing?" You will describe a food and partners will discuss whether it is appetizing or unappetizing and why they think so.

Begin by asking:

 Q *Spaghetti with meatballs and cheese: appetizing or unappetizing? Why?* [Click ❸ to reveal the prompt.] *Turn to your partner.*

PROMPT 3: "I think it is [appetizing/unappetizing] because . . ."

After partners have talked, have a few volunteers use the prompt to share their thinking with the class.

Using the same procedure, discuss:

 Q *A slice of cold pizza: appetizing or unappetizing? Why?* [Point to prompt 3.] *Turn to your partner.*

Q *A slice of cold, juicy watermelon: appetizing or unappetizing? Why?* [Point to prompt 3.] *Turn to your partner.*

Q *A bowl of oatmeal: appetizing or unappetizing? Why?* [Point to prompt 3.] *Turn to your partner.*

Point to the words *appetizing* and *unappetizing* and review the pronunciation and meaning of each word.

Review *Customary, Energize,* and *Appetizing* | Day 2

In this lesson, the students:

- Review and practice using the words *customary, energize,* and *appetizing* from Day 1
- Build their speaking and listening skills
- Work in a responsible way

Words Reviewed

customary
Customary means "usual or normal or happening regularly."

energize
Energize means "give energy or strength."

appetizing
Appetizing means "tasty or good to eat."

Materials

- Daily review cards (WA4)

REVIEW THE WORDS

1 Briefly Review the Words

Display the daily review cards (WA4). Review the pronunciation and meaning of each word.

Ask:

Q *Which of the words we learned yesterday was the most fun to talk about? Why?* [Click ❶ on WA4 to reveal the first prompt.] *Turn to your partner.*

WA4

| customary | energize | appetizing |

PROMPT 1: The word _____ was the most fun to talk about because . . .

❶ ❷ ❸ ❹ ❺

PROMPT 1: "The word [*appetizing*] was the most fun to talk about because . . ."

After partners have talked, have a few volunteers use the prompt to share their thinking with the class.

PRACTICE USING THE WORDS

2 Play "Which Word Goes With?"

Explain that partners will play "Which Word Goes With?" You will write a word where everyone can see it, and they will discuss which of this week's words goes with the word you wrote and why they think so.

Write the word *dinner* where everyone can see it and read it aloud.

Ask:

Q *Which of this week's words goes with* dinner*? Why?* [Click ❷ on WA4 to reveal the prompt.] *Turn to your partner.*

PROMPT 2: "I think [*appetizing*] goes with *dinner* because . . ."

Teacher Note

If the students have trouble making associations, call for their attention and think aloud about an association you might make, or ask questions such as [*customary*] "How might the word *customary* go with *dinner*?" "What foods are customary for you to eat for dinner?" "When is it customary for you to eat dinner?" [*energize*] "How might the word *energize* go with *dinner*?" "What do you eat at dinner that might energize you?" and [*appetizing*] "How might the word *appetizing* go with *dinner*?" "What appetizing foods do you like to eat for dinner?"

After partners have talked, have a few volunteers use the prompt to share their thinking with the class.

Using the same procedure, discuss:

- *holiday*

PROMPT 3: "I think [*customary*] goes with *holiday* because . . ."

- *exercise*

PROMPT 4: "I think [*energize*] goes with *exercise* because . . ."

- *delicious*

PROMPT 5: "I think [*appetizing*] goes with *delicious* because . . ."

Introduce *Plain, Differ, and Refreshing*

Day 3

In this lesson, the students:

- Learn and use the words *plain, differ,* and *refreshing*
- Review words with multiple meanings
- Review the prefix *re-*
- Build their speaking and listening skills
- Contribute ideas that are different from their partners' ideas

Words Taught

plain (p. 6)
Plain means "without anything added or without decoration." If something is plain, it is simple, not fancy. *Plain* also means a "large area of flat land."

differ
Differ means "is different."

refreshing (p. 22)
If something is refreshing, it makes you feel fresh (lively or not tired) and strong again.

Materials

- *Morning Meals Around the World*
- Word card 106 (WA5)
- Word card 107 (WA6)
- Word card 108 (WA7)

Teacher Note

To discuss the word *differ*, identify two areas of the classroom that are different and easy for the students to see from the rug area (for example, the front of the room and back of the room, the book nook and the writing center, or the bulletin board next to the door and the bulletin board next to the window). See Step 5.

INTRODUCE AND USE *PLAIN*

1 Introduce and Define *Plain*

Show page 6 of *Morning Meals Around the World* and reread the first two sentences aloud, emphasizing the word *plain*.

Explain that *plain* means "without anything added or without decoration." If something is plain, it is simple, not fancy. Explain that some people like to eat their cereal plain, or without anything, such as sugar or fruit, added.

Display word card 106 (WA5) and have the students say the word *plain*.

2 Play "Plain or Not Plain?"

Explain that partners will play "Plain or Not Plain?" You will describe something and partners will discuss whether it is plain or not plain and why they think so.

Begin by asking:

Q *A birthday cake decorated with roses and the words "Happy Birthday": plain or not plain? Why?* [Click ❶ on WA5 to reveal the first prompt.] *Turn to your partner.*

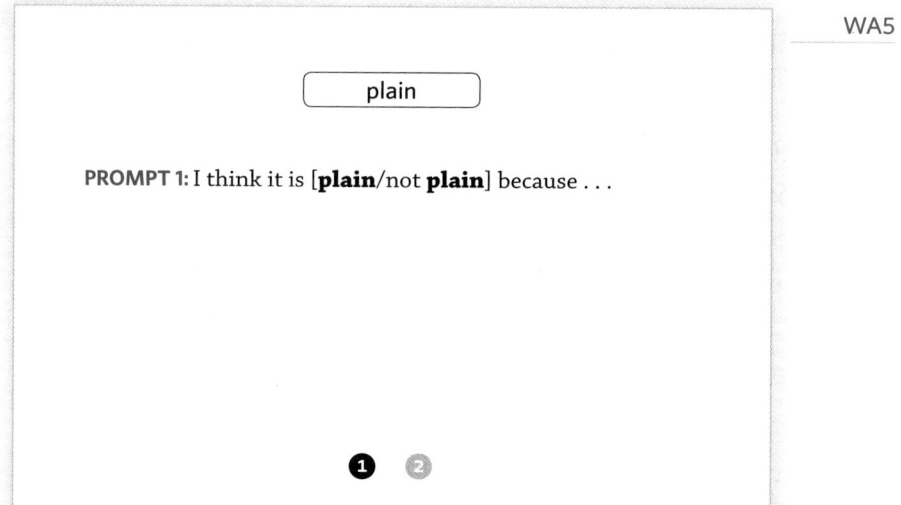

WA5

plain

PROMPT 1: I think it is [**plain**/not **plain**] because . . .

❶ ❷

PROMPT 1: "I think it is [plain/not plain] because . . ."

After partners have talked, have a few volunteers use the prompt to share their thinking with the class.

Using the same procedure, discuss:

Q *A hamburger with nothing on the bun: plain or not plain? Why?* [Point to prompt 1.] *Turn to your partner.*

Q *A T-shirt with a picture of a spider and a web on it: plain or not plain? Why?* [Point to prompt 1.] *Turn to your partner.*

Point to the word *plain* and review the pronunciation and meaning of the word.

3 Discuss Another Meaning of *Plain*

Remind the students that words often have more than one meaning and sometimes the meanings are very different. Point to the word *plain*, pronounce it, and review that *plain* means "without anything added or without decoration."

Explain that *plain* can also mean a "large area of flat land." Explain that parts of the American West are plains and that many years ago millions of buffalo lived on the plains where grass for grazing was plentiful. Explain that parts of Africa are plains and that giraffes, lions, and other animals live on the African plains.

Remind the students that if they hear or read a word that has more than one meaning, they can usually figure out the correct meaning by thinking about how the word is used. Explain that you will read a story that includes the word *plain*. Partners will decide whether *plain* means "without anything added" or a "large area of flat land" in the story and explain why they think so.

Read the following aloud twice:

- *During our travels, we crossed an immense plain. The flat land stretched before us for miles. There were no trees, only acres and acres of grass moving with the wind.*

Ask:

 Q *In the story, does* plain *mean "without anything added" or a "large area of flat land"? Why do you think that?* [Click ❷ on WA5 to reveal the prompt.] *Turn to your partner.*

PROMPT 2: "We think *plain* means [a 'large area of flat land'] because . . ."

After partners have talked, have a few volunteers use the prompt to share their thinking with the class.

Using the same procedure, discuss:

- *During our travels, we ate plain food: bread without jam, meat without salt or pepper, and potatoes without butter. We were hungry, so even plain food was delicious.*

INTRODUCE AND USE *DIFFER*

4 Introduce and Define *Differ*

Tell the students that the next word they will learn today is *differ*, and explain that *differ* means "is different." Display word card 107 ( WA6) and have the students say the word *differ*.

Show pages 10–11 of *Morning Meals Around the World* and review that morning meals differ, or are different, from country to country. Explain that as you read about morning meals in France and Italy, you want the students to listen for how the meals differ.

 **ELL Note**
You might show a picture of a plain.

🌐 **ELL Note**
The Spanish cognate of *differ* is *diferir*.

Read pages 10–11 aloud.

Ask and discuss as a class:

Q *How do morning meals in France and Italy differ?*

Click ❶ on word card 107 (WA6) to reveal the first prompt. Have a few volunteers use the prompt to share their thinking with the class.

PROMPT 1: "The morning meals differ because . . ."

Point out that you can see part of the word *different* in the word *differ* and explain that the words *different* and *differ* are related.

5 Discuss Things That Differ

Direct the students' attention to the two classroom areas you identified and explain that you want the students to quietly look at the areas and think about how they differ.

After a few moments, ask:

 Q *How does [the book nook] differ from [the writing center]?* [Click ❷ on WA6 to reveal the prompt.] *Turn to your partner.*

PROMPT 2: "[The book nook] differs from [the writing center] because . . ."

After partners have talked, have a few volunteers use the prompt to share their thinking with the class.

Ask:

 Q *How does a weekend day differ from a school day?* [Click ❸ on WA6 to reveal the prompt.] *Turn to your partner.*

PROMPT 3: "A weekend day differs from a school day because . . ."

After partners have talked, have a few volunteers use the prompt to share their thinking with the class.

Point to the word *differ* and review the pronunciation and meaning of the word.

INTRODUCE AND USE *REFRESHING*

6 Introduce and Define *Refreshing* and Review the Prefix *re-*

Show and read page 22 of *Morning Meals Around the World* aloud, emphasizing the word *refreshing*. Display word card 108 (WA7) and have the students say the word *refreshing*.

Explain that if something is refreshing, it makes you feel fresh (lively or not tired) and strong again. Explain that many people enjoy a refreshing drink, or a drink that makes them feel fresh and strong again, at their morning meal.

Explain that many people also enjoy a refreshing drink during the day, especially if they are hot or tired. Refreshing drinks cool them off and give them energy again.

Ask:

Q *When you are hot or tired, what refreshing drink do you like?* [Click **1** on WA7 to reveal the first prompt.] *Turn to your partner.*

PROMPT 1: "When I am [hot/tired], a refreshing drink I like is . . ."

After partners have talked, have a few volunteers use the prompt to share their thinking with the class.

Point to the prefix *re-* in *refreshing* and remind the students that they learned the prefix earlier. Review that *re-* means "again." Explain that adding the prefix *re-* to the word *fresh* makes the word *refresh*, which means "make fresh again."

7 Review the Game "Make a Choice"

Explain that partners will play "Make a Choice." You will describe two things and partners will discuss which is refreshing and why they think so.

Ask:

Q *Which is refreshing after you have worked hard: more hard work or a nap? Why?* [Click **2** on WA7 to reveal the prompt.] *Turn to your partner.*

PROMPT 2: "I think [a nap] is refreshing because . . ."

After partners have talked, have a few volunteers use the prompt to share their thinking with the class.

Using the same procedure, discuss:

Q *Which is refreshing when you are dirty: a shower or going shopping? Why?* [Point to prompt 2.] *Turn to your partner.*

Q *Which is refreshing when you are hungry: a snack or a nap? Why?* [Point to prompt 2.] *Turn to your partner.*

Point to the word *refreshing* and review the pronunciation and meaning of the word.

ELL Note

You may wish to discuss each choice individually by asking "After you work hard, is doing more hard work refreshing? Why?" and "After you work hard, is taking a nap refreshing? Why?"

- Chart paper and a marker

MORE STRATEGY PRACTICE

Review the Prefix *re-* and Discuss the Word *Reenergize*

Prepare a sheet of chart paper titled "Words with the Prefix *re-*." On the paper write these four vocabulary words: *reunite, reuse, reconsider,* and *refreshing.* Remind the students that the prefix *re-* is used in each of the words and that the prefix means "again." Review the pronunciation and meaning of each word:

- Reunite *means "come together again after being separated."*
- Reuse *means "use again."*
- Reconsider *means "think again about a decision."*
- *If something is refreshing, it makes you feel fresh and strong again.*

Remind the students that knowing that *re-* means "again" can help them figure out the meaning of a word that begins with the prefix. Write the word *reenergize* on the chart and explain that *reenergize* is a word made by adding the prefix *re-* to the word *energize.* Remind the students that *energize* means "give energy or strength." Then ask:

Q *Based on what you know about the prefix* re- *and the word* energize, *what do you think the word* reenergize *means? If something reenergizes you, what does it do?*

If necessary, explain that *reenergize* means "give energy or strength again." Explain that if something reenergizes you, it energizes you again.

Ask:

Q *If you are tired, what might reenergize you?* [Show the prompt.] *Turn to your partner.*

PROMPT: "If I am tired, [taking a nap] might reenergize me."

Have a few volunteers use the prompt to share their thinking with the class.

Ask the students to listen and watch for other words that use the prefix *re-*, and discuss any examples they find.

Teacher Note

You might post and save the "Words with the Prefix *re-*" chart to add to and use throughout the year.

 MORE ELL SUPPORT

Draw a Plain Object and Not Plain Object

Remind the students that *plain* means "without anything added or without decoration." If something is plain, it is simple, not fancy. Tell the students they will pick an object and draw it plain, or without any decoration, and then they will draw that same object with decoration. (For example, a student might draw a plain pair of sneakers and a pair of sneakers with lights on the back and lightning bolts on the sides.)

Ask the students to use the following prompts to explain their drawings to a partner:

PROMPT: "I drew a plain [pair of sneakers]. Then I drew a [pair of sneakers with lightning bolts on the side]."

Review *Plain, Differ, and Refreshing* — Day 4

In this lesson, the students:

- Review and practice using the words *plain, differ,* and *refreshing* from Day 3
- Build their speaking and listening skills
- Work in a responsible way

Words Reviewed

plain
Plain means "without anything added or without decoration." If something is plain, it is simple, not fancy. Plain also means "a large area of flat land."

differ
Differ means "is different."

refreshing
If something is refreshing, it makes you feel fresh (lively or not tired) and strong again.

Materials

- Daily review cards (WA8)
- Daily review activity (WA9)
- Copy of this week's family letter (BLM1) for each student
- (Optional) Copy of the "Week 18 Crossword Puzzle" (BLM3) for each student

REVIEW THE WORDS

1 Briefly Review The Words

Display the daily review cards (WA8). Review the pronunciation and meaning of each word.

Ask:

Q *Which of the words we learned yesterday might you use when you talk with your friends? How might you use the word?* [Click ❶ on WA8 to reveal the prompt.] *Turn to your partner.*

```
┌─────────────────────────────────────────────────────────┐
│   ┌──────────┐    ┌──────────┐    ┌─────────────┐        │
│   │  plain   │    │  differ  │    │ refreshing  │        │
│   └──────────┘    └──────────┘    └─────────────┘        │
│                                                           │
│   PROMPT 1: I might use the word _____.         │
│   I might say . . .                                       │
│                                                           │
│                                                           │
│                                                           │
│                            ❶                              │
└─────────────────────────────────────────────────────────┘
```

PROMPT 1: "I might use the word [*refreshing*]. I might say . . ."

After partners have talked, have a few volunteers use the prompt to share their thinking with the class.

PRACTICE USING THE WORDS

❷ Play "Finish the Story"

Tell the students that they are going to play "Finish the Story." Explain that you are going to read some stories and that you will leave off the last word of each story. Review that partners will decide which word makes the best ending for the story.

Display the daily review activity (◖ WA9) and begin playing the game.

1. Click ❶ to reveal the first story and the word choices. Point to the story and read it aloud twice, slowly and clearly.

   ▪ Story 1: *Raymond and Jesse are hot after playing basketball at the park. They go to Jesse's house to drink something _____.*

   Point out that the ending is missing.

2. Give the students a few moments to think about the story. Then point to the words and read each word aloud. Ask:

   Q *Which word makes the best ending for the story? Why?* [Click ❶ again and read the prompt.] *Turn to your partner.*

   PROMPT: "I think [*refreshing*] makes the best ending because . . ."

   After partners have talked, have a few volunteers use the prompt to share their thinking with the class.

Teacher Note

Each story on the weekly review activity (WA9) has a corresponding number: the first story is ❶; the second story is ❷; the third story is ❸. To play the game, click the corresponding number four times:

▪ The first click reveals the story and the word choices.

▪ The second click reveals the prompt.

▪ The third click reveals the correct answer.

▪ The fourth click clears the screen.

---

3. Conclude the discussion of this story by clicking ❶ a third time to highlight the correct vocabulary word and reveal the sentence with the correct word in place. Then reread the story with the word *refreshing* at the end.

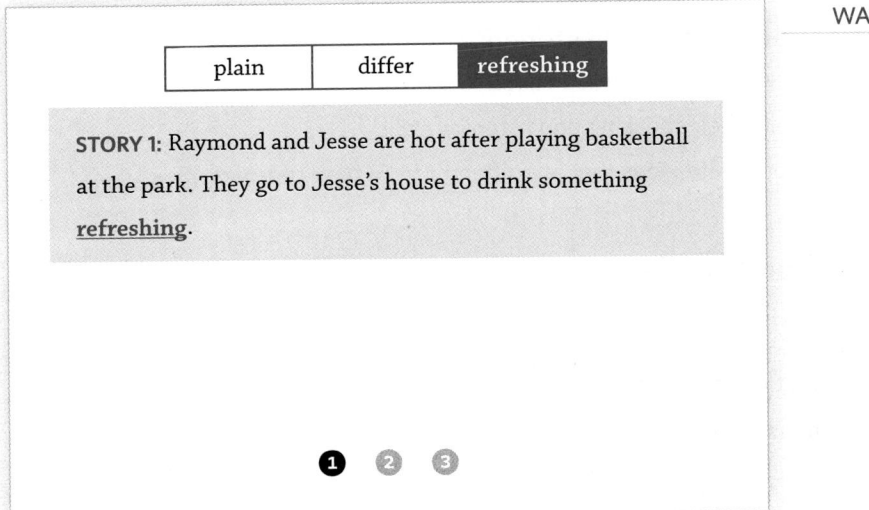

WA9

4. Click ❶ to clear the screen.

Repeat the procedure to discuss the following stories:

- Story 2: *Layla asked for a doll like her sister's. When she got the doll, Layla saw that it had blond hair instead of brown hair like her sister's doll. "The dolls don't match," she said. "They _____."* (differ)

- Story 3: *Zack doesn't like anything on his hot dog—no ketchup, mustard, relish, or onions. He likes his hot dog _____.* (plain)

EXTENSION

Discuss *Plain* and *Plane* and Other Homophones

Write the words *plain* and *plane* on chart paper or where everyone can see them. Ask the students what they notice about the words.

Explain that *plain* and *plane* are homophones and that *homophones* are "words that are pronounced the same way but are spelled differently and have different meanings." Have the students discuss the meanings of *plain* and *plane*. Then have them discuss the meanings of these homophones: *ate, eight; blew, blue; knight, night; meat, meet; one, won;* and *right, write.* Have the students watch for other homophones in their reading, and discuss the examples they find.

Teacher Note

If you are not using an interactive whiteboard, you might write the words and stories where everyone can see them.

Teacher Note

Send home with each student a copy of this week's family letter (BLM1). Encourage the students to talk about this week's words with their families.

Teacher Note

To provide students with additional review of words taught during Weeks 17 and 18, you might distribute a copy of the "Week 18 Crossword Puzzle" (BLM3) to each student.

Materials

- Ongoing review cards (WA10)
- "Class Vocabulary Assessment Record" sheet (CA1)

In this lesson, the students:

- Review words learned earlier
- Build their speaking and listening skills
- Contribute ideas that are different from their partners' ideas

Words Reviewed

cherish
Cherish means "care for something deeply." If you cherish something, you treat it with great care because it is very important to you.

industrious
Industrious means "hardworking."

lively
Lively means "active." Someone who is lively is energetic and full of life.

persist
Persist means "keep doing something, even though it is difficult." If you persist, you refuse to give up.

sorrowful
Sorrowful means "full of sorrow or very sad."

REVIEW THE WORDS

1 Briefly Review the Words

Display the ongoing review cards (☾ WA10). Review the pronunciation and meaning of each word.

PRACTICE USING THE WORDS

2 Play "Which Word Am I?"

Explain that partners will play "Which Word Am I?" You will give a clue about one of the words and partners will figure out the word.

Begin by saying:

- *I'm how you describe a person who is very excited and has a lot of energy.*

Ask:

 Q *Which word am I? Why?* [Click ❶ on WA10 to reveal the prompt.] *Turn to your partner.*

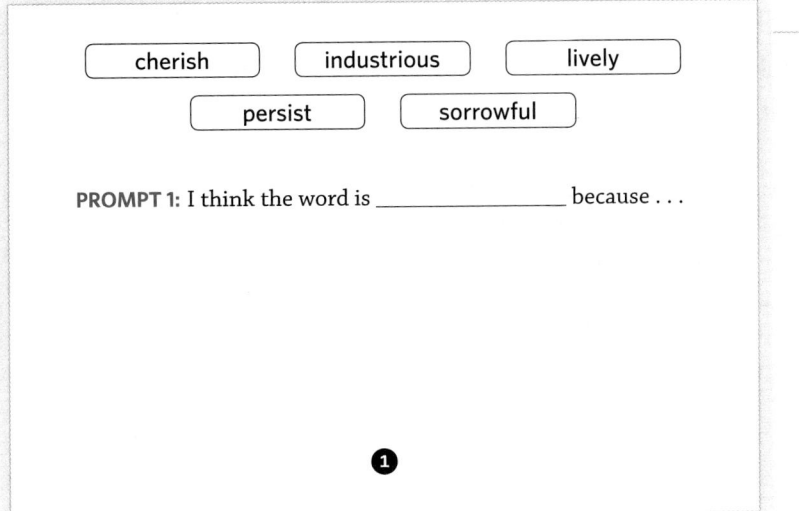

PROMPT 1: "I think the word is [*lively*] because . . ."

After partners have talked, have a few volunteers use the prompt to share their thinking with the class.

Using the same procedure, discuss:

- *I'm how you would feel if your pet goldfish died.* (sorrowful)

- *I mean "care for something deeply."* (cherish)

- *I'm what you do when you keep trying to learn something even if it is hard.* (persist)

- *I'm how you describe a person who stays up late to do her homework.* (industrious)

- *I'm a synonym for* sad. (sorrowful)

 CLASS VOCABULARY ASSESSMENT NOTE

Observe the students and ask yourself:

- Do the students' responses indicate that they understand the words' meanings?

- Can they identify the words in "Which Word Am I?" and explain why a word is the best choice?

- Are they using independent word-learning strategies to figure out word meanings when they read independently?

Record your observations on the "Class Vocabulary Assessment Record" sheet (CA1); see page 187 of the *Assessment Resource Book*.

(continues)

CLASS VOCABULARY ASSESSMENT NOTE

(continued)

Use the following suggestions to support struggling students:

- If **only a few students** understand a word's meaning, reteach the word using the vocabulary lesson in which it was first taught as a model.

- If **about half of the students** understand a word's meaning, provide further practice by inviting the students to tell or write a story in which they use the word.

Week 19

RESOURCES

Read-aloud
- *Homes* by Chris Oxlade

More Strategy Practice
- "Discuss Using a Glossary"

Extension
- "Explore Domain-specific Words: *Wire*"
- "Explore Related Words: *Detect*, *Detector*, and *Detective*"

 Online Resources

Visit the CCC Learning Hub (ccclearninghub.org) to find your online resources for this week.

Whiteboard Activities
- WA1–WA10

Reproducibles
- Week 19 family letter (BLM1)
- (Optional) "Week 19 Word Cards" (BLM2)

OVERVIEW

Words Taught	Words Reviewed
secure	comfy
durable	energize
texture	exhilarated
hazardous	memorable
convenient	unexpected
detect	

Word-learning Strategies

- Recognizing antonyms (review)
- Recognizing synonyms (review)
- Using a glossary to determine word meanings (review)

Vocabulary Focus

- Students learn and use six words from or about the book.
- Students review synonyms and antonyms.
- Students use a glossary to determine word meanings.
- Students review words learned earlier.
- Students build their speaking and listening skills.

Social Development Focus

- Students work in a responsible way.
- Students develop the skill of contributing ideas that are different from their partners' ideas.

DO AHEAD

✓ (Optional) Prior to Day 1, review the more strategy practice activity "Discuss Using a Glossary" on page 395.

✓ Prior to Day 4, visit the CCC Learning Hub (ccclearninghub.org) to access and print this week's family letter (BLM1). Make enough copies to send one letter home with each student.

✓ (Optional) Visit the CCC Learning Hub (ccclearninghub.org) to access and print "Week 19 Word Cards" (BLM2). These cards can be used to provide your students with more opportunities to review the words.

In this lesson, the students:

- Learn and use the words *secure, durable,* and *texture*
- Review antonyms
- Discuss using a glossary to determine word meanings
- Build their speaking and listening skills
- Work in a responsible way

Words Taught

secure
Secure means "safe and protected."

durable
If something is durable, it is tough. It can last a long time even if it is used a lot.

texture (p. 8)
Texture is "how a material feels—for example, rough or smooth."

INTRODUCE AND USE *SECURE*

1 Introduce and Define *Secure*

Briefly review *Homes.*

Show pages 4–5 and review that the first chapter tells us that science is at work everywhere in our homes. Point to the words "What is a home?" on page 4 and explain that the first paragraph on page 4 tells what a home is. Read the first paragraph aloud. Tell the students that the first word they will learn today is *secure* and that *secure* means "safe and protected." Explain that your home is a place where you feel secure, or safe and protected.

Display word card 109 (◖ WA1) and have the students say the word *secure.*

2 Play "Would You Feel Secure?"

Tell the students that partners will play a game called "Would You Feel Secure?" Explain that you will describe a situation and partners will discuss whether or not they would feel secure, or safe and protected, in that situation and why they think so.

Materials

- *Homes*
- Word card 109 (WA1)
- Word card 110 (WA2)
- Word card 111 (WA3)

 **ELL Note**
The Spanish cognate of *secure* is *seguro/a.*

Begin by saying:

- *Riding on a roller coaster*

Ask:

 Q *Would you feel secure, or safe and protected, riding on a roller coaster? Why?* [Click ❶ on WA1 to reveal the first prompt.] *Turn to your partner.*

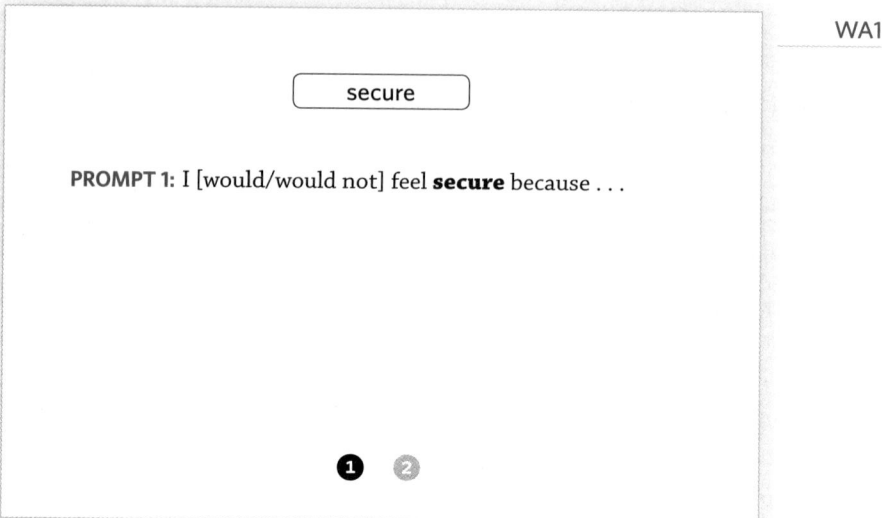

PROMPT 1: "I [would/would not] feel secure because . . ."

After partners have talked, have a few volunteers use the prompt to share their thinking with the class.

Using the same procedure, discuss one or more of the following:

- *Hiking in the woods with your family*
- *Eating lunch in the school cafeteria with your friends*
- *Riding on a boat during a storm*

Follow up by asking:

Q *What is a place you always feel secure? Why?*

Click ❷ on word card 109 (WA1) to reveal the prompt. Have one or two volunteers use the prompt to share their thinking with the class.

PROMPT 2: "I always feel secure . . ."

Point to the word *secure* and review the pronunciation and meaning of the word.

INTRODUCE AND USE *DURABLE*

3 Introduce and Define *Durable* and Review Antonyms

Show pages 6–7 of *Homes* and review that this part of the book tells about the materials that are used to build homes. Read the last paragraph on page 6 aloud.

Explain that *durable* is the next word the students will learn today. Tell the students that if something is durable, it is tough. It can last a long time even if it is used a lot. Explain that the walls of homes are built of stone, brick, or concrete, which are durable materials, or materials that are tough and last a long time. Explain that home builders use durable materials so that houses will be safe and strong.

Remind the students that earlier this year they learned the word *flimsy* and that *flimsy* means "thin and weak." Explain that *flimsy* and *durable* are *antonyms*, or "words with opposite meanings." Point out that home builders would not use flimsy materials because those materials would not be durable, or tough and long lasting.

Display word card 110 ( WA2) and have the students say the word *durable*.

ELL Note

The Spanish cognate of *durable* is *durable*.

Teacher Note

If you started an antonym chart, add *durable* and *flimsy* to it.

4 Discuss Durable Objects in the Classroom

Give examples of some objects in the classroom that are made of durable materials.

> **You might say:**
>
> "My desk is made of metal, which is durable, or tough and meant to last a long time. The walls of our classroom are made of stone, which is durable. Our curtains are made of a strong, durable fabric."

Use "Think, Pair, Share" to discuss:

 Q *What are some other durable objects in our classroom? Why do you say they are durable?* [Pause; click **1** on WA2 to reveal the first prompt.] *Turn to your partner.*

PROMPT 1: "[My chair] is durable because . . ."

After partners have talked, have a few volunteers use the prompt to share their thinking with the class.

Then briefly discuss as a class:

Q *What are some objects in our classroom that are not durable?*

Click **2** on WA2 to reveal the next prompt. Have a few volunteers use the prompt to share their thinking with the class.

PROMPT 2: "[The tissues in the tissue box] are not durable because . . ."

Point to the word *durable* and review the pronunciation and meaning of the word.

INTRODUCE AND USE *TEXTURE*

5 Introduce and Define *Texture*

Show pages 8–9 of *Homes* and explain that this part of the book tells more about the materials used to build homes. Read page 8 aloud, emphasizing the word *texture*.

Explain that *texture* is "how a material feels—for example, rough or smooth." Point out that building materials have different textures. Point to the house in the photograph on page 8 and talk about the textures of the materials the home is built with.

> **You might say:**
>
> [Point to the stone.] "The stone on the house has a bumpy texture." [Point to the wood posts on the front porch.] "The wood posts on the front porch have a smooth texture." [Point to the windows.] "The windows have a smooth and slippery texture because they are made of glass." [Point to the roof.] "The roof shingles have a rough texture."

Display word card 111 (◖ WA3) and have the students say the word *texture*.

6 Look for Different Textures in the Classroom

Tell the students that every object has a texture—it feels a particular way. Explain that some objects, such as a desktop or wooden floor, have a smooth texture. Other objects, such as sandpaper or tree bark, have a rough texture. An object's texture might also be described as sticky or slick, scratchy or bumpy, hard or soft, or lumpy, sandy, rocky, furry, or fuzzy.

Have the students feel their shirts. Then discuss as a class:

Q *How would you describe the texture of your shirt?*

Click **1** on word card 111 (WA3) to reveal the first prompt. Have a few volunteers use the prompt to share their thinking with the class.

PROMPT 1: "The texture of my shirt is . . ."

ELL Note

The Spanish cognate of *texture* is *textura*.

Ask the students to quietly look around the classroom for objects that have a smooth texture. After a few moments, ask:

Q *What do you see that has a smooth texture?* [Click  on WA3 to reveal the prompt.] *Turn to your partner.*

PROMPT 2: "[The wall] has a smooth texture."

After partners have talked, have a few volunteers use the prompt to share their thinking with the class.

Point to the word *texture* and review the pronunciation and meaning of the word.

MORE STRATEGY PRACTICE

Discuss Using a Glossary

Show the glossary on pages 28–29 of *Homes*. Tell the students that a *glossary* is "a list of words the author of a book thinks readers might need to know to understand the book." Explain that a glossary is usually found at the end of a book and is organized like a dictionary—it lists the words in alphabetical order and tells what each word means. Tell the students that if they come across a word that they do not understand in a nonfiction book, they can often look it up in the glossary to find out what it means.

Show page 8 and point to the words *properties* and *texture*. Explain that authors often use bold type to help readers know which words in a book can be found in the glossary. Point out that both *properties* and *texture* appear in bold type, which tells readers that they can look up their meanings in the glossary. Turn back to the glossary and model using it by looking up *property* and *texture* alphabetically and reading the definitions.

Then show page 22 and ask:

Q *What words on this page might we find in the glossary? Why do you say that?*

If necessary, point out that we can find the words *appliances*, *electricity*, and *detergent* in the glossary. We know that because they are in bold type. Turn to the glossary on pages 28–29 of the book and read the definitions of *appliance*, *electricity*, and *detergent*. Encourage the students to watch for and use the glossary in books they are reading independently.

Teacher Note

If the students need further practice with the word *texture*, have them name objects in the classroom that have a rough, bumpy, sticky, or scratchy texture.

🌐 **ELL Note**

You might have the students walk around the classroom, school, or playground to touch objects and identify or describe their textures.

Materials

- *Homes*

Day 2

Review *Secure, Durable,* and *Texture*

Materials

- Daily review cards (WA4)

In this lesson, the students:

- Review and practice using the words *secure, durable,* and *texture* from Day 1
- Build their speaking and listening skills
- Work in a responsible way
- Contribute ideas that are different from their partners' ideas

Words Reviewed

secure
Secure means "safe and protected."

durable
If something is durable, it is tough. It can last a long time even if it is used a lot.

texture
Texture is "how a material feels—for example, rough or smooth."

REVIEW THE WORDS

1 Briefly Review the Words

Display the daily review cards (WA4). Review the pronunciation and meaning of each word.

Ask:

Q *Which of the words you learned yesterday was the most fun to talk about? Why? [Click ❶ on WA4 to reveal the first prompt.] Turn to your partner.*

WA4

| secure | durable | texture |

PROMPT 1: I think _____ was the most fun to talk about because . . .

❶ ② ③ ④

PROMPT 1: "I think [*texture*] was the most fun to talk about because . . ."

After partners have talked, have a few volunteers use the prompt to share their thinking with the class.

PRACTICE USING THE WORDS

2 Discuss "Would You?" Questions

Explain that you will ask some questions that partners will discuss.

Ask:

 Q *Would you build a tree house out of durable materials? Why?* [Click **2** on WA4 to reveal the prompt.] *Turn to your partner.*

PROMPT 2: "I [would/would not] build a tree house out of durable materials because . . ."

After partners have talked, have a few volunteers use the prompt to share their thinking with the class.

Using the same procedure, discuss:

 Q *Would you feel secure riding your bike down a steep hill? Why?* [Click **3** to reveal the prompt.] *Turn to your partner.*

PROMPT 3: "I [would/would not] feel secure riding my bike down a steep hill because . . ."

 Q *Would you be comfortable wearing a T-shirt with a rough texture? Why?* [Click **4** to reveal the prompt.] *Turn to your partner.*

PROMPT 4: "I [would/would not] be comfortable wearing a T-shirt with a rough texture because . . ."

EXTENSION

Explore Domain-specific Words: *Wire*

Show the cover of *Homes* and review that homes are made up of many different parts and materials.

Write the word *wire* on the board. Tell the students that as you read a sentence from the chapter "Electricity" in the book, you want them to listen for and think about what they know about the word *wire*. Then read this sentence from page 15 aloud: "It passes through a small wire inside the bulb, then it heats up and glows bright." Ask:

Q *What do you know about wires?*

Have volunteers share their thinking. If necessary, explain that wires are strings of metal that help conduct, or transmit, electricity. Review that electricity is a form of energy used to make light and heat, and to power machines. Follow up by asking:

Q *What are some other things that have wires?*

Teacher Note

Academic language is the language necessary for success in school. It includes general academic words commonly found across content areas and in many different kinds of texts as well as content area or domain-specific words and terms. Knowledge of academic language is important for all students' success in school and is especially critical for English Language Learners.

Introduce *Hazardous, Convenient,* and *Detect*

Materials

- *Homes*
- Word card 112 (WA5)
- Word card 113 (WA6)
- Word card 114 (WA7)

In this lesson, the students:

- Learn and use the words *hazardous, convenient,* and *detect*
- Review synonyms
- Build their speaking and listening skills
- Contribute ideas that are different from their partners' ideas

Words Taught

hazardous
Hazardous means "dangerous."

convenient
If something is convenient, it is useful because it makes our lives easier or more comfortable.

detect (p. 25)
Detect means "discover or notice something that is not easy to see, hear, or feel."

INTRODUCE AND USE *HAZARDOUS*

1 Introduce and Define *Hazardous* and Review Synonyms

Show pages 10–11 of *Homes* and review that this part of *Homes* tells how heating systems keep homes warm. Review that some heating systems use radiators to provide heat to rooms. Explain that because radiators become hot, people need to be careful around them. Then read "Stay safe" on page 11 aloud.

Tell the students that *hazardous* is the first word they will learn today. Explain that *hazardous* means "dangerous." Explain that *hazardous* and *dangerous* are synonyms. Review that radiators and other heaters can be hazardous, or dangerous.

Display word card 112 (❰ WA5) and have the students say the word *hazardous*.

2 Talk About Hazardous Things

Explain that things that seem safe or harmless can be hazardous, or dangerous, if not used properly. For example, a ladder is harmless if you use it properly. However, if you are not careful when you climb a ladder or are careless while standing on it, a ladder can be hazardous. Ask:

 Q *In what ways might a pencil be hazardous?* [Click ❶ on WA5 to reveal the first prompt.] *Turn to your partner.*

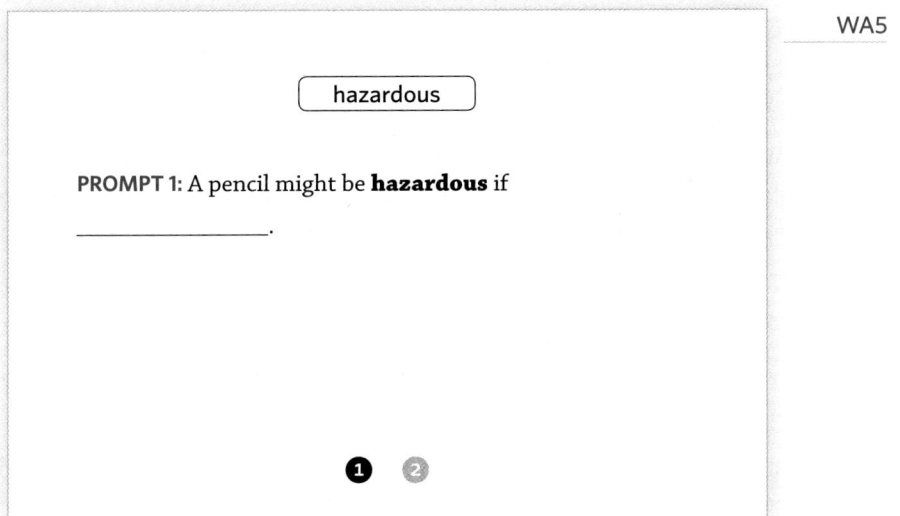

WA5

> hazardous
>
> **PROMPT 1:** A pencil might be **hazardous** if
>
> _____ .
>
> ❶ ❷

PROMPT 1: "A pencil might be hazardous if [you poked someone with it]."

After partners have talked, have a few volunteers use the prompt to share their thinking with the class.

Ask the students to look around the classroom for things that, if misused, might be hazardous. Then discuss as a class:

Q *What other things in our classroom might be hazardous? In what ways might they be hazardous?*

Click ❷ on word card 112 (WA5) to reveal the next prompt. Have one or two volunteers use the prompt to share their thinking with the class.

PROMPT 2: "[The pencil sharpener] might be hazardous if . . ."

Point to the word *hazardous* and review the pronunciation and meaning of the word.

INTRODUCE AND USE
CONVENIENT

3 Introduce and Define *Convenient*

Show pages 16–17 of *Homes* and tell the students that this part of the book explains where the water in our homes comes from. Read page 16 aloud.

Explain that having water available in our homes at the turn of a faucet is convenient, and tell the students that *convenient* is the next word they will learn today. Explain that if something is convenient, it is useful because it makes our lives easier or more comfortable.

Show pages 20–21 and review that this part of the book tells about tools that people use around their homes. Point to the can opener in the picture on page 20 and discuss as a class:

Q *How is a can opener convenient? How does it make our lives easier or more comfortable?*

Q *What other tools or appliances in our homes are convenient? Why are they convenient?*

Display word card 113 (◖ WA6) and have the students say the word *convenient*.

4 Discuss Things That Are Convenient

Remind the students that things that are convenient are useful because they make our lives easier or more comfortable. Give some examples of things in the classroom that you find convenient.

> **You might say:**
>
> "I think having a library in our classroom is convenient because it makes it easier to get our hands on a good book. I also think having computers in the classroom is convenient, because we can use computers to find information quickly, communicate with people far away, or create presentations. The pencil sharpener is a convenient device because it sharpens pencils quickly. The clock is convenient, too, because it makes it easy to know what time it is."

Ask:

 Q *What other things in our classroom are convenient? Why are they convenient?* [Click ❶ on WA6 to reveal the prompt.] *Turn to your partner.*

PROMPT 1: "The [recycling boxes] are convenient because . . ."

After partners have talked, have a few volunteers use the prompt to share their thinking with the class.

Follow up by briefly discussing as a class:

Q *What is something you own or have at home that you think is especially convenient? Why is it convenient?*

Point to the word *convenient* and review the pronunciation and meaning of the word.

INTRODUCE AND USE *DETECT*

5 Introduce and Define *Detect*

Show page 25 of *Homes* and explain that this part of the book tells about a convenient device found in many homes—a smoke alarm. Read "Stay safe" on page 25 aloud, emphasizing the word *detect*.

Explain that *detect* means "discover or notice something that is not easy to see, hear, or feel." Point out that smoke alarms detect, or discover or notice, smoke from fires and make a loud sound to warn us.

Display word card 114 (WA7) and have the students say the word *detect*.

6 Detect Sounds

Explain that you are going to ask the students to close their eyes, sit very quietly, and notice what sounds they detect inside or outside the classroom. Emphasize that it will be very important for them to sit quietly so that everyone has an opportunity to detect, or notice, sounds.

Have the students close their eyes, sit quietly, and detect sounds. After several moments, have the students open their eyes. Ask:

 Q *What sounds did you detect?* [Click ❶ on WA7 to reveal the prompt.] *Turn to your partner.*

PROMPT 1: "I detected [the sound of the clock ticking]."

Point to the word *detect* and review the pronunciation and meaning of the word.

EXTENSION

Explore Related Words: *Detect, Detector,* and *Detective*

Write the word *detect* where everyone can see it, and review that *detect* means "discover or notice something that is not easy to see, hear, or feel." Tell the students that knowing the meaning of *detect* can help them figure out the meaning of a word that is related to *detect*.

🌐 **ELL Note**
The Spanish cognate of *detect* is *detectar*.

Teacher Note
You might explain that *detect, discover,* and *notice* are synonyms and add them to the synonym chart.

Teacher Note
You might make some sounds; for example, you might clear your throat, tap on your desk, or rustle paper.

Tell the students that the word *detective* is a form of the word *detect*, and write *detective* next to *detect*. Explain that a *detective* is a "person who investigates and tries to solve crimes." Discuss as a class:

Q *At the scene of a crime, what does a detective try to detect, or discover or notice?*

PROMPT: "A detective tries to detect [clues]."

Tell the students that *detector* is also a form of the word *detect*, and write it where everyone can see. Explain that a *detector* is a "machine that detects, or discovers or notices, something." For example, a *lie detector* is a "machine that detects whether or not someone is telling a lie."

Discuss as a class:

Q *What does a smoke detector detect? A motion detector? A metal detector?*

PROMPT: "A [smoke detector/motion detector/metal detector] detects . . ."

Day 4 | Review *Hazardous, Convenient,* and *Detect*

Materials

- Daily review cards (WA8)
- Daily review activity (WA9)
- Copy of this week's family letter (BLM1) for each student

In this lesson, the students:

- Review and practice using the words *hazardous, convenient,* and *detect* from Day 3
- Build their speaking and listening skills
- Work in a responsible way

Words Reviewed

hazardous
Hazardous means "dangerous."

convenient
If something is convenient, it is useful because it makes our lives easier or more comfortable.

detect
Detect means "discover or notice something that is not easy to see, hear, or feel."

REVIEW THE WORDS

1 Briefly Review the Words

Display the daily review cards (WA8). Review the pronunciation and meaning of each word.

Ask:

 Q *Which of the words you learned yesterday do you think is particularly interesting? Why? [Click ❶ on WA8 to reveal the prompt.] Turn to your partner.*

---

hazardous   convenient   detect

PROMPT 1: I think _____ is particularly
interesting because . . .

❶

PROMPT 1: "I think [*convenient*] is particularly interesting because . . ."

After partners have talked, have a few volunteers use the prompt to share their thinking with the class.

PRACTICE USING THE WORDS

2 Play "Find Another Word"

Tell the students that partners will play the game "Find Another Word." Remind the students that you will show a sentence with one or more words underlined. You will read each sentence aloud, and partners will decide which vocabulary word can replace the underlined part of the sentence.

Display the daily review activity (◖ WA9) and begin playing the game:

1. Click ❶ to reveal the first sentence. Point to the sentence and read it aloud, emphasizing the underlined words.

   ▪ Sentence 1: *The pot of boiling water is <u>dangerous</u> and should not be touched without an oven mitt.*

2. Give the students a few moments to think about the sentence and the underlined word. Then point to the three word choices and ask:

 Q *Which vocabulary word could replace the underlined word? Why? [Click ❶ again and point to the prompt.] Turn to your partner.*

Teacher Note

You might explain that the students may need to change the form of the word to complete the sentence by adding an ending such as *-s*, *-ing*, or *-ed*.

Teacher Note

Each sentence in the daily review activity (WA9) has a corresponding number: the first sentence is ❶; the second sentence is ❷; and the third sentence is ❸. To play the game, click the corresponding number four times:

▪ The first click reveals the sentence.

▪ The second click reveals the prompt.

▪ The third click highlights the correct answer and reveals the sentence with the correct answer in place.

▪ The fourth click clears the screen.

PROMPT 1: "I think the word [*hazardous*] could replace *dangerous* because . . ."

After partners have talked, have a few volunteers use the prompt to share their thinking with the class.

3. Conclude the discussion by clicking ❶ a third time to highlight the correct vocabulary word and reveal the sentence with the correct word in place.

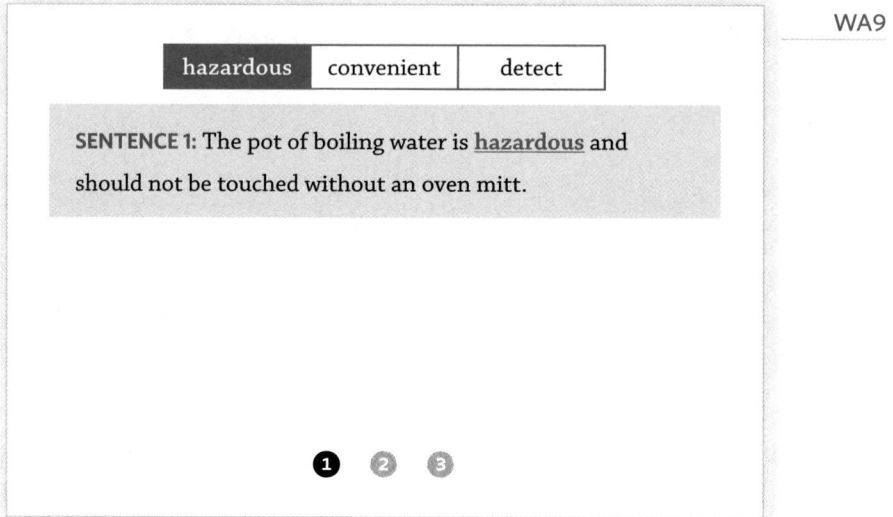

4. Click ❶ to clear the screen.

Use the same procedure to discuss the following sentences:

- Sentence 2: *During fire safety week, the class learned that they must have an alarm in their home to <u>notice</u> smoke from fires.* (detect)

- Sentence 3: *A grocery store is opening up a block away from Lyle's house. He is excited because he can walk there whenever he needs anything. "It is so <u>useful</u>!" Lyle exclaims.* (convenient)

Teacher Note

Send home with each student a copy of this week's family letter (BLM1). Encourage the students to talk about this week's words with their families.

Materials

- Ongoing review cards (WA10)

In this lesson, the students:

- Review words learned earlier
- Build their speaking and listening skills
- Work in a responsible way

Words Reviewed

comfy
Comfy means "comfortable."

energize
Energize means "give energy or strength."

exhilarated
Exhilarated means "very happy and excited."

memorable
Memorable means "worth remembering." Something that is memorable is not easy to forget.

unexpected
Unexpected means "not expected." If something is unexpected it is surprising. You did not expect, or think, that it would happen.

REVIEW THE WORDS

1 Briefly Review the Words

Display the ongoing review cards (WA10) and review the pronunciation and meaning of each word.

PRACTICE USING THE WORDS

2 Play "Make a Choice"

Explain that partners will use the words to play "Make a Choice." Point to the word *exhilarated* and tell the students that they will play the first round of the game with this word. Remind the students that you will describe two things and ask them to decide which one they think would make them feel exhilarated and tell why they think so. Explain that partners may not always agree and that is OK. What is important is that they explain their thinking.

Ask:

 Q *Which of these would be exhilarating: a ride on a roller coaster or cleaning your room? Why?* [Click ❶ on WA10 to reveal the first prompt.] *Turn to your partner.*

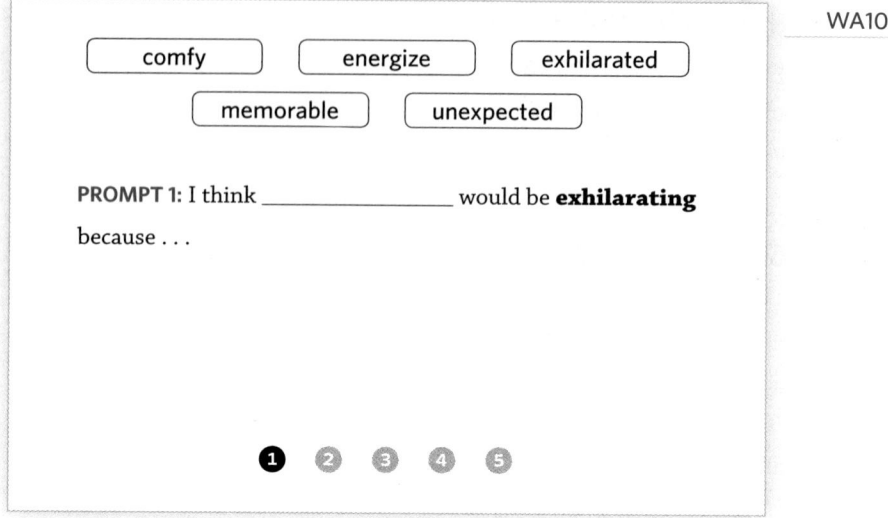

WA10

comfy   energize   exhilarated

memorable   unexpected

PROMPT 1: I think _____ would be **exhilarating** because . . .

❶ ❷ ❸ ❹ ❺

PROMPT 1: "I think [riding on a roller coaster] would be exhilarating because . . ."

After partners have talked, have one or two volunteers use the prompt to share their thinking with the class.

Using the same procedure, discuss:

[comfy]

 Q *Which of these is comfy: a soft, fluffy pillow or a pillow full of rocks? Why?* [Click ❷ to reveal the prompt.] *Turn to your partner.*

PROMPT 2: "I think [a soft, fluffy pillow] is comfy because . . ."

[energize]

 Q *Which of these would make you feel energized: a long bike ride or a long nap? Why?* [Click ❸ to reveal the prompt.] *Turn to your partner.*

PROMPT 3: "I think [a long bike ride] would make me feel energized because . . ."

[memorable]

 Q *Which of these would be memorable: meeting your favorite author or meeting your friend at the park? Why?* [Click ❹ to reveal the prompt.] *Turn to your partner.*

PROMPT 4: "I think [meeting my favorite author] would be memorable because . . ."

[unexpected]

 Q *Which of these would be unexpected: seeing a lion in your backyard or seeing a lion at the zoo? Why?* [Click ➎ to reveal the prompt.] *Turn to your partner.*

PROMPT 5: "I think [seeing a lion in my backyard] would be unexpected because . . ."

Week 20

RESOURCES

Read-aloud

- "Origami: The Art of Japanese Paper Folding" (see pages 428–429)

More Strategy Practice

- "Review the Suffix -ful and Discuss Painful and Delightful"
- "Play 'Use the Clues'"

Assessment Resource Book

- Week 20 vocabulary assessments

 Online Resources

Visit the CCC Learning Hub (ccclearninghub.org) to find your online resources for this week.

Whiteboard Activities

- WA1–WA10

Assessment Forms

- "Class Vocabulary Assessment Record" sheet (CA1)
- "Individual Vocabulary Assessment: Word Check 5" answer sheet (IA1)
- "Individual Vocabulary Assessment Student Record" sheet (SR1)
- "Individual Vocabulary Assessment Class Record" sheet (CR1)
- (Optional) "Student Self-assessment" response sheet (SA1)

Reproducibles

- Week 20 family letter (BLM1)
- (Optional) "Week 20 Word Cards" (BLM2)
- (Optional) "Week 20 Crossword Puzzle" (BLM3)

OVERVIEW

Words Taught	Words Reviewed
graceful	convenient
spectacular	durable
original	intense
achieve	refreshing
challenge	secure
determination	

Word-learning Strategies

- Using the suffix *-ful* to determine word meanings (review)
- Using context to determine word meanings (review)

Vocabulary Focus

- Students learn and use six words from the article.
- Students review the suffix *-ful*.
- Students review using context to determine word meanings.
- Students review words learned earlier.
- Students build their speaking and listening skills.

Social Development Focus

- Students work in a responsible way.
- Students develop the skill of contributing ideas that are different from their partners' ideas.

Ⓙ DO AHEAD

✓ (Optional) Prior to Day 1, review the more strategy practice activity "Review the Suffix *-ful* and Discuss *Painful* and *Delightful*" on page 415.

✓ (Optional) Prior to Day 3, review the more strategy practice activity "Play 'Use the Clues'" on page 421.

(continues)

⏱ DO AHEAD *(continued)*

✓ Prior to Day 4, visit the CCC Learning Hub (ccclearninghub.org) to access and print this week's family letter (BLM1). Make enough copies to send one letter home with each student.

✓ Prior to Day 5, make a copy of the "Class Vocabulary Assessment Record" sheet (CA1); see page 188 of the *Assessment Resource Book*.

✓ Prior to Day 5, make a class set of the "Individual Vocabulary Assessment: Word Check 5" answer sheet (IA1); see page 192 of the *Assessment Resource Book*. Make enough copies for each student to have one; set aside a reference copy for yourself.

✓ (Optional) Prior to Day 5, make a master copy of the "Student Self-assessment" response sheet (SA1); see page 195 of the *Assessment Resource Book*. Write the words you have chosen to be assessed on the master copy. Then make enough copies for each student to have one.

✓ (Optional) Visit the CCC Learning Hub (ccclearninghub.org) to access and print the following materials: "Week 20 Word Cards" (BLM2) and "Week 20 Crossword Puzzle" (BLM3). These materials can be used to provide your students with more opportunities to review the words.

In this lesson, the students:

- Learn and use the words *graceful, spectacular,* and *original*
- Review the suffix *-ful*
- Build their speaking and listening skills
- Work in a responsible way

Words Taught

graceful (p. 428)
Graceful means "moving in a smooth and beautiful way."

spectacular (p. 428)
Spectacular means "amazing to look at."

original (p. 429)
Original means "completely new and different." If something is original, it is not like anything else.

Materials

- "Origami: The Art of Japanese Paper Folding" (see pages 428–429)
- Word card 115 (WA1)
- Word card 116 (WA2)
- Word card 117 (WA3)

INTRODUCE AND USE *GRACEFUL*

1 Introduce and Define *Graceful* and Review the Suffix *-ful*

Briefly review "Origami: The Art of Japanese Paper Folding."

Read the first sentence of the article aloud, emphasizing the word *graceful*: "Could you fold a square of paper into a graceful fish or a long-stemmed flower?"

Tell the students that *graceful* means "moving in a smooth and beautiful way."

Explain that fish are often the subject of origami artists because they are colorful creatures and graceful swimmers. They move through the water in a smooth and beautiful way. Ask the students to picture in their mind a fish swimming gracefully through the water.

Explain that many other animals are graceful, and name some graceful animals (for example, dolphins, deer, horses, cats, and eagles). Explain that many people are also graceful, including dancers, ice-skaters, and athletes such as runners and swimmers.

Display word card 115 (WA1) and have students say the word *graceful*.

Point to the word *grace* in *graceful* and explain that *grace* means "smoothness and beauty of movement." Point to the suffix *-ful* and review that *-ful* is a suffix that means "full of." Explain that *graceful* means "full of grace or full of smoothness and beauty of movement."

2 Play "Graceful or Not Graceful?"

Remind the students that some animals and people are graceful, and explain that other animals and people are *not* graceful. They are clumsy; they move in a way that is not smooth and beautiful.

Tell the students that partners will play "Graceful or Not Graceful?" Explain that you will describe an animal or person and partners will discuss whether or not the animal or person is graceful and why they think so.

Begin by asking:

 Q *A chicken walking across a barnyard: graceful or not graceful? Why?* [Click ❶ on WA1 to reveal the first prompt.] *Turn to your partner.*

WA1

> graceful
>
> **PROMPT 1:** The chicken [is/is not] **graceful** because . . .
>
> ❶ ② ③ ④

PROMPT 1: "The chicken [is/is not] graceful because . . ."

After partners have talked, have a few volunteers use the prompt to share their thinking with the class.

Using the same procedure, discuss:

 Q *A leopard running smoothly and beautifully across a plain: graceful or not graceful? Why?* [Click ❷ to reveal the next prompt.] *Turn to your partner.*

PROMPT 2: "The leopard [is/is not] graceful because . . ."

Q *A skateboarder rolling swiftly and steadily down the sidewalk: graceful or not graceful? Why? [Click ❸ to reveal the next prompt.] Turn to your partner.*

PROMPT 3: "The skateboarder [is/is not] graceful because . . ."

 Q *A skateboarder wobbling from side to side as she bounces down the sidewalk: graceful or not graceful? Why? [Click ❹ to reveal the next prompt.] Turn to your partner.*

PROMPT 4: "The wobbling skateboarder [is/is not] graceful because . . ."

Point to the word *graceful* and review the pronunciation and meaning of the word.

INTRODUCE AND USE *SPECTACULAR*

3 Introduce and Define *Spectacular*

Read this sentence from the first paragraph of the article aloud, emphasizing the word *spectacular*: "In origami, a simple sheet of paper can become a spectacular piece of art."

Explain that *spectacular* means "amazing to look at." Explain that some origami objects are spectacular. Remind the students that artists have made origami sailboats and butterflies. Explain that origami objects like these would be spectacular, or amazing to look at.

Explain that something can be fun or interesting to look at but not be spectacular. For example, watching a single sparkler burn on the Fourth of July might be fun or interesting, but it is not spectacular, or amazing. Explain that seeing a gigantic explosion of colorful fireworks in the sky would be spectacular.

Display word card 116 (◖ WA2) and have the students say the word *spectacular*.

4 Play "Spectacular or Not Spectacular?"

Explain that partners will play "Spectacular or Not Spectacular?" You will describe something and partners will discuss whether or not it is spectacular and why.

Begin by saying:

 Q *An immense orca leaps out of the water right next to your boat: spectacular or not spectacular? Why? [Click ❶ on WA2 to reveal the first prompt.] Turn to your partner.*

PROMPT 1: "An orca [would/would not] be spectacular because . . ."

 ELL Note
The Spanish cognate of *spectacular* is *espectacular*.

After partners have talked, have one or two volunteers use the prompt to share their thinking with the class.

Using the same procedure, discuss:

 Q *A plastic toy whale floats in your bath water: spectacular or not spectacular?* [Click ❷ to reveal the next prompt.] *Why?*

PROMPT 2: "A toy whale [would/would not] be spectacular because . . ."

Point to the word *spectacular* and review the pronunciation and meaning of the word.

INTRODUCE AND USE *ORIGINAL*

5 Introduce and Define *Original*

Remind the students that there are origami contests, and read these sentences from the article (page 429) aloud, emphasizing the word *original*: "Some origami contests have a theme such as plants or prehistoric animals. In other contests, there are categories such as best original design, best technical folding, and best miniature model."

Tell the students that *original* means "completely new and different." Explain that if something is original, it is not like anything else. Explain that some origami objects are original. For example, precise models of butterflies and sailboats are original because they are not like any other origami designs. They are completely new and different.

Display word card 117 ( WA3) and have the students say the word *original*.

6 Discuss Creating Original Things

Use "Think, Pair, Share" to discuss:

 Q *If you wanted to make a pizza that was original, or completely new and different, what toppings would you use?* [Pause; click ❶ on WA3 to reveal the first prompt.] *Turn to your partner.*

PROMPT 1: "To make an original pizza, I would use . . ."

After partners have talked, have a few volunteers use the prompt to share their thinking with the class.

Ask the students to imagine that they have written a story. A friend reads the story and says, "Your story is original."

Ask:

 Q *Would you be pleased if your friend said your story was original? Why?* [Click ❷ to reveal the next prompt.] *Turn to your partner.*

PROMPT 2: "If my friend said my story was original, I [would/would not] be pleased because . . ."

🌐 ELL Note

The Spanish cognate of *original* is *original*.

Teacher Note

You might want to explain that if you add the prefix *un-* to *original*, you make the word *unoriginal*, which means "not new and different." *Original* and *unoriginal* are antonyms.

After partners have talked, have one or two volunteers use the prompt to share their thinking with the class.

Point to the word *original* and review the pronunciation and meaning of the word.

MORE STRATEGY PRACTICE

Review the Suffix *-ful* and Discuss *Painful* and *Delightful*

Write the word *graceful* where everyone can see it. Point to the suffix *-ful* in *graceful* and review that *-ful* is a suffix that means "full of." Review that when you add *-ful* to the word *grace* you make the word *graceful*, which means "full of grace or full of smoothness and beauty of movement."

Write the word *pain* next to *graceful* and ask:

Q *What word do you make when you add the suffix* -ful *to the word* pain?

Remind the students that knowing the meaning of the suffix *-ful* can help them figure out the meaning of a word that uses the suffix.

Ask:

Q *Based on what you know about the suffix* -ful *and the word* pain, *what do you think the word* painful *means? If something is painful, how does it feel?*

If necessary, explain that *painful* means "full of pain." Explain that something that is painful hurts a lot.

Write the word *delight* and ask:

Q *What word do you make when you add the suffix* -ful *to the word* delight?

Explain that *delight* means "great happiness or pleasure."

Ask:

Q *Based on what you know about the suffix* -ful *and the word* delight, *what do you think the word* delightful *means? If you are having a delightful time at a party, what kind of time are you having?*

If necessary, explain that *delightful* means "full of delight or very happy or pleasant." If you are having a delightful time at a party, you are having a very pleasant time.

Materials

- Daily review cards (WA4)

In this lesson, the students:

- Review and practice using the words *graceful, spectacular,* and *original* from Day 1
- Build their speaking and listening skills

Words Reviewed

graceful
Graceful means "moving in a smooth and beautiful way."

spectacular
Spectacular means "amazing to look at."

original
Original means "completely new and different." If something is original, it is not like anything else.

REVIEW THE WORDS

1 Briefly Review the Words

Display the daily review cards (◗ WA4). Review the pronunciation and meaning of each word.

Use "Think, Pair, Share" to discuss:

 Q *Which of the words we learned yesterday might you use when you talk to your friends? How might you use the word?* [Pause; click ❶ on WA4 to reveal the first prompt.] *Turn to your partner.*

WA4

graceful	spectacular	original

PROMPT 1: I might use the word _____.

I might say . . .

❶ ❷

PROMPT 1: "I might use the word [*spectacular*]. I might say . . ."

After partners have talked, have a few volunteers use the prompt to share their thinking with the class.

PRACTICE USING THE WORDS

2 Play "Which Word Am I?"

Explain that partners will play "Which Word Am I?" You will give a clue about one of the words and they will figure out the word.

Begin by saying:

- *I'm how you describe something that is not like anything else.*

Ask:

 Q *What word am I? Why do you think so?* [Click ❷ on WA4 to reveal the prompt.] *Turn to your partner.*

PROMPT 2: "We think the word is [*original*] because . . ."

Using the same procedure, discuss:

- *I'm how you describe a ballet dancer who moves beautifully.* (graceful)
- *I'm how you describe something that is amazing to see.* (spectacular)
- *I'm an antonym of the word* clumsy. (graceful)
- *I'm how you might describe something you've never seen before.* (spectacular *or* original)

Materials

- "Origami: The Art of Japanese Paper Folding"
  (see pages 428–429)
- Word card 118 (WA5)
- Word card 119 (WA6)
- Word card 120 (WA7)

In this lesson, the students:

- Learn and use the words *achieve, challenge,* and *determination*
- Build their speaking and listening skills
- Work in a responsible way
- Contribute ideas that are different from their partners' ideas

Words Taught

achieve (p. 428)
Achieve means "do something successfully, especially something that requires a lot of effort."

challenge (p. 429)
A *challenge* is "something that is hard to do or requires a lot of work or effort."

determination (p. 429)
Determination is "deciding you will do something and then doing it, even if it is difficult."

INTRODUCE AND USE *ACHIEVE*

1 Introduce and Define *Achieve*

Remind the students that in "Origami: The Art of Japanese Paper Folding," they learned that origami artists fold paper to create objects. Read this sentence from the article aloud, emphasizing the word *achieve*: "Some artists use wet paper to achieve a more rounded look; others experiment with unusual materials, such as cloth, wire, sheet metal, and even toilet paper."

Explain that *achieve* means "do something successfully, especially something that requires a lot of effort." Explain that some origami artists achieve, or successfully create, a more rounded look in their objects by using wet paper.

Display word card 118 (WA5) and have the students say the word *achieve*.

2 Discuss Things We Have Achieved

Remind the students that achieving something, or doing it successfully, often requires a lot of effort or work. Give a couple of examples of things you have achieved.

Teacher Note

You may want to explain that the word *achievement* is related to the word *achieve* and that an *achievement* is "something you achieve, or do successfully."

You might say:

"When I was your age, I wanted to make my school's basketball team. I practiced and practiced, and I finally achieved my goal of making the team. Recently, I set a goal for myself of reading three books every month. This month I achieved my goal by reading three books."

Use "Think, Pair, Share" to discuss:

 Q *What is something you have achieved, or done successfully? How did you feel when you achieved it?* [Pause; click ❶ on WA5 to reveal the prompt.] *Turn to your partner.*

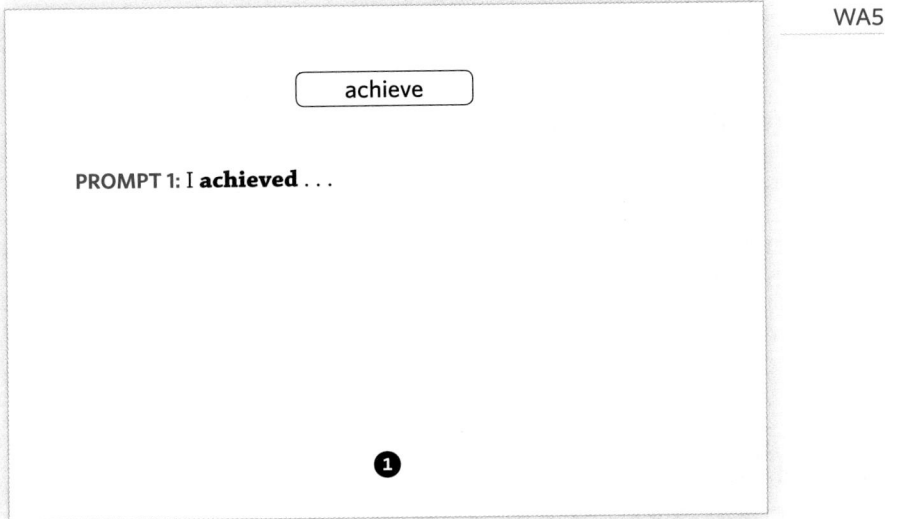

WA5

achieve

PROMPT 1: I **achieved** . . .

❶

PROMPT 1: "I achieved . . ."

After partners have talked, have a few volunteers use the prompt to share their thinking with the class.

Point to the word *achieve* and review the pronunciation and meaning of the word.

INTRODUCE AND USE *CHALLENGE*

3 Introduce and Define *Challenge*

Read this sentence from the first photo caption aloud, emphasizing the word *challenge*: "Folding origami can be a fun challenge."

Explain that a *challenge* is "something that is hard to do or requires a lot of work or effort." Explain that many people enjoy origami because turning a piece of paper into a beautiful object is a challenge. It is hard to do and requires a lot of effort.

Display word card 119 (🌙 WA6) and ask the students to say the word *challenge*.

4 Discuss Challenges

Explain that all of us face challenges, and give a few examples of things that are or were challenges for you.

> **You might say:**
>
> "Learning to square-dance was a challenge for me. It was hard to learn the steps. Sometimes talking to strangers is a challenge for me. It's hard because I feel shy and I worry that I might say something silly. I've had to work hard to overcome that challenge."

Use "Think, Pair, Share" to discuss:

 Q *What is something that is a challenge for you? What is something that is hard for you to do or requires a lot of work?* [Pause; click **1** on WA6 to reveal the prompt.] *Turn to your partner.*

PROMPT 1: "[Doing division] is a challenge because . . ."

After partners have talked, have one or two volunteers use the prompt to share their thinking with the class.

Point to the word *challenge* and review the pronunciation and meaning of the word.

INTRODUCE AND USE *DETERMINATION*

5 Introduce and Define *Determination*

Review that Sadako was a Japanese girl who became ill with leukemia. She believed that if she folded a thousand paper cranes, she would get well. Reread the last paragraph of the article aloud, emphasizing the word *determination*.

Explain that *determination* is "deciding you will do something and then doing it, even if it is difficult." Explain that Sadako had determination. Even though she was very sick, she decided she would fold a thousand paper cranes, and she persisted, or kept making the paper cranes, until she died.

Display word card 120 (WA7) and have the students say the word *determination*.

6 Play "Does Olive Have Determination?"

Tell the students that partners will play "Does Olive Have Determination?" Explain that you will describe something our imaginary third-grade friend Olive is doing, and partners will discuss whether or not Olive has determination and why they think so.

Teacher Note

Support struggling students by asking questions such as "What is a game or sport that is a challenge for you because it is hard to play?" "What is something we do in school that is a challenge and requires you to think and work hard?" and "What is something that takes you a long time to do?"

 **ELL Note**

The Spanish cognate of *determination* is *determinación*.

Teacher Note

You may want to remind the students that they learned the word *persist* earlier and that *persist* means "keep doing something, even though it is difficult." If you persist, you refuse to give up.

Begin by saying:

- *Olive wants to learn to dive. At the pool, her friend Sam shows her how to dive, and Olive gives it a try. She lands on her stomach with a loud smack. "Ouch!" Olive shouts. "That hurt! I'm through with diving! It's not for me!"*

Ask:

 Q *Does Olive have determination? Why?* [Click ❶ on WA7 to reveal the first prompt.] *Turn to your partner.*

PROMPT 1: "Olive [does/does not] have determination because . . ."

After partners have talked, have one or two volunteers use the prompt to share their thinking with the class.

Follow up by discussing as a class:

Q *If Olive had determination, what might she do to learn to dive?*

Click ❷ on word card 120 (WA7) to reveal the next prompt. Have a few volunteers use the prompt to share their thinking with the class.

PROMPT 2: "If Olive had determination, she might . . ."

Using the same procedure, discuss:

- *Olive is working on a jigsaw puzzle. The puzzle is a challenge because there are lots of pieces. After a few minutes, Olive throws up her hands in frustration. "This is a stupid puzzle!" she shouts. "None of the pieces fit!" She gathers up the pieces and puts the puzzle away.*

Point to the word *determination* and review the pronunciation and meaning of the word.

MORE STRATEGY PRACTICE

Play "Use the Clues"

Display the "Use the Clues" chart (◖ WA8).

WA8

> ### Use the Clues
>
> When Alana's friend told her that her painting was spectacular, Alana felt _____. "I'm glad you like it," said Alana with a big smile.
>
> The actor wasn't very graceful. As he was walking across the stage, he _____. Unfortunately, some people in the audience laughed.

Materials

- "Use the Clues" chart (WA8)

Teacher Note

Alternatively, you may wish to write the "Use the Clues" sentences on a sheet of chart paper or where everyone can see them.

Remind the students that when you are reading and you come to a word you do not know, you can sometimes figure out the meaning of the word by reading the sentence that includes the word, or the sentence before or after it, and looking for clues. Explain that the students will play a game called "Use the Clues," in which they look for clues to a word that is missing from a sentence.

Direct the students' attention to the first story on the chart. (Cover up the second set of sentences.) Point to the blank and explain that as you read the sentences aloud, you want them to think about what the missing word might be and which words in the sentences are clues to the missing word. Tell the students that more than one word might make sense as the missing word and that the word does not need to be a vocabulary word. Explain that the students may disagree about the missing word, and that is fine. What is important is that they explain their thinking.

Read the sentences aloud, saying "blank" for the missing word. Ask:

Q *What do you think the missing word might be?*

Have a volunteer share his thinking. Follow up by asking:

Q *Why do you think the missing word is [wonderful]? What words in the sentences are clues that tell you the missing word is [wonderful]?*

Then ask:

Q *Who has a different idea about what the missing word might be?*

Have one or two volunteers share their thinking. Ask each volunteer to explain her thinking about clues to the missing word.

If necessary, explain that the missing word might be *proud, great,* or *exhilarated* and that *spectacular,* "*I'm glad you like it,*" and *with a big smile* are clues to the missing word.

Discuss the second story in the same way. If necessary, explain that the missing word might be *tripped, stumbled, slipped,* or *fell* and that "wasn't very graceful," "As he was walking," and "some people in the audience laughed" are clues to the missing word.

Teacher Note

Accept all words the students can support with context clues from the sentences. If the students cannot suggest a word, or if they suggest words that are not supported by the context, provide a word (such as *pleased*) and point out the context clues that support it.

In this lesson, the students:

- Review and practice using the words *achieve*, *challenge*, and *determination* from Day 3
- Build their speaking and listening skills
- Work in a responsible way

Words Reviewed

achieve
Achieve means "do something successfully, especially something that requires a lot of effort."

challenge
A *challenge* is "something that is hard to do or requires a lot of work or effort."

determination
Determination is "deciding you will do something and then doing it, even if it is difficult."

REVIEW THE WORDS

1 Briefly Review the Words

Display the daily review cards (WA9). Review the pronunciation and meaning of each word.

Use "Think, Pair, Share" to discuss:

 Q *If you were writing a story about something you've done that you are proud of, which of the words might you use? How might you use it?* [Pause; click ❶ on WA9 to reveal the first prompt.] *Turn to your partner.*

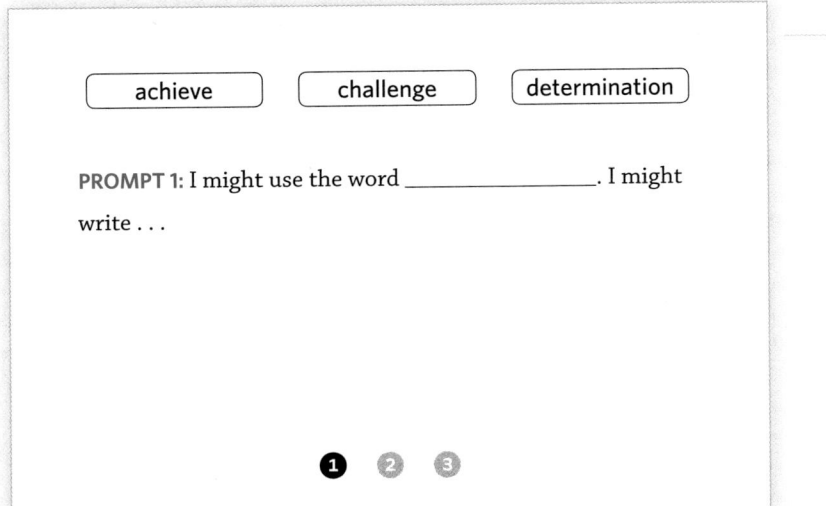

WA9

achieve   challenge   determination

PROMPT 1: I might use the word _____. I might write . . .

❶ ❷ ❸

Materials

- Daily review cards (WA9)
- Copy of this week's family letter (BLM1) for each student
- (Optional) Copy of the "Week 20 Crossword Puzzle" (BLM3) for each student

PROMPT 1: "I might use the word [*challenge*]. I might write . . ."

After partners have talked, have a few volunteers use the prompt to share their thinking with the class.

PRACTICE USING THE WORDS

2 Answer Questions About the Words

Ask:

 Q *Does it take determination to achieve something? Why?* [Click **2** on WA9 to reveal the prompt.] *Turn to your partner.*

PROMPT 2: "It [does/does not] take determination to achieve something because . . ."

After partners have talked, have one or two volunteers use the prompt to share their thinking with the class.

Using the same procedure, discuss:

 Q *Does it take determination to deal with a challenge? Why?* [Click **3** to reveal the next prompt.] *Turn to your partner.*

PROMPT 3: "It [does/does not] take determination to deal with a challenge because . . ."

Teacher Note

Send home with each student a copy of this week's family letter (BLM1). Encourage the students to talk about this week's words with their families.

Teacher Note

To provide students with additional review of words taught during Weeks 19 and 20, you might distribute a copy of the "Week 20 Crossword Puzzle" (BLM3) to each student.

In this lesson, the students:

- Review words learned earlier
- Build their speaking and listening skills
- Contribute ideas that are different from their partners' ideas

Words Reviewed

convenient
If something is convenient, it is useful because it makes our lives easier or more comfortable.

durable
If something is durable, it is tough. It can last a long time even if it is used a lot.

intense
Intense means "very great or strong."

refreshing
If something is refreshing, it makes you feel fresh (lively or not tired) and strong again.

secure
Secure means "safe and protected."

REVIEW THE WORDS

1 Briefly Review the Words

Display the ongoing review cards (◗ WA10). Review the pronunciation and meaning of each word.

PRACTICE USING THE WORDS

2 Introduce the Game "Does That Make Sense?"

Tell the students that partners will play a game called "Does That Make Sense?" Explain that you will read a sentence that includes one or more of the vocabulary words. Partners will decide whether the word makes sense in the sentence and explain why they think so.

Tell the students that before they play the game in pairs, they will practice playing as a class. Point to the words *durable* and *secure* on the ongoing review cards (WA10) and explain that the first sentence includes the words *durable* and *secure*.

Materials

- Ongoing review cards (WA10)
- "Class Vocabulary Assessment Record" sheet (CA1)
- Class set of the "Individual Vocabulary Assessment: Word Check 5" answer sheet (IA1)
- Class set of the "Individual Vocabulary Assessment Student Record" sheet (SR1)
- "Individual Vocabulary Assessment Class Record" sheet (CR1)
- (Optional) Class set of the "Student Self-assessment" response sheet (SA1)

Read the following sentence aloud twice:

- *Alan felt secure walking across the durable wooden bridge.*

Ask:

Q *Do the words* durable *and* secure *make sense in the sentence? Why do you think that?*

Give the students a few moments to think about the questions. Then click ❶ on the ongoing review cards (WA10) to reveal the prompt and have one or two volunteers use the prompt to share their thinking with the class.

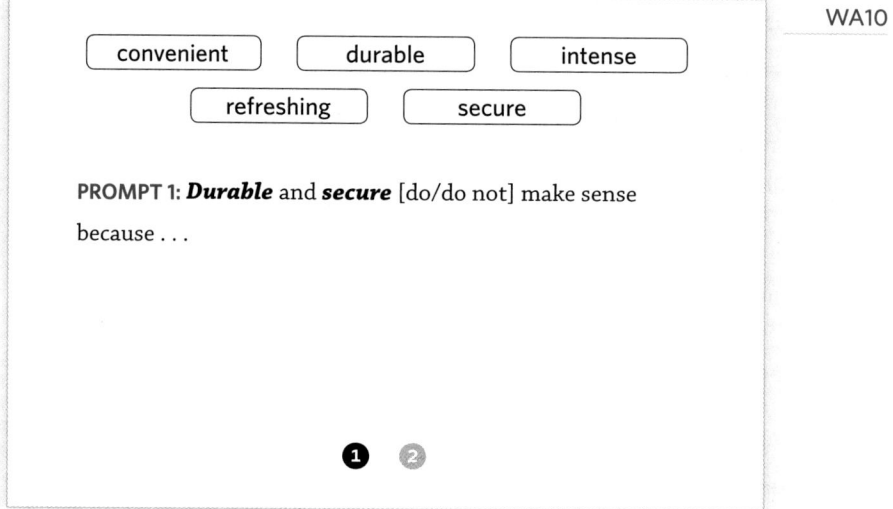

PROMPT 1: "*Durable* and *secure* [do/do not] make sense because . . ."

❸ Play the Game in Pairs

Now play the game in pairs. Point to the word *convenient* and explain that the next sentence includes the word *conveniently*. Remind the students that as they listen to the sentence, they are to think about whether the word *conveniently* makes sense in the sentence. Then partners will share their thinking with each other.

Read the following scenario aloud twice:

- *The new playground is conveniently located across town from Maya's house.*

Ask:

 Q *Does the word* conveniently *make sense in the sentence? Why do you think that?* [Click ❷ to reveal the next prompt.] *Turn to your partner.*

PROMPT 2: "The word [*conveniently*] [does/does not] make sense because . . ."

After partners have talked, have a few volunteers use the prompt to share their thinking with the class.

Use the same procedure to discuss the following scenarios:

[refreshing]

- *On a hot summer day, David has a refreshing bowl of warm soup to cool down.*

[intense]

- *The intense wind knocked down power lines and trees.*

 Assessment Notes

CLASS VOCABULARY ASSESSMENT NOTE

Observe the students and ask yourself:

- Are the students able to explain why the vocabulary words do or do not make sense in the sentences?
- Do they use the vocabulary words to explain their thinking?
- Are they using the words in their writing?

Record your observations on the "Class Vocabulary Assessment Record" sheet (CA1); see page 188 of the *Assessment Resource Book*.

Use the following suggestions to support struggling students:

- If **only a few students** understand a word's meaning, reteach the word using the vocabulary lesson in which it was first taught as a model.
- If **about half of the students** understand a word's meaning, provide further practice by having the students play "Imagine That!" (see Week 1, Day 5, Step 2).

INDIVIDUAL VOCABULARY ASSESSMENT NOTE

Before continuing with the week 21 lesson, take this opportunity to assess individual students' understanding of words taught in Weeks 17–20 by using the "Individual Vocabulary Assessment: Word Check 5" answer sheet (IA1) on page 192 of the *Assessment Resource Book*. For instructions on administering this assessment, see "Completing the Individual Vocabulary Assessment" on page 189 of the *Assessment Resource Book*.

STUDENT SELF-ASSESSMENT NOTE

In addition to or in place of the Individual Vocabulary Assessment, you might have each student evaluate her understanding of words taught in Weeks 17–20 using the "Student Self-assessment" response sheet (SA1). For instructions on administering this assessment, see "Completing the Student Self-assessment" on page 193 of the *Assessment Resource Book*.

Origami

The Art of Japanese Paper Folding

Could you fold a square of paper into a graceful fish or a long-stemmed flower? Origami, or Japanese paper folding, is an art form practiced by many people. In origami, a simple sheet of paper can become a spectacular piece of art.

Japan

Japan is an island country that lies near the east coasts of Russia, Korea, and China. It is made up of four major islands.

Ancient Art Form, Modern Appeal

Paper was invented in China and brought to Japan around the year 500. Because paper was rare back then, paper decorations were reserved for special ceremonies. As paper became more common, people started to make paper models for fun. By the 1800s, children in Japan and Europe were learning the art of folding paper into interesting shapes.

Traditionally, origami objects are created using square pieces of paper that range in size from 1 to 15 inches wide. Six inches is one of the most common sizes. The paper is usually colored or patterned on one or both sides. The paper square is not usually cut or glued but is shaped by making a series of creases and folds. Some artists use wet paper to achieve a more rounded look; others experiment with unusual materials, such as cloth, wire, sheet metal, and even toilet paper.

A Worldwide Craze

Today, there are fans of origami worldwide. The most popular shapes are still traditional Japanese models, such as flowers and birds, but many people are inspired by more unusual-looking life-forms, such as scorpions, armadillos, and horned beetles.

Some people submit their paper creations to origami contests. Some origami contests have a theme such as plants or prehistoric animals. In other contests, there are categories such as best original design, best technical folding, and best miniature model. Winners of the Massachusetts Institute of Technology origami contest have included precise models of a butterfly, a sailboat, and a gold-colored beaver.

Origami is a tradition that has been passed on through many generations. Artists fold origami to express themselves. Scientists and engineers use it to explore shapes and angles to invent new technology. Teachers sometimes use origami as a tool to help kids learn math. And many people fold paper just because it's fun.

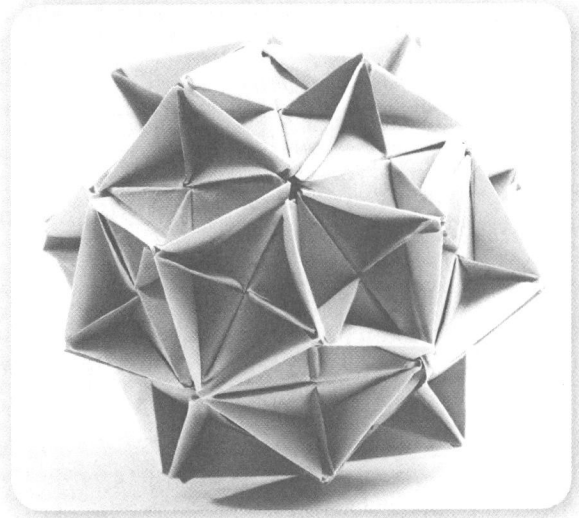

Folding origami can be a fun challenge. Some complicated origami figures are constructed using several sheets of paper.

One Thousand Paper Cranes

In the city of Hiroshima, Japan, people bring thousands of paper cranes to a memorial park every year. They do this to remember a girl

A 1,000-crane chain takes a long time for one person to make, but it can be completed quickly if many people join in.

named Sadako Sasaki. After World War II (1939–1945), Sadako became ill with leukemia, a form of cancer. She had heard the legend that if a person folds 1,000 paper cranes, he or she will be granted one wish. Her wish was to become healthy again.

Sadako decided to fold 1,000 paper cranes. For months, she kept folding and folding, but on October 25, 1955, she died, with 350 cranes left to make. Her friends completed the remaining cranes for her. Sadako's determination to finish her project has come to stand for a wish for peace. Today, people across the world fold paper cranes and string them into chains. They send them to the memorial park to remember Sadako's dream.

RESOURCES

Read-aloud

- *Morning Meals Around the World* by Maryellen Gregoire, illustrated by Jeff Yesh

Functional Texts

- "Lincoln School Lunch Calendar for the week of May 21–25" (see page 447)
- "How to Make a Paper Airplane" (see page 448)

More Strategy Practice

- "Discuss Another Meaning of *Tip*"

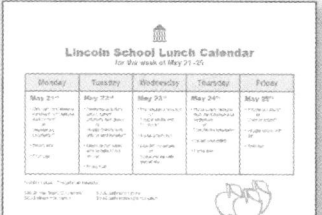

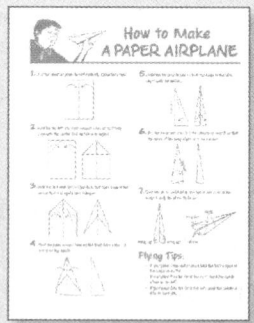

 ## Online Resources

Visit the CCC Learning Hub (ccclearninghub.org) to find your online resources for this week.

Whiteboard Activities

- WA1–WA9

Reproducibles

- Week 21 family letter (BLM1)
- (Optional) "Week 21 Word Cards" (BLM2)

OVERVIEW

Words Taught	Words Reviewed
require	graceful
serve	lively
prefer	mature
vertical	successful
horizontal	unsuccessful
tip	

Word-learning Strategies

- Recognizing synonyms (review)
- Recognizing antonyms (review)
- Recognizing words with multiple meanings (review)

Vocabulary Focus

- Students learn and use six words from or about a book and functional texts.
- Students review synonyms and antonyms.
- Students review words with multiple meanings.
- Students review words learned earlier.
- Students build their speaking and listening skills.

Social Development Focus

- Students develop the skill of asking clarifying questions.
- Students listen respectfully to the thinking of others and share their own.

⏱ DO AHEAD

✓ Prior to Day 3, collect two pieces of paper to fold during the discussion of the words *vertical* and *horizontal*.

✓ (Optional) Prior to Day 3, review the more strategy practice activity "Discuss Another Meaning of *Tip*" on page 442.

✓ Prior to Day 4, visit the CCC Learning Hub (ccclearninghub.org) to access and print this week's family letter (BLM1). Make enough copies to send one letter home with each student.

✓ (Optional) Visit the CCC Learning Hub (ccclearninghub.org) to access and print "Week 21 Word Cards" (BLM2). These cards can be used to provide your students with more opportunities to review the words.

Materials

- *Morning Meals Around the World*
- "Lincoln School Lunch Calendar for the week of May 21–25" (see page 447)
- Word card 121 (WA1)
- Word card 122 (WA2)
- Word card 123 (WA3)
- (Optional) *Making Meaning Student Response Book*

In this lesson, the students:

- Learn and use the words *require, serve,* and *prefer*
- Review synonyms
- Build their speaking and listening skills
- Listen respectfully to the thinking of others and share their own
- Ask clarifying questions

Words Taught

require
Require means "need."

serve (p. 23)
Serve means "give someone food or drink."

prefer
Prefer means "like better." If you prefer something, you like it better than something else.

INTRODUCE AND USE *REQUIRE*

1 Introduce and Define *Require* and Review Synonyms

Show page 23 of *Morning Meals Around the World* and review that this is a recipe for Mexican breakfast quesadillas. Remind the students that a recipe gives directions for how to make or cook something.

Point to the words "What you need" in the recipe and explain that this part of the recipe lists what is required, or needed, to make Mexican breakfast quesadillas. Tell the students that *require* is the first word they will discuss today, and explain that *require* and *need* are *synonyms*, or "words that mean the same thing or almost the same thing." Remind the students that some of the things that are required, or needed, to make a Mexican breakfast quesadilla are 2 flour tortillas, 1 onion, and 2 thin slices of ham.

Display word card 121 (WA1) and have the students say the word *require.*

2 Play "What Is Required?"

Tell the students that they will play a game called "What Is Required?" Explain that you will describe a fun event the students might attend, and partners will discuss what is required, or needed, for the event.

🌐 ELL Note

The Spanish cognate of *require* is *requerir.*

Teacher Note

If you started a synonym chart, add *require* and *need* to it.

Begin by saying:

- *A day at the beach*

Ask:

 Q *What are things that are required to spend a fun day at the beach?* [Click ❶ on WA1 to reveal the first prompt.] *Turn to your partner.*

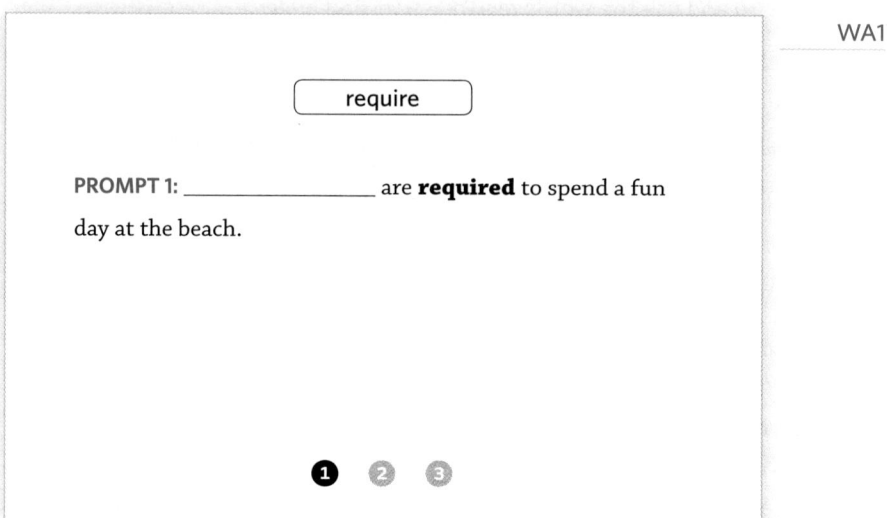

PROMPT 1: "[Sunscreen, towels, and swimsuits] are required to spend a fun day at the beach."

After partners have talked, have a few volunteers use the prompt to share their thinking with the class.

Using the same procedure, discuss one or both of the following:

- *A picnic in the park*

 Q *What are things that are required for a picnic in the park?* [Click ❷ to reveal the next prompt.] *Turn to your partner.*

PROMPT 2: "[Blankets, food, and plates] are required for a picnic in the park."

- *A camping trip*

 Q *What are things that are required for a camping trip?* [Click ❸ to reveal the prompt.] *Turn to your partner.*

PROMPT 3: "[A tent, firewood, and flashlights] are required for a camping trip."

Point to the word *require* and review the pronunciation and meaning of the word.

INTRODUCE AND USE *SERVE*

3 Introduce and Define *Serve*

Show the recipe again, point to "What to do," and review that this part of the recipe lists the steps you follow to make Mexican breakfast quesadillas. Ask the students to listen carefully as you read the last step. Then read step 8 aloud, emphasizing the word *serve*.

Tell the students that the next word they will learn today is *serve* and that *serve* means "give someone food or drink." Explain that after you make the quesadillas, you serve them, or give them to someone to eat, with sour cream and salsa.

Display word card 122 (WA2) and have the students say the word *serve*.

ELL Note

The Spanish cognate of *serve* is *servir*.

4 Discuss Foods Served

Give some examples of foods or drinks you have recently served to family or friends or been served.

> **You might say:**
>
> "When my parents came over for dinner this weekend, I served, or gave them to eat, a delicious vegetable stir-fry with broccoli and tofu. Last night I went out to dinner with my son. I ordered a big plate of spaghetti with a salad and garlic bread, and a waiter served me my food."

Ask:

 Q *What food does our cafeteria serve, or give us, for lunch?* [Click ❶ on WA2 to reveal the first prompt.] *Turn to your partner.*

PROMPT 1: "Our cafeteria serves [sandwiches and apples] for lunch."

After partners have talked, have a few volunteers use the prompt to share their thinking with the class.

Then discuss as a class:

Q *If you were planning a party, what foods would you serve?* [Click ❷ to reveal the next prompt.] *Turn to your partner.*

PROMPT 2: "I would serve [lasagna and salad] at my party."

After partners have talked, have a few volunteers use the prompt to share their thinking with the class.

Point to the word *serve* and review the pronunciation and meaning of the word.

INTRODUCE AND USE *PREFER*

5 Introduce and Define *Prefer*

Teacher Note

You might have the students bring their *Making Meaning Student Response Books* to the rug to refer to as you discuss the functional text used in today's lesson.

Show the "Lincoln School Lunch Calendar," and review that this functional text shows a week of lunches being served at Lincoln School. Review that on some days the students at Lincoln School have a choice of what to eat. For example, on Monday they might have a "Deli ham and cheese sandwich with lettuce and tomato" or a "Vegetarian sandwich." On Wednesday, they might have "Fish nuggets with dip" or "Veggie sticks with hummus."

Explain that when the students at Lincoln School have a choice of foods to eat, they can select the foods that they prefer, and tell the students that *prefer* is the last word they will learn today. Explain that *prefer* means "like better" and that if you prefer something, you like it better than something else. Remind the students that on Monday the students at Lincoln School can choose either a ham and cheese sandwich or a vegetarian sandwich, whichever they prefer, or like better.

 **ELL Note**

The Spanish cognate of *prefer* is *preferir*.

Display word card 123 (WA3) and have students say the word *prefer*.

6 Play "Which Do You Prefer?"

Tell the students that they will play a game called "Which Do You Prefer?" Explain that you will describe two things and partners will discuss which one they prefer, or like better, and why.

Begin by saying:

* *Reading a book or writing a story*

Ask:

 Q *Which do you prefer: reading a book or writing a story? Why?* [Click ❶ on WA3 to reveal the prompt.] *Turn to your partner.*

PROMPT 1: "I prefer [writing a story] because . . ."

After partners have talked, have a few volunteers use the prompt to share their thinking with the class.

Using the same procedure, discuss one or more of the following:

* *Spring or winter*
* *Riding a bike or swimming*
* *Breakfast or dinner*

Point to the word *prefer* and review the pronunciation and meaning of the word.

In this lesson, the students:

- Review and practice using the words *require*, *serve*, and *prefer* from Day 1
- Build their speaking and listening skills
- Listen respectfully to the thinking of others and share their own

Words Reviewed

require
Require means "need."

serve
Serve means "give someone food or drink."

prefer
Prefer means "like better." If you prefer something, you like it better than something else.

REVIEW THE WORDS

1 Briefly Review the Words

Display the daily review cards (WA4). Review the pronunciation and meaning of each word.

Ask:

 Q *Which of the words would you use when ordering something from a restaurant? Why?* [Click **1** on WA4 to reveal the first prompt.] *Turn to your partner.*

WA4

| require | serve | prefer |

PROMPT 1: I would use the word _____.

I might say . . .

1 **2** **3** **4**

Materials

- Daily review cards (WA4)

PROMPT 1: "I would use the word [*prefer*]. I might say . . ."

After partners have talked, have a few volunteers use the prompt to share their thinking with the class.

PRACTICE USING THE WORDS

2 Discuss "Would You?" Questions

Explain that you will ask some questions that partners will discuss.

Ask:

Q *Would you serve foods you prefer at a family party? Why?* [Click ❷ on WA4 to reveal the prompt.] *Turn to your partner.*

PROMPT 2: "I [would/would not] serve foods I prefer at a family party because . . ."

After partners have talked, have a few volunteers use the prompt to share their thinking with the class.

Using the same procedure, discuss:

Q *What is required to build a sand castle? Why?* [Click ❸ to reveal the prompt.] *Turn to your partner.*

PROMPT 3: "[Sand, shovels, and water] are required to build a sand castle because . . ."

Q *What games do you prefer to play? Why?* [Click ❹ to reveal the prompt.] *Turn to your partner.*

PROMPT 4: "I prefer to play [kickball] because . . ."

In this lesson, the students:

- Learn and use the words *vertical, horizontal,* and *tip*
- Review antonyms
- Review words with multiple meanings
- Build their speaking and listening skills
- Ask clarifying questions

Words Taught

vertical (p. 448)
If something is vertical, it is positioned up and down rather than from side to side.

horizontal
If something is horizontal, it is positioned from side to side rather than up and down.

tip (p. 448)
A *tip* is a "piece of advice or useful information."

INTRODUCE AND USE *VERTICAL* AND *HORIZONTAL*

1 Introduce and Define *Vertical*

Show the functional text "How to Make a Paper Airplane," and remind the students that this is a list of steps for making a paper airplane.

Point to step 1 and read it aloud, emphasizing the word *vertically.* Tell the students that the word *vertical* can be found in *vertically,* and that *vertical* is the first word they will learn today. Explain that if something is vertical it is positioned up and down rather than from side to side. Explain that the first step in making a paper airplane is to fold a piece of paper vertically, or so that the folded paper is positioned up to down rather than side to side. Model folding a piece of paper vertically. Point out that the crease, or fold, is vertical, or up and down.

Display word cards 124–125 ( WA5) and reveal word card 124. Have the students say the word *vertical.*

Materials

- "How to Make a Paper Airplane" (see page 448)
- Word cards 124–125 (WA5)
- Word card 126 (WA6)
- Two pieces of paper (prepared ahead)
- (Optional) *Making Meaning Student Response Book*

🌐 ELL Note

The Spanish cognate of *vertical* is *vertical.*

Teacher Note

You might have the students bring their *Making Meaning Student Response Books* to the rug to refer to as you discuss the functional text used in today's lesson.

Teacher Note

If you started an antonym chart, add *vertical* and *horizontal* to it.

2 Introduce and Define *Horizontal* and Review Antonyms

Tell the students that *horizontal* is the next word they will learn today, and explain that *horizontal* and *vertical* are *antonyms*, or "words with opposite meanings." Explain that if something is horizontal, it is positioned from side to side rather than up and down. Model folding the second piece of paper horizontally, pointing out that the fold is horizontal, or side to side. Show the two folded pieces of paper together.

Click to reveal word card 125 on word cards 124–125 (WA5) and have the students say the word *horizontal*.

3 Play "Vertical or Horizontal?"

Tell the students that they will play a game called "Vertical or Horizontal?" Explain that you will ask the students to picture something in their minds, and then you will ask them if the position of the thing they pictured is vertical (up and down) or horizontal (side to side).

Begin by having the students picture the following:

- *A tree standing straight and tall in the school yard*

Ask:

 Q *Is a tree standing straight and tall vertical or horizontal?* [Click ❶ on WA5 to reveal the prompt.] *Turn to your partner.*

WA5

> vertical   horizontal
>
> **PROMPT 1:** _____ is [**vertical/horizontal**].
>
> ❶

PROMPT 1: "[A tree standing straight and tall] is [vertical]."

After partners have talked, have a few volunteers use the prompt to share their thinking with the class.

Then have the students picture the following scenario:

- *A tree lying flat on the ground after a storm*

Q *Is a tree lying flat on the ground vertical or horizontal?* [Click to reveal the prompt.] *Turn to your partner.*

Have the students picture one or more of the following pairs:

- *A soldier standing straight and tall at attention*
- *A soldier lying flat on her back, asleep on a cot*

- *A mountain rising high into the air*
- *A flat stretch of desert going on for miles and miles*

- *A table top*
- *A table leg*

Point to the words *vertical* and *horizontal* and review the pronunciation and meaning of each word.

INTRODUCE AND USE *TIP*

4 Introduce and Define *Tip*

Point to the "Flying Tips" section of "How to Make a Paper Airplane" and explain that the directions for making a paper airplane include a section called "Flying Tips." Ask the students to listen as you read the tips. Then read "Flying Tips" aloud.

Explain that *tip* is the last word the students will learn today and that a *tip* is a "piece of advice or useful information." Explain that this section has tips, or advice or useful information, about what to do if your paper airplane is not flying properly.

Display word card 126 (◖ WA6) and have the students say the word *tip*.

5 Discuss Tips the Students Would Give

Explain that you will describe a situation in which people need tips, or advice, and partners will discuss the tips they might give.

Begin by describing this situation:

- *Vinnie is a new student at our school. He wants to make friends, but he is shy.*

Q *What tips, or advice, would you give Vinnie to make new friends?* [Click ❶ on WA6 to reveal the prompt.] *Turn to your partner.*

PROMPT 1: "My tip would be . . ."

After partners have talked, have a few volunteers use the prompt to share their thinking with the class.

Using the same procedure, discuss:

* *Your friend wants to learn to ride a bike.*

Q *What tips would you give your friend who wants to learn to ride a bike?* [Point to the prompt.] *Turn to your partner.*

Point to the word *tip* and review the pronunciation and meaning of the word.

MORE STRATEGY PRACTICE

Discuss Another Meaning of *Tip*

Remind the students that words often have more than one meaning and sometimes the meanings are very different. Write the word *tip* where everyone can see it, pronounce it, and review that a *tip* is a "piece of advice or useful information."

Ask and discuss as a class:

Q *What else do you know about the word* tip?

If necessary, follow up by asking:

Q *What do you mean when you say the tip of the pencil is sharp?*

Q *What do you mean when you say you gave the waiter a tip?*

Q *What do you mean when you say that something is about to tip over?*

PROMPTS: "*Tip* also means . . ." or "If the tip of the pencil is sharp . . ."

Have a few volunteers use the prompt to share their thinking with the class.

Explain that *tip* can also mean "the end point of something," "an extra amount of money," or "to fall or cause something to fall."

In this lesson, the students:

- Review and practice using the words *vertical, horizontal,* and *tip* from Day 3
- Build their speaking and listening skills
- Listen respectfully to the thinking of others and share their own

Words Reviewed

vertical
If something is vertical, it is positioned up and down rather than from side to side.

horizontal
If something is horizontal, it is positioned from side to side rather than up and down.

tip
A *tip* is a "piece of advice or useful information."

REVIEW THE WORDS

1 Briefly Review the Words

Display the daily review cards (WA7). Review the pronunciation and meaning of each word.

Ask:

 Q *Which of the words you learned yesterday do you think is particularly interesting? Why?* [Click ❶ on WA7 to reveal the first prompt.] *Turn to your partner.*

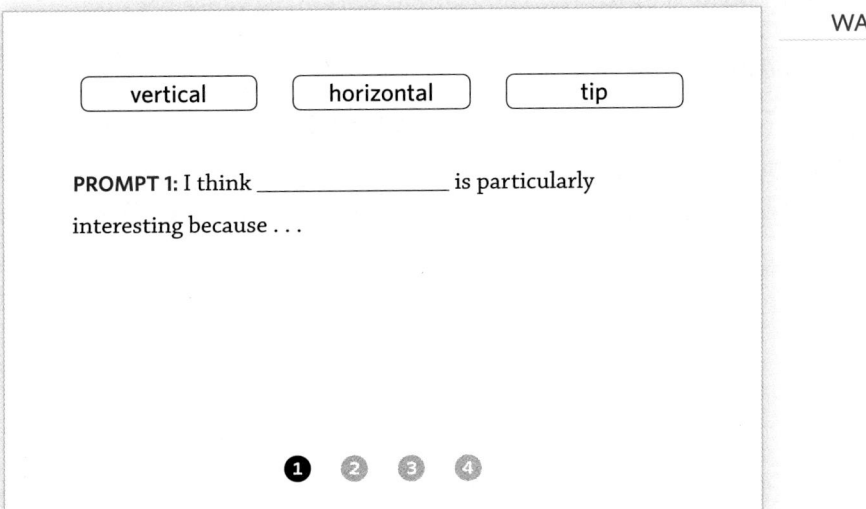

WA7

vertical   horizontal   tip

PROMPT 1: I think _____ is particularly
interesting because . . .

❶ ② ③ ④

PROMPT 1: "I think [*tip*] is particularly interesting because . . ."

After partners have talked, have a few volunteers use the prompt to share their thinking with the class.

PRACTICE USING THE WORDS

2 Review the Game "Does That Make Sense?"

Tell the students that partners will play a game called "Does That Make Sense?" Remind the students that you will read a sentence that includes one of the vocabulary words. Partners will decide whether the word makes sense in the sentence and explain why they think so.

Read the following sentences aloud twice:

- *The lamp had fallen over. When we stood it upright, it was horizontal.*

Ask:

 Q *Does the word* horizontal *make sense in the sentence? Why do you think that?* [Click **2** on WA7 to reveal the next prompt.] *Turn to your partner.*

PROMPT 2: "The word *horizontal* [does/does not] make sense because . . ."

After partners have talked, have a few volunteers use the prompt to share their thinking with the class.

Use the same procedure to discuss the following sentences:

[tip]

- *While Chloe was packing for her camping trip, her mom gave her a tip to bring warm socks and a hat.*

 Q *Does the word* tip *make sense in the sentence? Why do you think that?* [Click **3** to reveal the prompt.] *Turn to your partner.*

PROMPT 3: "The word *tip* [does/does not] make sense because . . ."

[horizontal]

- *During my nap, I was lying vertical on my bed.*

 Q *Does the word* vertical *make sense in the sentence? Why do you think that?* [Click **4** to reveal the prompt.] *Turn to your partner.*

PROMPT 4: "The word *vertical* [does/does not] make sense because . . ."

Teacher Note

If the students struggle to answer the questions, call for their attention. Reread the sentence aloud, and explain that *horizontal* does not make sense in the sentence because the lamp would be vertical, or positioned up and down, after it was returned to an upright position. If it were horizontal, it would be lying flat. Then read the next sentence and discuss it as a class, rather than in pairs.

Teacher Note

Send home with each student a copy of this week's family letter (BLM1). Encourage the students to talk about this week's words with their families.

In this lesson, the students:

- Review words learned earlier
- Build their speaking and listening skills
- Listen respectfully to the thinking of others and share their own
- Ask clarifying questions

Words Reviewed

graceful
Graceful means "moving in a smooth and beautiful way."

lively
Lively means "active." Someone who is lively is energetic and full of life.

mature
Mature means "grown up or adult." A mature person is sensible and reasonable. He or she is not being immature or childish.

successful
If you are successful, you do what you set out to do or do something well.

unsuccessful
Unsuccessful means "not successful." If you are unsuccessful, you do not accomplish what you set out to do.

REVIEW THE WORDS

1 Briefly Review the Words

Display the ongoing review cards (WA8) and review the pronunciation and meaning of each word.

PRACTICE USING THE WORDS

2 Review the Activity "Describe the Character"

Tell the students that partners will do an activity called "Describe the Character." Remind the students that you will read a story aloud, and partners will decide which vocabulary word best describes the main character of the story and explain why they think so.

1. Display the ongoing review activity (WA9) and click ❶ to reveal the first story. Point to the story and read it aloud twice, slowly and clearly.

   - Story 1: *Oliver wants to learn how to play the flute, but after his first lesson he is frustrated. He doesn't practice and finally stops going to his lessons. He never learns to play the flute.*

Materials

- Ongoing review cards (WA8)
- Ongoing review activity (WA9)

Teacher Note

Each sentence on the weekly review activity (WA9) has a corresponding number: the first story is ❶; the second story is ❷; the third story is ❸; and so on. To play the game, click the corresponding number four times:

- The first click reveals the story.
- The second click reveals the prompt.
- The third click highlights the correct answer.
- The fourth click clears the screen.

2. Point to the vocabulary words and ask:

   Q *Which vocabulary word best describes Oliver? Why?* [Click **❶** again and read the prompt aloud.] *Turn to your partner.*

   PROMPT 1: "[*Unsuccessful*] best describes Oliver because . . ."

3. After partners have talked, have a few volunteers use the prompt to share their thinking with the class. After they have shared, conclude the discussion by clicking **❶** a third time to highlight the correct vocabulary word.

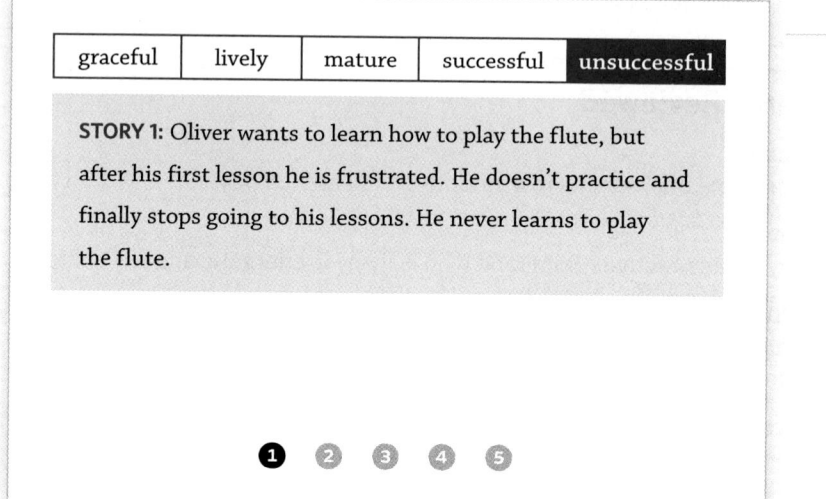

WA9

| graceful | lively | mature | successful | **unsuccessful** |

STORY 1: Oliver wants to learn how to play the flute, but after his first lesson he is frustrated. He doesn't practice and finally stops going to his lessons. He never learns to play the flute.

❶ ② ③ ④ ⑤

Teacher Note

If you are not using an interactive whiteboard, write each story and the words where everyone can see them.

4. Finally, click **❶** to clear the screen.

Using the same procedure, discuss the following stories:

- Story 2: *Laura danced beautifully across the stage. She spun around lightly on her toes while her arms flowed through the air to the sound of the music.* (graceful)

- Story 3: *Otis was full of energy. He ran and jumped and skipped and somersaulted hour after hour. He never seemed to grow tired.* (lively)

- Story 4: *Maria wanted to build a model plane for her grandpa's birthday present. She spent hours and hours working on it, and finally got the airplane built. Her grandpa loved his gift.* (successful)

- Story 5: *Grady is reading quietly at the library. His friend Orlando yells and makes a funny face at him, but Grady ignores Orlando and continues to read.* (mature)

Lincoln School Lunch Calendar
for the week of May 21–25

Monday	Tuesday	Wednesday	Thursday	Friday
May 21	**May 22**	**May 23**	**May 24**	**May 25**
• Deli ham and cheese sandwich with lettuce and tomato* or Vegetarian sandwich**	• Homemade turkey with mashed potatoes and gravy or Veggie burger with lettuce and tomato**	• Fish nuggets with dip or Veggie sticks with hummus**	• Homemade lasagna with meat sauce and vegetable or Vegetarian lasagna**	• Pepperoni pizza* or Cheese pizza**
• Snack mix	• Mixed green salad with veggie sticks on top	• Dinner roll	• Breadstick	• Veggie sticks with dip
• Fruit cup	• Fresh fruit	• Low-fat ice cream or Strawberries with yogurt dip	• Fresh fruit	• Fruit cup

*contains pork   **vegetarian selection

How to Make
A PAPER AIRPLANE

1. Fold the sheet of paper in half vertically. Open the paper.

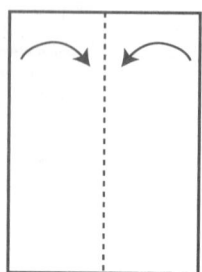

2. Fold the top left and right corners down so that they align with the center fold and form triangles.

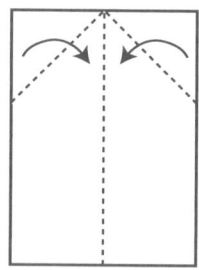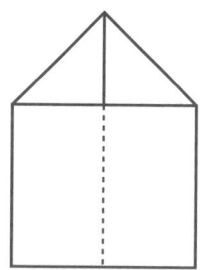

3. Fold the left and right corners in so that they align at the center fold and again form triangles.

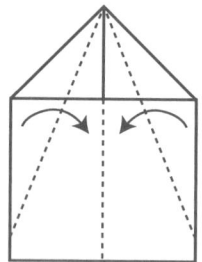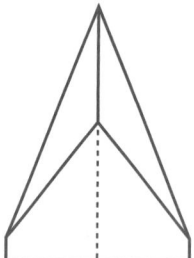

4. Fold the paper in half, keeping the folds from steps 1, 2, and 3 on the inside.

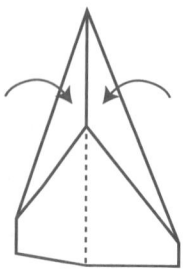

5. Fold the top wing in half so that the edge of the wing aligns with the rudder.

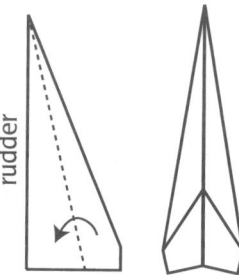

6. Flip the plane over and fold the other wing in half so that the edge of the wing aligns with the rudder.

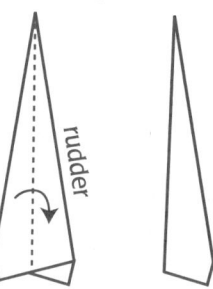

7. Open the plane and fold up the tips at the back of the wings to help the plane fly better.

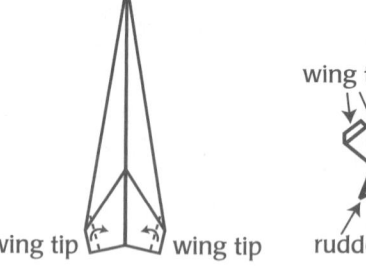

wing tip   wing tip   wings
            wing tips
                             rudder

Flying Tips:

- If your plane dives and crashes, fold the back edges of the wings up a little.
- If your plane flies too far to the right, bend the rudder a little to the left.
- If your plane flies too far to the left, bend the rudder a little to the right.

448

Week 22

RESOURCES

Read-aloud

- *Flashy Fantastic Rain Forest Frogs* by Dorothy Hinshaw Patent, illustrated by Kendahl Jan Jubb

More Strategy Practice

- "Discuss Another Meaning of *Fantastic*"

Extensions

- "Discuss the Compound Word *Painkiller*"
- "Explore Domain-specific Words: *Rain Forests*"

More ELL Support

- "Discuss a Pair of Illustrations in *Flashy Fantastic Rain Forest Frogs*"

Assessment Resource Book

- Week 22 vocabulary assessment

 ## Online Resources

Visit the CCC Learning Hub (ccclearninghub.org) to find your online resources for this week.

Whiteboard Activities

- WA1–WA11

Assessment Form

- "Class Vocabulary Assessment Record" sheet (CA1)

Reproducibles

- Week 22 family letter (BLM1)
- (Optional) "Week 22 Word Cards" (BLM2)
- (Optional) "Week 22 Crossword Puzzle" (BLM3)

OVERVIEW

Words Taught	Words Reviewed
flashy	challenge
fantastic	prefer
diverse	require
avoid	serve
deadly	spectacular
threatened	

Word-learning Strategy

- Recognizing words with multiple meanings (review)

Vocabulary Focus

- Students learn and use six words from or about the book.
- Students review words with multiple meanings.
- Students review words learned earlier.
- Students build their speaking and listening skills.

Social Development Focus

- Students develop the skill of asking clarifying questions.
- Students listen respectfully to the thinking of others and share their own.
- Students share their partners' thinking.

⏱ DO AHEAD

✓ (Optional) Prior to Day 1, review the more strategy practice activity "Discuss Another Meaning of *Fantastic*" on page 457.

✓ Prior to Day 4, visit the CCC Learning Hub (ccclearninghub.org) to access and print this week's family letter (BLM1). Make enough copies to send one letter home with each student.

(continues)

⏱ DO AHEAD *(continued)*

✓ Prior to Day 5, make a copy of the "Class Vocabulary Assessment Record" sheet (CA1); see page 196 of the *Assessment Resource Book*.

✓ (Optional) Visit the CCC Learning Hub (ccclearninghub.org) to access and print the following materials: "Week 22 Word Cards" (BLM2) and "Week 22 Crossword Puzzle" (BLM3). These materials can be used to provide your students with more opportunities to review the words.

In this lesson, the students:

- Learn and use the words *flashy*, *fantastic*, and *diverse*
- Review recognizing words with multiple meanings
- Build their speaking and listening skills
- Share their partners' thinking
- Ask clarifying questions

Words Taught

flashy (p. 3)
Flashy means "very big, bright, or expensive."
Something that is flashy catches your attention.

fantastic (p. 3)
Fantastic means "strange, unusual, or unbelievable."

diverse
Diverse means "different from one another."

INTRODUCE AND USE *FLASHY*

1 Introduce and Define *Flashy*

Briefly review *Flashy Fantastic Rain Forest Frogs*.

Show pages 2–3 and read the first paragraph on page 3 aloud, emphasizing the word *flashy*.

Explain that *flashy* means "very big, bright, or expensive." Point to the frogs in the illustration and explain that the author describes rain forest frogs as flashy because they are brightly colored. Point out that these flashy frogs are much more colorful than ordinary green or brown frogs.

Display word card 127 (WA1) and have the students say the word *flashy*.

2 Talk About Flashy Things

Explain that something that is flashy catches your attention. You notice it because it is very big, bright, or expensive. Give some examples of flashy things you have seen or own.

> **You might say:**
>
> "My neighbor has a flashy motorcycle. It is very big, bright red, and has lots of shiny chrome. People stop and look at it whenever she rides it. I have a flashy dress that I wear to parties. It is bright green with gold sparkles. People always notice the dress when I wear it."

Materials

- *Flashy Fantastic Rain Forest Frogs*
- Word card 127 (WA1)
- Word card 128 (WA2)
- Word card 129 (WA3)

Ask:

 Q *What do you have or what have you seen that is flashy? Why do you think it is flashy? [Click ❶ on WA1 to reveal the first prompt.] Turn to your partner.*

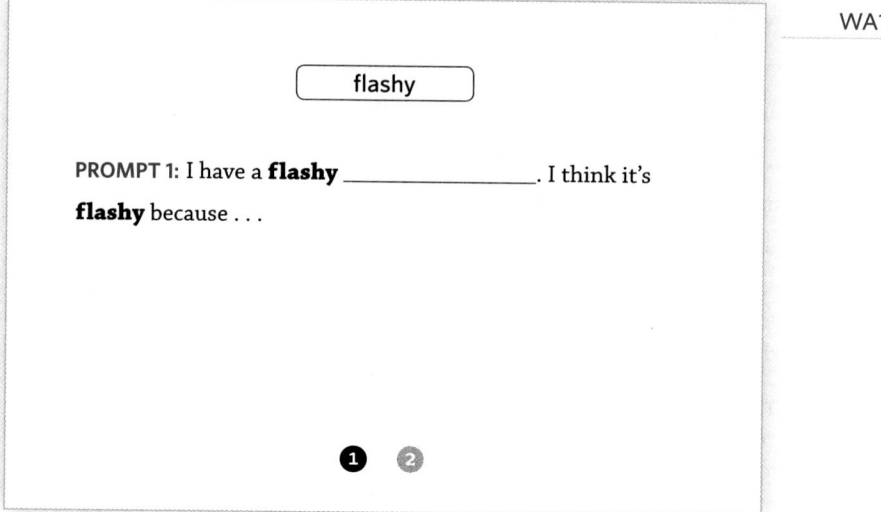

WA1

flashy

PROMPT 1: I have a **flashy** _____. I think it's **flashy** because . . .

❶ ❷

PROMPT 1: "I have a flashy [belt]. I think it's flashy because . . ."

After partners have talked, have a few volunteers use the prompt to share their thinking with the class.

Use "Think, Pair, Share" to discuss:

 Q *If you were to design a flashy bike, how would it look? [Pause; click ❷ to reveal the next prompt.] Turn to your partner.*

PROMPT 2: "My flashy bike would . . ."

After partners have talked, have one or two volunteers use the prompt to share their thinking.

Point to the word *flashy* and review the pronunciation and meaning of the word.

INTRODUCE AND USE *FANTASTIC*

3 Introduce and Define *Fantastic*

Tell the students that *fantastic* is the next word they will learn today and that *fantastic* means "strange, unusual, or unbelievable." Display word card 128 (⟨ WA2) and have the students say the word *fantastic*. Explain that you will reread the paragraph they heard earlier and they are to listen for how rain forest frogs are fantastic, or strange or unusual.

Reread the first paragraph on page 3 aloud, emphasizing the word *fantastic*.

Teacher Note

Support struggling students by asking questions such as "What clothing or costume do you own that is very colorful?" and "What bike, scooter, or toy do you own or have you seen that is brightly colored or shiny?"

Teacher Note

Support struggling students by asking questions such as "What would you do to make sure people noticed the bike?" "What bright colors would you paint it?" and "What mirrors, baskets, special seat, streamers, or other things would you have on the bike to make it stand out?"

Teacher Note

You may want to explain that *fantastic*, *strange*, *unusual*, and *unbelievable* are synonyms.

 **ELL Note**

The Spanish cognate of *fantastic* is *fantástico/a.*

Ask and discuss as a class:

Q *What are some ways that rain forest frogs are fantastic, or strange or unusual?*

Click ❶ on word card 128 (WA2) to reveal the first prompt. Have a few volunteers use the prompt to share their thinking with the class.

PROMPT 1: "The frogs are fantastic because . . ."

4 Discuss Fantastic Creatures

Explain that sometimes TV shows, movies, and books have fantastic creatures—strange and unbelievable creatures such as monsters, giants, dragons, and aliens from outer space.

Ask and discuss as a class:

Q *What fantastic creature have you read about in a book or seen on TV or in a movie? What made it fantastic?*

Click ❷ to reveal the next prompt. Have one or two volunteers use the prompt to share their thinking with the class.

PROMPT 2: "A fantastic creature I have [read about/seen] is . . ." or "It is fantastic because . . ."

5 Make Up a Fantastic Creature

Tell the students that you want them to use their imaginations to make up their own fantastic creatures. Explain that they should think about what their creature looks like and how it acts and that the creature can be scary or silly. Explain that partners will describe their creatures to each other. After partners talk, you will ask a few students to tell the class about their partner's fantastic creature.

Use "Think, Pair, Share" to discuss:

 Q *If you were to make up your own fantastic creature, what would it look like? How would it act?* [Pause; click ❸ on WA2 to reveal the prompt.] *Turn to your partner.*

After partners have talked, have a few volunteers use the prompt to share their partner's thinking with the class.

PROMPT 3: "[Ronny's] fantastic creature . . ."

Point to the word *fantastic* and review the pronunciation and meaning of the word.

INTRODUCE AND USE *DIVERSE*

6 Introduce and Define *Diverse*

ELL Note

The Spanish cognate of *diverse* is *diverso/a*.

Explain that *diverse* is the last word the students will learn today and that *diverse* means "different from one another." Display word card 129 (◖ WA3) and have the students say the word *diverse*.

Show pages 2–3 again and point to the pictures of the frogs.

Ask and discuss as a class:

Q *How are these frogs diverse, or different from one another?*

Click ❶ on word card 129 (WA3) to reveal the first prompt. Have a few volunteers use the prompt to share their thinking with the class.

PROMPT 1: "The frogs are diverse because . . ."

7 Discuss How Dogs Are Diverse

Explain that other kinds of animals are diverse and give an example.

> **You might say:**
>
> "Cats are diverse, or different from one another. Some have long hair, and some have short hair. Some have black hair; others have brown or yellow hair or spots or stripes. Some have long tails and others have short tails or no tail at all."

Ask:

 Q *How are dogs diverse? In what ways are they different?* [Click ❷ on WA3 to reveal the prompt.] *Turn to your partner.*

PROMPT 2: "Dogs are diverse because . . ."

After partners have talked, have a few volunteers use the prompt to share their thinking with the class.

8 Discuss Our Diverse Interests

Tell the students that people are also diverse. Explain that people have diverse interests, and give some examples.

> **You might say:**
>
> "For fun, some people like to draw. Some like to ride bikes. Others like to go bowling."

Ask and discuss as a class:

Q *What is something that you like to do for fun?*

Have a few volunteers share their thinking.

Then follow up by asking and discussing as a class:

Q *Are our interests diverse? Why or why not?*

Click ❸ on word card 129 to reveal the prompt. Have one or two volunteers use the prompt to share their thinking with the class.

PROMPT 3: "Our interests [are/are not] diverse because . . ."

Point to the word *diverse* and review the pronunciation and meaning of the word.

MORE STRATEGY PRACTICE

Discuss Another Meaning of *Fantastic*

Remind the students that words often have more than one meaning and sometimes the meanings are very different. Write the word *fantastic* where everyone can see it, pronounce it, and review that *fantastic* means "strange, unusual, or unbelievable."

Ask and discuss as a class:

Q *What else do you know about the word* fantastic? *What do you mean when you say you had a fantastic time at a party?*

PROMPTS: "*Fantastic* also means . . ." or "If I had a fantastic time, I . . ."

Have a few volunteers use the prompt to share their thinking with the class.

Explain that *fantastic* can also mean "very good, wonderful, or terrific."

MORE ELL SUPPORT

Discuss a Pair of Illustrations in *Flashy Fantastic Rain Forest Frogs*

Show pages 18–19 of *Flashy Fantastic Rain Forest Frogs* and review that this part of the book tells how tadpoles grow into tiny frogs. Read page 19 aloud. Then have the students look carefully at the illustrations on the pages. Ask and have the students discuss in pairs:

Q *What interesting things do you notice in these illustrations?*

PROMPT: "I notice that . . ."

Teacher Note

If the students struggle to answer the question, you might point out that tadpoles look like fish and swim in the water. Once they grow front and back legs and their tails shrink, they leave the water and become little frogs.

Day 2 | Review *Flashy, Fantastic,* and *Diverse*

Materials

- Daily review cards (WA4)
- "Tell Me a Story" chart (WA5)

In this lesson, the students:

- Review and practice using the words *flashy*, *fantastic*, and *diverse* from Day 1
- Build their speaking and listening skills
- Listen respectfully to the thinking of others and share their own
- Ask clarifying questions

Words Reviewed

flashy
Flashy means "very big, bright, or expensive." Something that is flashy catches your attention.

fantastic
Fantastic means "strange, unusual, or unbelievable."

diverse
Diverse means "different from one another."

REVIEW THE WORDS

1 Briefly Review the Words

Display the daily review cards (WA4). Review the pronunciation and meaning of each word.

Ask:

 Q *Which of these words might you use to describe a plant that talks? Why?* [Click ❶ on WA4 to reveal the prompt.] *Turn to your partner.*

PROMPT 1: "I might use [*fantastic*] because . . ."

After partners have talked, have a few volunteers use the prompt to share their thinking with the class.

Using the same procedure, discuss:

Q *Which of these words might you use to discuss how butterflies are different from one another? Why?* [Point to prompt 1.] *Turn to your partner.* (diverse)

Q *Which of these words might you use to describe a brightly colored, sparkly sweater? Why?* [Point to prompt 1.] *Turn to your partner.* (flashy)

PRACTICE USING THE WORDS

2 Do the Activity "Tell Me a Story"

Explain that partners will do the activity "Tell Me a Story." Remind the students that you will tell them the beginning of a story that includes a vocabulary word. They will use what they know about the word and their imaginations to make up an ending for the story.

Display the "Tell Me a Story" chart (WA5). Point to story 1 and begin by reading the story aloud twice, slowly and clearly. Point to the word *fantastic* and explain that you will tell the beginning of a story that includes the word *fantastic*.

- Story 1: *Jenna and her friends were exploring a dark cave. Jenna stopped suddenly, pointed her flashlight, and shouted, "Look at this! I've never seen anything like it. It's fantastic!" The fantastic thing Jenna saw in the cave was . . .*

Ask:

Q *How might you finish the story? What fantastic thing did Jenna see?* [Point to prompt 1.] *Turn to your partner.*

WA5

Tell Me a Story

Jenna and her friends were exploring a dark cave. Jenna stopped suddenly, pointed her flashlight, and shouted, "Look at this! I've never seen anything like it. It's fantastic!" The fantastic thing Jenna saw in the cave was . . .

PROMPT 1: The **fantastic** thing Jenna saw was . . .

PROMPT 1: "The fantastic thing Jenna saw was. . ."

After partners have talked, have one or two volunteers use the prompt to share their thinking with the class.

Using the same procedure, discuss:

[flashy]

- Story 2: *Paulo was invited to a costume party. He said, "I need to wear something flashy." Paulo arrives at the party wearing . . .*

Ask:

Q *How might you finish the story? What is Paulo wearing that is flashy?* [Point to prompt 2.] *Turn to your partner.*

PROMPT 2: "Paulo is wearing a flashy . . ."

Teacher Note

If the students have difficulty thinking of an ending, review the definition of *fantastic* and think aloud about an ending. (For example, say "The fantastic thing Jenna saw was a giant bat hanging over her head!") Then reread the beginning of the story and repeat the question.

 ELL Note

You might explain that a *costume party* is a "party in which people dress up in costumes, or clothes that make them look like another person or an animal or thing."

[diverse]

- Story 3: *Marta is a bug collector. She loves to tell her friends about the diverse bugs in her collection. She says that her diverse bugs are . . .*

Ask:

 Q *How might you finish the story? What might Marta say about the diverse bugs she has collected?* [Point to prompt 3.] *Turn to your partner.*

PROMPT 3: "When Marta talks about the diverse bugs in her collection, she might say . . ."

EXTENSION

Explore Domain-specific Words: *Rain Forests*

Show the cover of *Flashy Fantastic Rain Forest Frogs* and review that many different types of frogs live in tropical rain forests. Ask:

Q *What else do you know about rain forests?*

Have a few volunteers share their thinking.

Tell the students that you will read a description of the rain forest from the book and that as you read, you want them to close their eyes and picture the rain forest. Then read the second paragraph on page 5 of the book aloud, without showing the illustration. Ask:

Q *What did you learn about the rain forest from the part I just read?*

Have volunteers share their thinking. If necessary, point out that rain forests are full of plants and have three layers—the canopy, the understory, and the forest floor. Review that some rain forest frogs live their whole lives in the canopy and understory. Others never leave the forest floor.

In this lesson, the students:

- Learn and use the words *avoid, deadly,* and *threatened*
- Build their speaking and listening skills
- Listen respectfully to the thinking of others and share their own

Words Taught

avoid (p. 12)
Avoid means "keep away from."

deadly
Deadly means "dangerous and likely to cause death."

threatened (p. 28)
If something is threatened, it is in danger or likely to be harmed or destroyed.

INTRODUCE AND USE *AVOID*

1 Introduce and Define *Avoid*

Show pages 12–13 of *Flashy Fantastic Rain Forest Frogs* and review that frogs have ways to hide from and escape predators. Read page 12 aloud, emphasizing the word *avoid*.

Explain that *avoid* means "keep away from." Point to the pictures of the frogs on pages 12–13 and review that the webbing between their toes and flaps of skin on their sides act like wings and help them avoid, or keep away from, birds and other predators.

Display word card 130 (WA6) and have the students say the word *avoid*.

2 Discuss Avoiding Things

Explain that sometimes we avoid, or keep away from, certain foods because we do not like how they taste or because eating them makes us sick.

Ask:

Q *What is a food you avoid? Why?* [Click ❶ on WA6 to reveal the first prompt.] *Turn to your partner.*

PROMPT 1: "I avoid [peanuts] because . . ."

Materials

- *Flashy Fantastic Rain Forest Frogs*
- Word card 130 (WA6)
- Word card 131 (WA7)
- Word card 132 (WA8)

After partners have talked, have a few volunteers use the prompt to share their thinking with the class.

Explain that sometimes we avoid doing something because it is difficult, boring, or not much fun. Give examples of things you avoid doing now or avoided doing when you were younger.

> **You might say:**
>
> "Sometimes I avoid doing housework even though the house needs to be cleaned. It's just no fun, and I'd rather be reading or visiting with friends. When I was your age, I avoided playing baseball with my brother because he would tease me when I didn't catch the ball."

Use "Think, Pair, Share" to discuss:

 Q *When have you avoided doing something? Why?* [Pause; click ❷ on WA6 to reveal the prompt.] *Turn to your partner.*

PROMPT 2: "I avoided [cleaning my room] because . . ."

After partners have talked, have a few volunteers use the prompt to share their thinking with the class.

Point to the word *avoid* and review the pronunciation and meaning of the word.

INTRODUCE AND USE *DEADLY*

3 Introduce and Define *Deadly*

Show pages 14–15 and review that predators stay away from poison dart frogs because their skin contains poisonous chemicals. Read page 15 aloud.

Explain that *deadly* is the next word the students will learn and that *deadly* means "dangerous and likely to cause death." Explain that the poison in the skin of some frogs is deadly. It is dangerous and can kill people.

Display word card 131 (🔊 WA7) and have the students say the word *deadly*.

4 Discuss Deadly Things

Explain that things other than animals can be deadly, or dangerous and likely to cause death.

Ask:

 Q *Why might a storm, such as a hurricane or tornado, be deadly?* [Click ❶ on WA7 to reveal the first prompt.] *Turn to your partner.*

PROMPT 1: "A storm might be deadly because . . ."

Teacher Note

You might point to the word *dead* in *deadly* and explain that *dead* and *deadly* are related and that *dead* is a clue to the meaning of *deadly*.

After partners have talked, have one or two volunteers use the prompt to share their thinking with the class.

 Q *Why might crossing a street without looking both ways be deadly?* [Click ❷ to reveal the next prompt.] *Turn to your partner.*

PROMPT 2: "It might be deadly because . . ."

After partners have talked, have a few volunteers use the prompt to share their thinking with the class.

Point to the word *deadly* and review the pronunciation and meaning of the word.

INTRODUCE AND USE
THREATENED

5 Introduce and Define *Threatened*

Show pages 28–29 and read page 28 aloud, emphasizing the word *threatened*.

Explain that if something is threatened, it is in danger or likely to be harmed or destroyed. Explain that frogs such as the blue poison frog are threatened, or in danger, because they live in a small area of the forest. If that part of the forest is destroyed by people cutting down trees, the frogs will have no shelter or food and will die.

Display word card 132 (WA8) and have the students say the word *threatened*.

6 Discuss Threatening Situations

Ask:

 Q *If there were a forest fire, what would be threatened? What would be in danger or likely to be harmed or destroyed? Why?* [Click ❶ on WA8 to reveal the first prompt.] *Turn to your partner.*

PROMPT 1: "If there were a forest fire, [animals] would be threatened because . . ."

After partners have talked, have a few volunteers use the prompt to share their thinking with the class.

Using the same procedure, discuss:

Q *If you felt threatened by a growling dog, what might you do? Why?* [Click ❷ to reveal the next prompt.] *Turn to your partner.*

PROMPT 2: "If I felt threatened by a dog, I might . . ."

Point to the word *threatened* and review the pronunciation and meaning of the word.

EXTENSION

Discuss the Compound Word *Painkiller*

Write this sentence from page 27 of *Flashy Fantastic Rain Forest Frogs* where everyone can see it: "One chemical from poison dart frog skin is a more powerful painkiller than morphine."

Direct the students' attention to the sentence and explain that it is a sentence from *Flashy Fantastic Rain Forest Frogs*. Tell them that the sentence contains a *compound word*, or a "word made up of two or more shorter words." Then read the sentence aloud.

Ask and discuss as a class:

Q *What compound word do you see in the sentence?*

If necessary, tell the students that the compound word is *painkiller*.

Remind the students that they can figure out the meaning of a compound word by identifying the shorter words that make up the compound word and thinking about what each word means.

Ask and discuss as a class:

Q *What are the shorter words that make up the compound word* painkiller?

Q *What do you think the word* painkiller *means? What is a painkiller?*

If necessary, explain that a *painkiller* is a "pill or other medicine that is taken to stop pain."

Teacher Note

For a list of common compound words, visit the CCC Learning Hub (ccclearninghub.org) to view the "Compound Words" list in the General Resources section.

In this lesson, the students:

- Review and practice using the words *avoid*, *deadly*, and *threatened* from Day 3
- Build their speaking and listening skills
- Listen respectfully to the thinking of others and share their own

Words Reviewed

avoid
Avoid means "keep away from."

deadly
Deadly means "dangerous and likely to cause death."

threatened
If something is threatened, it is in danger or likely to be harmed or destroyed.

REVIEW THE WORDS

1 Briefly Review the Words

Display the daily review cards (WA9). Review the pronunciation and meaning of each word.

Ask:

 Q *If you were walking in the woods and saw a deadly snake, would you feel threatened? Why?* [Click ❶ on WA9 to reveal the first prompt.] *Turn to your partner.*

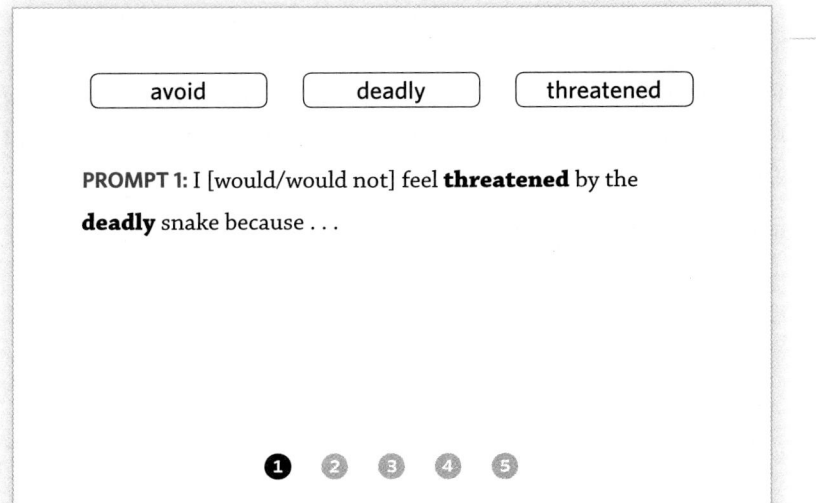

WA9

| avoid | deadly | threatened |

PROMPT 1: I [would/would not] feel **threatened** by the **deadly** snake because . . .

❶ ② ③ ④ ⑤

Materials

- Daily review cards (WA9)
- Copy of this week's family letter (BLM1) for each student
- (Optional) Copy of the "Week 22 Crossword Puzzle" (BLM3) for each student

PROMPT 1: "I [would/would not] feel threatened by the deadly snake because . . . "

After partners have talked, have a few volunteers use the prompt to share their thinking with the class.

Using the same procedure, discuss:

Q *On a hot day, what do you avoid?* [Click ❷ to reveal the next prompt.] *Turn to your partner.*

PROMPT 2: "On a hot day, I avoid . . ."

PRACTICE USING THE WORDS

2 Play "Make a Choice"

Explain that partners will play "Make a Choice."

Point to the word *avoid* and ask:

Q *Which would you avoid on a cold day: a hot bath or a cold shower? Why?* [Click ❸ on WA9 to reveal the prompt.] *Turn to your partner.*

PROMPT 3: "I would avoid a [cold shower] because . . ."

After partners have talked, have a few volunteers use the prompt to share their thinking with the class.

Using the same procedure, discuss:

[deadly]

Q *Which might be deadly for a young kitten: losing its mother or playing with a toy mouse? Why?* [Click ❹ to reveal the next prompt.] *Turn to your partner.*

PROMPT 4: "[Losing its mother] might be deadly because . . ."

[threatened]

Q *Which would cause you to feel threatened: meeting a bear in the woods or meeting a rabbit in the woods? Why?* [Click ❺ to reveal the prompt.] *Turn to your partner.*

PROMPT 5: "[Meeting a bear] would cause me to feel threatened because . . ."

Teacher Note

Send home with each student a copy of this week's family letter (BLM1). Encourage the students to talk about this week's words with their families.

Teacher Note

To provide students with additional review of words taught during Weeks 21 and 22, you might distribute a copy of the "Week 22 Crossword Puzzle" (BLM3) to each student.

In this lesson, the students:

- Review words learned earlier
- Build their speaking and listening skills
- Listen respectfully to the thinking of others and share their own
- Ask clarifying questions

Words Reviewed

challenge
A *challenge* is "something that is hard to do or requires a lot of work or effort."

prefer
Prefer means "like better." If you prefer something, you like it better than something else.

require
Require means "need."

serve
Serve means "give someone food or drink."

spectacular
Spectacular means "amazing to look at."

REVIEW THE WORDS

1 Briefly Review the Words

Display the ongoing review cards (WA10). Review the pronunciation and meaning of each word.

PRACTICE USING THE WORDS

2 Do the Activity "Tell Me a Story"

Explain that partners will do the activity "Tell Me a Story." Remind the students that you will tell them the beginning of a story that includes a vocabulary word. They will use what they know about the word and their imaginations to make up an ending for the story.

Display the "Tell Me a Story" chart (WA11). Point to story 1 and begin by reading the story aloud twice, slowly and clearly.

- Story 1: *Arman's class is having a picnic to celebrate the end of the school year. They will serve . . .*

Materials

- Ongoing review cards (WA10)
- "Tell Me a Story" chart (WA11)
- "Class Vocabulary Assessment Record" sheet (CA1)

Q *How might you finish the story?* [Point to prompt 1.] *Turn to your partner.*

Tell Me a Story

Arman's class is having a picnic to celebrate the end of the school year. They will serve . . .

_____

PROMPT 1: They will **serve** . . .

PROMPT 1: "They will serve . . ."

After partners have talked, have one or two volunteers use the prompt to share their thinking with the class.

Discuss the following stories using the same procedure:

- Story 2: *Paula is learning how to ride a bike. To overcome the challenge, she must . . .*

 Q *How might you finish this story?* [Point to prompt 2.] *Turn to your partner.*

PROMPT 2: "To overcome the challenge, she must . . ."

Follow up by asking:

Q *Why must Paula [practice riding every day] to overcome the challenge?*

Point to prompt 3. Have the volunteers use the prompt to share their thinking with the class.

PROMPT 3: "Paula must [practice riding every day] to overcome the challenge because . . ."

- Story 3: *Manny enjoyed his trip hiking through a national park. One spectacular thing he saw was . . .*

 Q *How might you finish this story?* [Point to prompt 4.] *Turn to your partner.*

PROMPT 4: "One spectacular thing he saw was . . ."

Follow up by asking:

Q *Why would [a giant waterfall] be spectacular?*

Point to prompt 5. Have the volunteers use the prompt to share their thinking with the class.

PROMPT 5: "[A giant waterfall] would be spectacular because . . ."

- Story 4: *My family is going to take a vacation this summer. I would prefer to go to . . .*

Teacher Note

If the students have difficulty thinking of an ending, review the definition of *serve* and think aloud about an ending. (For example, say "They will serve sandwiches, juice, and watermelon.") Then reread the beginning of the story and repeat the question.

Q *How might you finish this story?* [Point to prompt 6.] *Turn to your partner.*

PROMPT 6: "I would prefer to go to . . ."

Follow up by asking:

Q *Why would you prefer to go to [the beach]?*

Point to prompt 7. Have the volunteers use the prompt to share their thinking with the class.

PROMPT 7: "I would prefer to go to [the beach] because . . ."

- Story 5: *Gwen decides to plant flowers in her garden. She goes to the store with her father to get supplies. Her father explains that planting flowers requires . . .*

 Q *How might you finish this story?* [Point to prompt 8.] *Turn to your partner.*

PROMPT 8: "Planting flowers requires . . ."

Follow up by asking:

Q *Why does planting flowers require [seeds]?*

Point to prompt 9. Have the volunteers use the prompt to share their thinking with the class.

PROMPT 9: "Planting flowers requires [seeds] because . . ."

 ## ✓ CLASS VOCABULARY ASSESSMENT NOTE

Observe the students and ask yourself:

- Are the students able to complete the stories using the vocabulary words?
- Can they explain why they finished the stories the way they did?
- Are they using the vocabulary words in their speech and writing?

Record your observations on the "Class Vocabulary Assessment Record" sheet (CA1); see page 196 of the *Assessment Resource Book*.

Use the following suggestions to support struggling students:

- If *only a few students* understand a word's meaning, reteach the word using the vocabulary lesson in which it was first taught as a model.

- If *about half of the students* understand a word's meaning, provide further practice in using the word by reviewing the word's meaning and then asking a question that requires the student to talk about the word in terms of his own experiences. For example, ask questions such as "When have you overcome a challenge? How did you overcome it?" or "When have you seen something spectacular? What did it look like?"

RESOURCES

Read-aloud

- *Explore the Desert* by Kay Jackson

Extension

- "Explore Domain-specific Words: *Evaporate*"

 More ELL Support

- "Scan, Write About, and Draw an Object"

 ## Online Resources

Visit the CCC Learning Hub (ccclearninghub.org) to find your online resources for this week.

Whiteboard Activities

- WA1–WA10

Reproducibles

- Week 23 family letter (BLM1)
- (Optional) "Week 23 Word Cards" (BLM2)

OVERVIEW

Words Taught	Words Reviewed
adapt	diverse
depend	flashy
scan	flimsy
disrupt	hazardous
trample	plain
forbid	

Word-learning Strategies

- Recognizing synonyms (review)
- Recognizing words with multiple meanings (review)

Vocabulary Focus

- Students learn and use six words from or about the book.
- Students review synonyms.
- Students review words with multiple meanings.
- Students review words learned earlier.
- Students build their speaking and listening skills.

Social Development Focus

- Students develop the skill of asking clarifying questions.
- Students listen respectfully to the thinking of others and share their own.

⏱ DO AHEAD

✓ Prior to Day 4, visit the CCC Learning Hub (ccclearninghub.org) to access and print this week's family letter (BLM1). Make enough copies to send one letter home with each student.

✓ (Optional) Visit the CCC Learning Hub (ccclearninghub.org) to access and print "Week 23 Word Cards" (BLM2). These cards can be used to provide your students with more opportunities to review the words.

Materials

- *Explore the Desert*
- Word card 133 (WA1)
- Word card 134 (WA2)
- Word card 135 (WA3)

In this lesson, the students:

- Learn and use the words *adapt, depend,* and *scan*
- Review synonyms
- Review words with multiple meanings
- Build their speaking and listening skills
- Listen respectfully to the thinking of others and share their own

Words Taught

adapt (p. 6)
Adapt means "change to fit new situations or conditions." People adapt to new situations or conditions by changing their behavior or ideas.

depend (p. 6)
Depend means "rely on or need someone or something for help or support."

scan (p. 19)
Scan means "examine something, or look at something carefully and closely." *Scan* also means "read something quickly, without looking closely for details."

INTRODUCE AND USE *ADAPT*

1 Introduce and Define *Adapt*

Show pages 6–7 of *Explore the Desert* and review that the first chapter tells about the plants and animals that live in the desert. Read the last paragraph on page 7 aloud, emphasizing the word *adapted*.

Explain that *adapt* means "change to fit new situations or conditions." Tell the students that desert plants and animals have adapted, or changed, over thousands of years so that they can survive the hot, dry conditions. Review that the leaves of some desert trees have adapted, or changed, by curling up during the hottest times of the day. In this way, the leaves conserve water. Point to the picture of the owls on pages 6–7 and explain that these burrowing owls have adapted, or changed, to fit life in the hot, dry desert, as well. They have adapted by burrowing, or digging, and nesting in the ground where it is much cooler.

Display word card 133 (◖ WA1) and have the students say the word *adapt*.

🌐 ELL Note

The Spanish cognate of *adapt* is *adaptar*.

Teacher Note

You might explain that *conserve* means "keep something safe from being damaged or destroyed." The trees conserve, or save, the water by curling up their leaves.

2 Discuss Adapting

Tell the students that, like plants and animals, people adapt, or change, to fit new situations or conditions. Explain that people often adapt by changing their behavior or ideas. Tell about times you have adapted to a new situation and what you did to adapt.

> **You might say:**
>
> "I used to teach first grade. When I started teaching third grade, I had to adapt, or change, my teaching style and lesson plans. To adapt, I talked to other third-grade teachers and read through the third-grade textbooks. When I was your age, my family moved to a new city. I had to adapt to a new neighborhood. To adapt, I made new friends, and they showed me where the park and other fun places in the neighborhood were. Pretty soon the new neighborhood felt like home."

Use "Think, Pair, Share" to discuss:

 Q *When have you had to adapt to a new situation? What did you do to adapt?* [Pause; click ❶ on WA1 to reveal the first prompt.] *Turn to your partner.*

WA1

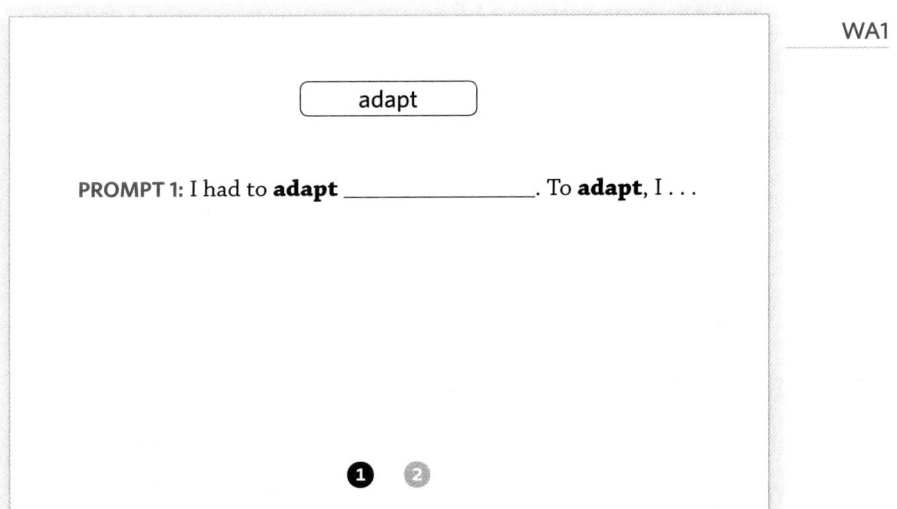

adapt

PROMPT 1: I had to **adapt** _____. To **adapt**, I . . .

❶ ❷

PROMPT 1: "I had to adapt [when my baby sister came home from the hospital]. To adapt, I . . ."

After partners have talked, have a few volunteers use the prompt to share their thinking with the class.

3 Discuss Ways the Students Would Adapt

Ask the students to imagine they have sprained (hurt) their wrist on the hand they write with, and it is in a cast.

Teacher Note

Support struggling students by asking questions such as "Have you ever had to adapt, or change your behavior, because you got a new baby brother or sister or a new stepmother or stepfather?" and "Have you ever had to adapt because you moved to a new place or changed schools?"

Discuss as a class:

Q *How would you adapt so that you could get your schoolwork done despite your hurt wrist?*

Click ❷ on WA1 to reveal the prompt and have a few volunteers use the prompt to share their thinking with the class.

PROMPT 2: "I would adapt by . . ."

Point to the word *adapt* and review the pronunciation and meaning of the word.

INTRODUCE AND USE *DEPEND*

4 Introduce and Define *Depend* and Review Synonyms

Show pages 6–7 again. Read these sentences from page 6, emphasizing the word *depend*: "Desert plants and animals depend on each other for survival. Desert plants provide shelter and food for desert animals. Animals help plants by spreading their seeds throughout the desert."

Explain that *depend* is the next word the students will learn today and that *depend* means "rely on or need someone or something for help or support." Tell the students that *depend*, *rely*, and *need* are synonyms. Explain that the plants and animals depend on, or rely on or need, each other to survive in the desert. Desert animals depend on desert plants to provide them with shelter from the hot sun and with food. Desert plants depend on desert animals to spread their seeds throughout the desert.

Display word card 134 ( WA2) and have the students say the word *depend*.

5 Discuss People We Depend On

Explain that people depend on, or rely on or need, other people to help them or support them. Give examples of people you depend on or have depended on, or examples of people who depend on or have depended on you.

> **You might say:**
>
> "When I was a child, I depended, or relied, on my parents to take care of me. I needed them to provide me with food, clothing, a place to live, and love. As a teacher, I depend on the other teachers I work with for support and advice. I also depend on you, my students, to help me by working hard and treating one another respectfully. When I was teaching my daughter to ride her bike, she depended on, or needed, me to help her learn and make sure she didn't fall down."

ELL Note

The Spanish cognate of *depend* is *depender*.

Teacher Note

If you started a synonym chart, add *depend*, *rely*, and *need* to it.

Use "Think, Pair, Share" to discuss:

 Q *Who is someone you depend on? How do you depend on that person?* [Pause; click ❶ on WA2 to reveal the first prompt.] *Turn to your partner.*

PROMPT 1: "I depend on [my brother Kim] to [help me with my homework when I'm stuck]."

After partners have talked, have one or two volunteers use the prompt to share their thinking with the class.

Follow up by discussing as a class:

Q *Who is someone that depends on you? How does that person depend on you?*

Click ❷ on WA2 to reveal the next prompt, and have one or two volunteers use the prompt to share their thinking with the class.

PROMPT 2: "[My mom] depends on me to [watch my little sister when my mom is on the telephone]."

Point to the word *depend* and review the pronunciation and meaning of the word.

INTRODUCE AND USE *SCAN*

6 Introduce and Define *Scan*

Show pages 18–19 of *Explore the Desert* and review that this part of the book describes desert animals that hunt at night. Read the first paragraph on page 19 aloud, emphasizing the word *scan*.

Explain that *scan* is the last word the students will learn today and that *scan* means "examine something, or look at something carefully and closely." Explain that the owl scans, or looks closely, at the ground while hunting. The owl is scanning for food.

Display word card 135 (WA3) and have the students say the word *scan*.

7 Do the Activity "Imagine That!"

Tell the students that they will do the activity "Imagine That!" You will describe an imaginary situation. The students will make pictures in their minds and then use the word *scan* to discuss what they imagined.

Have the students close their eyes and picture the following scene in their minds:

- *Caleb is swinging on the swings at the park. Suddenly, he leaps off the swing and shouts, "Oh no!" Caleb bends down and scans the ground near the swings.*

Use "Think, Pair, Share" to discuss:

 Q *Why is Caleb scanning, or examining or looking carefully at, the ground? [Pause.]* Open your eyes. [Click ❶ on WA3 to reveal the first prompt.] *Turn to your partner.*

PROMPT 1: "I think Caleb is scanning the ground because . . ."

After partners have talked, have a few volunteers use the prompt to share their thinking with the class. Follow up by asking:

Q *[Alexis], you said Caleb might be [scanning the ground for his glasses]. What might that look like? Please act out [scanning the ground] for us.*

Using the same procedure, discuss:

- *Brianna is at a popular amusement park. She is standing alone among a crowd of people near the park entrance. Brianna looks confused and a little frightened. She begins scanning the crowd.*

 Q *Why is Brianna scanning the crowd? [Pause.]* Open your eyes. [Click ❷ to reveal the prompt.] *Turn to your partner.*

PROMPT 2: "I think Brianna is scanning the crowd because . . ."

Point to the word *scan* and review the pronunciation and meaning of the word.

8 Discuss Another Meaning of *Scan*

Point to the word *scan* and review that in the book *scan* means "examine something, or look at something carefully and closely." Remind the students that words often have other meanings and that sometimes those meanings are very different. Explain that the word *scan* can also mean "read something quickly, without looking closely for details." Explain that sometimes people scan a book, newspaper article, or other text because they are in a hurry or because they are looking for one particular piece of information and do not want to read every word. Ask the students to watch as you act out scanning your *Vocabulary Teaching Guide*. Then scan a page or two of the guide. Ask:

Q *What did you see me do when I scanned the teacher's guide?*

Click ❸ on WA3 to reveal the next prompt and have a few volunteers use the prompt to share their thinking with the class.

PROMPT 3: "When you scanned the teacher's guide, you . . ."

Remind the students that if they hear or read a word that has more than one meaning, they can usually figure out the correct meaning by thinking about how the word is used. Explain that you will read a passage that includes the word *scan*. Partners will decide whether *scan* means "examine something, or look at something carefully and closely" or "read something quickly, without looking closely for details" and explain why they think so.

Read the following aloud twice:

- *The doctor spent several minutes scanning the patient's X-ray. She did not want to miss anything.*

Ask:

 Q *In the passage, does* scan *mean "examine something, or look at something carefully and closely" or "read something quickly, without looking closely for details"? Why do you think that?* [Click ❹ on WA3 to reveal the next prompt.] *Turn to your partner.*

PROMPT 4: "I think *scan* means [examine something closely] because . . ."

After partners have talked, have a few volunteers use the prompt to share their thinking with the class.

Using the same procedure, discuss:

- *Mr. Russell was in a hurry. He quickly scanned the headlines in the newspaper and then rushed out the door.*

 ## MORE ELL SUPPORT

Scan, Write About, and Draw an Object

Remind the students that one meaning of the word *scan* is to "examine something, or look at something carefully and closely." Explain that the students are to choose an object in the classroom, such as a book, a desk, a table, the globe, or the pencil sharpener. You will then give them a couple of minutes to scan the object, or look at it closely and carefully. Afterwards, they will write about what they saw when they scanned the object, and they will draw the object.

Have the students select an object and give them a minute or two to scan it. Then have them return to their desks or tables and write about and draw the object they scanned. When the students have finished, have them discuss their writing and drawing by asking:

Q *What did you see when you scanned [the pencil sharpener]?*

Have volunteers use the prompt to answer the question.

PROMPT: "When I scanned [the pencil sharpener], I saw [a round metal thing with a hole in it for the pencil]."

Materials

- Daily review cards (WA4)
- Daily review activity (WA5)

In this lesson, the students:

- Review and practice using the words *adapt, depend,* and *scan* from Day 1
- Build their speaking and listening skills
- Ask clarifying questions

Words Reviewed

adapt
Adapt means "change to fit new situations or conditions." People adapt to new situations or conditions by changing their behavior or ideas.

depend
Depend means "rely on or need someone or something for help or support."

scan
Scan means "examine something, or look at something carefully and closely." *Scan* also means "read something quickly, without looking closely for details."

REVIEW THE WORDS

1 Briefly Review the Words

Display the daily review cards (WA4). Review the pronunciation and meaning of each word.

Ask:

Q *Which of the words might you use if you were writing a story about moving with your family to a new town? What might you write?* [Click ❶ on WA4 to reveal the first prompt.] *Turn to your partner.*

WA4

adapt	depend	scan

PROMPT 1: I might use the word _____. I might write . . .

PROMPT 1: "I might use the word [*adapt*]. I might write . . ."

After partners have talked, have a few volunteers use the prompt to share their thinking with the class.

PRACTICE USING THE WORDS

2 Review the Game "What's the Missing Word?"

Tell the students that they will play the game called "What's the Missing Word?" Review that you will read some sentences aloud and that a word will be missing from each sentence. Explain that partners will decide which vocabulary word could replace the missing word and explain why they think so.

Display the daily review activity (◖ WA5) and begin playing the game:

1. Point to the words *adapt*, *depend*, and *scan*. Then click ❶ to reveal the first sentence and read it aloud. Point out that a word is missing.

   ▪ Sentence 1: *Regina _____ to living in a colder climate by wearing warm coats, gloves, and boots.*

2. Give the students a few moments to think about the sentence. Then use "Think, Pair, Share" to discuss:

   Q *What's the missing word? Why do you think so?* [Pause; click ❶ again to reveal the prompt.] *Turn to your partner.*

   PROMPT: "I think [*adapts*] is the missing word because . . ."

   After partners have talked, have one or two volunteers use the prompt to share their thinking with the class.

3. Conclude the discussion of this sentence by clicking ❶ a third time to highlight the correct vocabulary word and reveal the correct word in place. Read the sentence again with the word *adapts* replacing the missing word.

WA5

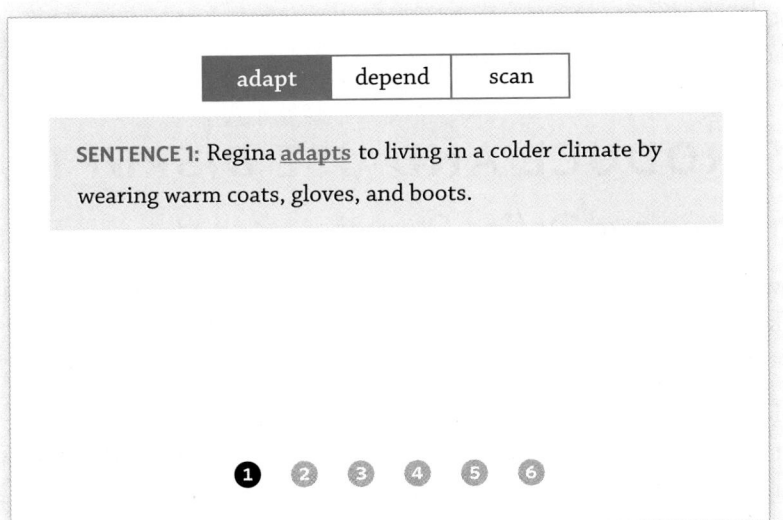

4. Click ❶ to clear the screen.

Repeat the procedure to discuss the following sentences:

- Sentence 2: *The squirrel _____ the ground for nuts.* (scans)
- Sentence 3: *The kitten _____ on its mother for milk.* (depends)
- Sentence 4: *After their first flight, the baby eagles must _____ to life outside the nest.* (adapt)
- Sentence 5: *Dominic _____ on the bus driver, Ms. Kunkel, to take him to school.* (depends)
- Sentence 6: *The lifeguard _____ the lake for swimmers.* (scans)

Day 3 | Introduce *Disrupt, Trample,* and *Forbid*

Materials

- *Explore the Desert*
- Word card 136 (WA6)
- Word card 137 (WA7)
- Word card 138 (WA8)

In this lesson, the students:

- Learn and use the words *disrupt, trample,* and *forbid*
- Build their speaking and listening skills
- Listen respectfully to the thinking of others and share their own

Words Taught

disrupt (p. 22)
Disrupt means "disturb or interrupt something that is happening."

trample (p. 23)
Trample means "damage or crush by walking or stepping on something heavily."

forbid
Forbid means "order someone not to do something."

INTRODUCE AND USE *DISRUPT*

1 Introduce and Define *Disrupt*

Show pages 22–23 of *Explore the Desert* and review that this part of the book describes how people affect the desert. Point to the box at the bottom of page 22 and read it aloud, emphasizing the word *disrupt*.

Explain that *disrupt* means "disturb or interrupt something that is happening." Explain that people should not go off trails in the desert because they can disrupt, or disturb, the plants and animals that live near the trails.

Display word card 136 (WA6) and have the students say the word *disrupt*.

2 Discuss Whether Olive Is Disrupting Something

Explain that you will describe something that the imaginary third-grader Olive is doing; then partners will decide whether or not she is disrupting something, or disturbing or interrupting something that is happening. Begin by reading the following scenario aloud twice:

- *It is quiet reading time. Olive is talking loudly to her friend Orlando. Students sitting nearby cannot concentrate on what they are reading.*

Ask:

Q *Is Olive disrupting quiet reading time? Why?* [Click ❶ on WA6 to reveal the first prompt.] *Turn to your partner.*

WA6

PROMPT 1: "I think Olive [is/is not] disrupting quiet reading time because . . ."

After partners have talked, have one or two volunteers use the prompt to share their thinking with the class.

Using the same procedure, discuss one or both of the following:

- *It's nap time for Olive's baby sister, Emma. Olive stays in her room and quietly reads while Emma is napping.*

 Q *Is Olive disrupting her sister's nap time? Why?* [Click ❷ to reveal the prompt.] *Turn to your partner.*

PROMPT 2: "I think Olive [is/is not] disrupting her sister's nap time because . . ."

- *Olive is watching her friend Orlando's play practice. Just as Orlando is about to speak his lines, Olive leaps up onto the stage and starts singing a song.*

Q *Is Olive disrupting play practice? Why?* [Click ❸ to reveal the prompt.] *Turn to your partner.*

PROMPT 3: "I think Olive [is/is not] disrupting play practice because . . ."

Point to the word *disrupt* and review the pronunciation and meaning of the word.

INTRODUCE AND USE *TRAMPLE*

3 Introduce and Define *Trample*

Show pages 22–23 of *Explore the Desert* again and review that this part of the book describes how people affect the desert. Read page 23 aloud, emphasizing the word *trample*.

Tell the students that the next word they will learn today is *trample* and that *trample* means "damage or crush by walking or stepping on something heavily." Point to the hikers on page 23 and explain that hikers like these can trample, or damage or crush, a plant such as a cactus or animals' homes by stepping heavily on them.

Display word card 137 (◖ WA7) and have the students say the word *trample*.

4 Do the Activity "Imagine That!"

Tell the students that they will do the activity "Imagine That!" Explain that you will describe an imaginary situation in which something has been trampled. The students will use what they know about the word and their imaginations to tell how they think the object might have been trampled.

Have the students close their eyes and picture the following scene in their minds:

- *You build a toothpick tower on your living room floor. You leave the living room to go to the kitchen for a snack. When you return, the tower has been trampled.*

Use "Think, Pair, Share" to discuss:

 Q *How might the toothpick tower have been trampled?* [Pause.] *Open your eyes.* [Click ❶ on WA7 to reveal the first prompt.] *Turn to your partner.*

PROMPT 1: "The toothpick tower might have been trampled [when/by] . . ."

After partners have talked, have one or two volunteers use the prompt to share their thinking with the class.

Follow up by discussing as a class:

Q *What might the trampled toothpick tower look like?*

In the same way, discuss:

- *You are at the circus. You see a trampled hat in the center ring.*

 Q *How might the hat have been trampled?* [Pause.] *Open your eyes.* [Click ❷ to reveal the next prompt.] *Turn to your partner.*

PROMPT 2: "The hat might have been trampled [when/by] . . ."

After partners have talked, have one or two volunteers use the prompt to share their thinking with the class.

Follow up by asking:

Q *What might the trampled hat look like?*

Point to the word *trample* and review the pronunciation and meaning of the word.

INTRODUCE AND USE *FORBID*

5 Introduce and Define *Forbid*

Show pages 24–25 of *Explore the Desert* and review that this part of the book is about protecting the desert. Read page 25 aloud.

Tell the students that the U.S. government creates national parks to protect areas like the desert. Explain that the government forbids people to build roads or homes in these areas and tell the students that *forbid* is the last word they will learn today. Explain that *forbid* means "order someone not to do something."

Display word card 138 (🌙 WA8) and have the students say the word *forbid*.

6 Discuss *Forbid*

Explain that forbidding people to build roads or homes in national parks is only one of many things that governments forbid, or order people not to do. The government typically forbids things by passing laws. For example, there are traffic laws that forbid speeding (driving faster than the speed limit). These laws protect pedestrians and help to prevent accidents. There are also laws that forbid stealing or doing damage to others' property. Discuss as a class:

Q *What is something else the law forbids?*

Click ❶ on word card 138 (WA8) to reveal the first prompt. Have a few volunteers use the prompt to share their thinking with the class.

PROMPT 1: "The law forbids . . ."

Teacher Note

If the students struggle to answer the question, give a few more examples of things the law forbids (for example, jaywalking, littering, and mistreating animals). Then follow up by asking questions such as "What does the law say people cannot do when they are riding a bike? Driving a car? Flying on an airplane? Picnicking in a park?"

Explain that your school also has rules that forbid students from doing certain things. Give a few examples of school rules that forbid something.

> **You might say:**
>
> "One of our school rules forbids students from running in the halls. Another school rule forbids students from being on campus before 7:30 in the morning."

Use "Think, Pair, Share" to discuss:

 Q *What is something else the school forbids? Why do you think the school forbids it?* [Pause; click ❷ on WA8 to reveal the next prompt.] *Turn to your partner.*

PROMPT 2: "The school forbids [throwing food in the cafeteria]. I think the school forbids it because . . ."

After partners have talked, have a few volunteers use the prompt to share their thinking with the class

Point to the word *forbid* and review the pronunciation and meaning of the word.

EXTENSION

Explore Domain-specific Words: *Evaporate*

Explain that authors who write about science topics such as different habitats and climates often use scientific words to discuss their subjects. Explain that in the book *Explore the Desert* author Kay Jackson uses the scientific word *evaporate* to describe the dry desert climate.

Write the word *evaporate* where everyone can see it. Tell the students that as you read the sentence from the book that includes the word *evaporate*, you want them to listen for the word and think about what it might mean. Then read these sentences aloud: "Deserts get less than 10 inches (25 centimeters) of rain each year. Desert air is so dry, raindrops often evaporate before they hit the ground." Ask:

Q *What do you think the word* evaporate *might mean?*

Have a few volunteers share their thinking. If necessary, explain that *evaporate* means "to change from liquid to gas." When something evaporates it changes from water to vapor in the air. Explain that because the desert climate is so dry, raindrops often evaporate, or change from water to vapor in the air, before they hit the ground.

In this lesson, the students:

- Review and practice using the words *disrupt, trample,* and *forbid* from Day 3
- Build their speaking and listening skills
- Ask clarifying questions

Words Reviewed

disrupt
Disrupt means "disturb or interrupt something that is happening."

trample
Trample means "damage or crush by walking or stepping on something heavily."

forbid
Forbid means "order someone not to do something."

REVIEW THE WORDS

1 Briefly Review the Words

Display the daily review cards (WA9). Review the pronunciation and meaning of each word.

Ask:

> **Q** *Which of the words would you use when telling a story about a deer sneaking into your garden? Why?* [Click ❶ on WA9 to reveal the first prompt.] *Turn to your partner.*

Materials

- Daily review cards (WA9)
- Copy of this week's family letter (BLM1) for each student

WA9

disrupt	trample	forbid

PROMPT 1: I would use the word _____.

I might say . . .

❶ ❷ ❸ ❹ ❺

PROMPT 1: "I would use the word [*trample*]. I might say . . ."

After partners have talked, have a few volunteers use the prompt to share their thinking with the class.

PRACTICE USING THE WORDS

2 Discuss "Would You?" Questions

Explain that you will ask some questions that partners will discuss.

Ask:

Q *Would you forbid your friend from trampling on your sand castle? Why?* [Click ❷ to reveal the prompt.] *Turn to your partner.*

PROMPT 2: "I [would/would not] forbid my friend from trampling on my sand castle because . . ."

After partners have talked, have a few volunteers use the prompt to share their thinking with the class.

Using the same procedure, discuss:

Q *Would you disrupt a school assembly? Why?* [Click ❸ to reveal the next prompt.] *Turn to your partner.*

PROMPT 3: "I [would/would not] disrupt a school assembly because . . ."

Q *Would you be exhilarated if someone disrupted a conversation you were having with a friend? Why?* [Click ❹ to reveal the next prompt.] *Turn to your partner.*

PROMPT 4: "I [would/would not] be exhilarated if someone disrupted a conversation I was having with a friend because . . ."

Q *Would you forbid your dog from trampling on your neighbor's flowers? Why?* [Click ❺ to reveal the next prompt.] *Turn to your partner.*

PROMPT 5: "I [would/would not] forbid my dog from trampling on my neighbor's flowers because . . ."

Teacher Note

You might remind the students that they learned the word *exhilarated* earlier and that it means "very happy and excited."

Teacher Note

Send home with each student a copy of this week's family letter (BLM1). Encourage the students to talk about this week's words with their families.

In this lesson, the students:

- Review words learned earlier
- Build their speaking and listening skills
- Listen respectfully to the thinking of others and share their own

Words Reviewed

diverse
Diverse means "different from one another."

flashy
Flashy means "very big, bright, or expensive." Something that is flashy catches your attention.

flimsy
Flimsy means "thin and weak." If something is flimsy, it is not sturdy or strong.

hazardous
Hazardous means "dangerous."

plain
Plain means "without anything added or without decoration." If something is plain, it is simple, not fancy. *Plain* also means a "large area of flat land."

REVIEW THE WORDS

1 Briefly Review the Words

Display the ongoing review cards (WA10) and review the pronunciation and meaning of each word.

PRACTICE USING THE WORDS

2 Play "Which Word Am I?"

Explain that partners will play "Which Word Am I?" You will give a clue about one of the words and partners will figure out the word.

Begin by saying:

- *I'm how you might describe a cake without any frosting or candles.*

Ask:

 Q *Which word am I? Why?* [Click ❶ on WA10 to reveal the prompt.]
Turn to your partner.

Materials

- Ongoing review cards (WA10)

| diverse | flashy | flimsy |
| hazardous | plain | |

PROMPT 1: I think the word is _____ because . . .

1

PROMPT 1: "I think the word is [*plain*] because . . ."

After partners have talked, have a few volunteers use the prompt to share their thinking with the class.

Using the same procedure, discuss:

- *I'm a word you might use to describe a table made of toothpicks.* (flimsy)

- *I'm another word for* different. (diverse)

- *I'm how you describe something that is not safe and could be dangerous.* (hazardous)

- *I'm how you describe a shiny new pair of bright red sunglasses with orange blinking lights on the side.* (flashy)

Week 24

RESOURCES

Read-aloud

- *Polar Bears* by Mark Newman

More Strategy Practice

- "Discuss Another Meaning of *Decline*"

Assessment Resource Book

- Week 24 vocabulary assessments

 ## Online Resources

Visit the CCC Learning Hub (ccclearninghub.org) to find your online resources for this week.

Whiteboard Activities

- WA1–WA10

Assessment Forms

- "Class Vocabulary Assessment Record" sheet (CA1)
- "Individual Vocabulary Assessment: Word Check 6" answer sheet (IA1)
- "Individual Vocabulary Assessment Student Record" sheet (SR1)
- "Individual Vocabulary Assessment Class Record" sheet (CR1)
- (Optional) "Student Self-assessment" response sheet (SA1)

Reproducibles

- Week 24 family letter (BLM1)
- (Optional) "Week 24 Word Cards" (BLM2)
- (Optional) "Week 24 Crossword Puzzle" (BLM3)

OVERVIEW

Words Taught	Words Reviewed
struggle	avoid
skill	customary
skillful	disrupt
opportunity	texture
generally	trample
decline	

Word-learning Strategies

- Using the suffix *-ful* to determine word meanings (review)
- Recognizing synonyms (review)
- Recognizing words with multiple meanings (review)

Vocabulary Focus

- Students learn and use six words from or about the book.
- Students review using the suffix *-ful* to determine word meanings.
- Students review synonyms and words with multiple meanings.
- Students review words learned earlier.
- Students build their speaking and listening skills.

Social Development Focus

- Students develop the skill of giving reasons for their opinions.
- Students listen respectfully to the thinking of others and share their own.

⏱ DO AHEAD

- ✓ (Optional) Prior to Day 3, review the more strategy practice activity "Discuss Another Meaning of *Decline*" on page 503.

- ✓ Prior to Day 4, visit the CCC Learning Hub (ccclearninghub.org) to access and print this week's family letter (BLM1). Make enough copies to send one letter home with each student.

(continues)

⏱ DO AHEAD   *(continued)*

✓ Prior to Day 5, make a copy of the "Class Vocabulary Assessment Record" sheet (CA1); see page 197 of the *Assessment Resource Book.*

✓ Prior to Day 5, make a class set of the "Individual Vocabulary Assessment: Word Check 6" answer sheet (IA1); see page 201 of the *Assessment Resource Book.* Make enough copies for each student to have one; set aside a reference copy for yourself.

✓ (Optional) Prior to Day 5, make a master copy of the "Student Self-assessment" response sheet (SA1); see page 204 of the *Assessment Resource Book.* Write the words you have chosen to be assessed on the master copy. Then make enough copies for each student to have one.

✓ (Optional) Visit the CCC Learning Hub (ccclearninghub.org) to access and print the following materials: "Week 24 Word Cards" (BLM2) and "Week 24 Crossword Puzzle" (BLM3). These materials can be used to provide your students with more opportunities to review the words.

In this lesson, the students:

- Learn and use the words *struggle, skill,* and *skillful*
- Review the suffix *-ful*
- Build their speaking and listening skills
- Share their partners' thinking with the class
- Listen respectfully to the thinking of others and share their own

Materials

- *Polar Bears*
- Word card 139 (WA1)
- Word cards 140–141 (WA2)

Words Taught

struggle (p. 10)
Struggle means "try very hard to do something."

skill (p. 10)
Skill is the "ability to do something well." A skill comes from training and practice.

skillful
Skillful means "good at doing something."

INTRODUCE AND USE *STRUGGLE*

1 Introduce and Define *Struggle*

Show pages 10–11 of *Polar Bears* and review that this part of the book tells about how baby polar bears grow up and learn to survive. Read page 10 aloud, emphasizing the word *struggle.*

Explain that *struggle* means to "try very hard to do something." Explain that life is hard and dangerous for baby polar bears. Because of this, baby polar bears must struggle, or try very hard, to survive. Polar bear mothers help their babies struggle to survive by teaching them what they need to know to make it to adulthood.

Display word card 139 (◖ WA1) and have the students say the word *struggle.*

2 Discuss Struggling

Give examples of times you have struggled to do or accomplish something or seen someone struggle.

> **You might say:**
>
> "I am struggling to learn to play the guitar. It is challenging, but I am trying very hard to learn. I struggled when I ran my first half marathon. Toward the end of the race, I was really, really tired, but I struggled to keep going and I finished. My son sometimes struggles with his homework. The homework is difficult and he has to work hard to finish all of it."

Use "Think, Pair, Share" to discuss the question that follows. Ask the students to be ready to share their partners' thinking with the class.

Q *When have you struggled, or tried very hard, to do something?* [Pause; click on WA1 to reveal the first prompt.] *Turn to your partner.*

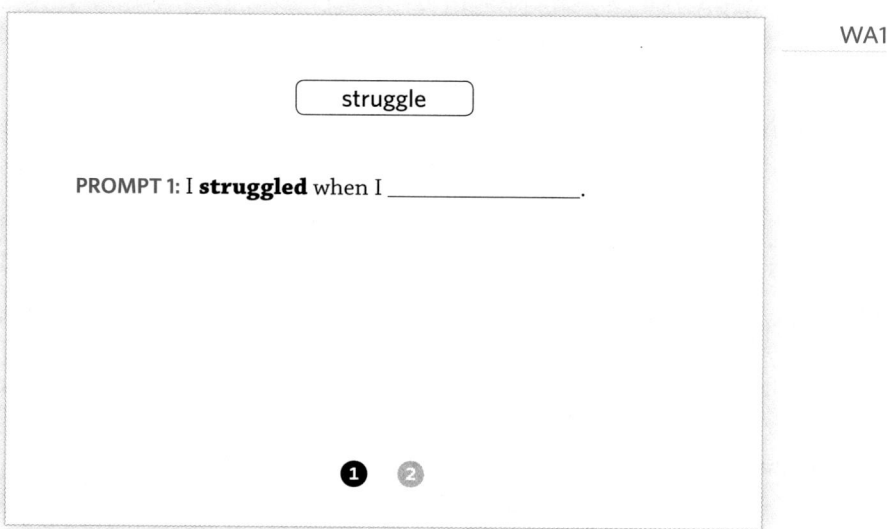

WA1

struggle

PROMPT 1: I **struggled** when I _____.

PROMPT 1: "I struggled when I [was learning to swim]."

After partners have talked, click **2** on WA1 to reveal the next prompt. Then have one or two volunteers use the prompt to share their partners' thinking with the class:

PROMPT 2: "[Leif] struggled when he [was learning to swim]."

Point to the word *struggle* and review the pronunciation and meaning of the word.

INTRODUCE AND USE *SKILL* AND *SKILLFUL*

3 Introduce and Define *Skill*

Show pages 10–11 of *Polar Bears* again and review that this part of the book tells about how baby polar bears grow up and learn to survive. Read the second sentence aloud, emphasizing the word *skill*.

Explain that *skill* is the "ability to do something well." A skill comes from training and practice. Tell the students that the polar bears learn skills, or abilities, to survive from their mother. Display word cards 140–141 (◖ WA2) and reveal word card 140. Have the students say the word *skill*.

Show pages 16–17 and explain that the polar bears on these pages are learning and practicing a very important skill. Ask the students to listen for what that skill is as you read page 17. Then read page 17 aloud. Ask:

Q *What skill, or ability, are the bears learning and practicing?*

Click ❶ on word card 140 (WA2) to reveal the first prompt. Have a few volunteers use the prompt to share their thinking with the class.

PROMPT 1: "The bears are learning and practicing the skill of [hunting]."

Teacher Note

For further practice with the word *skill*, you might show the students pages 22–23 and ask "What skill is this polar bear demonstrating?"

4 Discuss Skills

Give some example of skills learned in school.

> **You might say:**
>
> "In school, we learn many skills, or abilities. In school, I learned the skill of drawing and painting. Reading and writing are two skills, or abilities, you are learning in school."

Ask:

Q *What other skills, or abilities, do we learn in school?* [Click ❷ on WA2 to reveal the prompt.] *Turn to your partner.*

PROMPT 2: "We also learn the skill of [spelling] in school."

After partners have talked, have a few volunteers use the prompt to share their thinking with the class.

5 Introduce and Define *Skillful* and Review the Suffix *-ful*

Explain that the last word the students will learn today is *skillful*. Display word cards 140–141 (◖ WA2) and reveal word card 141. Have the students say the word *skillful*.

Point to the suffix *-ful* in *skillful* and review that *-ful* is a suffix and that the suffix *-ful* means "full of." Ask:

Q *Based on what you know about the word* skill *and the suffix* -ful, *what do you think the word* skillful *might mean?*

Click ❸ to reveal the prompt. Have one or two volunteers use the prompt to share their thinking with the class.

PROMPT 3: "I think *skillful* means . . ."

If necessary, explain that *skillful* means "full of skill" or "good at doing something." Explain that the polar bears need to be skillful, or good at skills such as hunting and swimming, to survive in the Arctic.

6 Discuss Being Skillful

Explain that each of us is skillful, or good at doing certain things, usually because we have learned to do them and have practiced doing them. Give some examples of things you or someone you know is skillful at doing.

> **You might say:**
>
> "I am skillful at painting. I've taken classes in which professional painters taught me techniques, or ways, to paint, and I practice every week. My daughter is skillful at ice-skating. She goes to lessons twice a week and is performing in the winter pageant. We have many skillful students in our class. Some of you are skillful storytellers. You tell and write wonderful stories. Others of you are skillful at drawing. I've watched you during recess, and I think many of you are skillful rope jumpers, four-square players, and soccer and basketball players."

Use "Think, Pair, Share" to discuss:

 Q *What is something you are skillful at doing? How did you become skillful?* [Pause; click ❹ to reveal the prompt.] *Turn to your partner.*

PROMPT 4: "I am skillful at [playing the piano]. I became skillful by . . ."

After partners have talked, have a few volunteers use the prompt to share their thinking with the class.

Use "Think, Pair, Share" to discuss:

 Q *What is something you would like to be skillful at doing? How would you become skillful?* [Pause; click ❺ to reveal the next prompt.] *Turn to your partner.*

PROMPT 5: "I would like to be skillful at [skateboarding]. To be skillful, I would need to . . ."

After partners have talked, have a few volunteers use the prompt to share their thinking with the class.

Point to the words *skill* and *skillful* and review the pronunciation and meaning of each word.

In this lesson, the students:

- Review and practice using the words *struggle, skill,* and *skillful* from Day 1
- Build their speaking and listening skills
- Give reasons for their thinking

Words Reviewed

struggle
Struggle means "try very hard to do something."

skill
Skill is the "ability to do something well." A skill comes from training and practice.

skillful
Skillful means "good at doing something."

REVIEW THE WORDS

1 Briefly Review the Words

Display the daily review cards (WA3). Review the pronunciation and meaning of each word.

Ask:

 Q *Which of these words might you use to describe a time when you learned something new? Why? [Click ❶ on WA3 to reveal the first prompt.] Turn to your partner.*

WA3

| struggle | skill | skillful |

PROMPT 1: I might use _____ because . . .

❶ ② ③ ④

Materials

- Daily review cards (WA3)

PROMPT 1: "I might use [*struggle*] because . . ."

After partners have talked, have a few volunteers use the prompt to share their thinking with the class.

PRACTICE USING THE WORDS

2 Play "Make a Choice"

Explain that partners will play the game "Make a Choice." Point to the word *skill* and ask:

Q *Which skill do you think would be harder to learn: skiing or playing the violin? Why?* [Click ❷ to reveal the prompt.] *Turn to your partner.*

PROMPT 2: "I think [playing the violin] would be a harder skill to learn because . . ."

After partners have talked, have a few volunteers use the prompt to share their thinking with the class.

Using the same procedure, discuss:

[struggle]

Q *Which might you struggle to do: take a nap or build a tree house? Why?* [Click ❸ to reveal the next prompt.] *Turn to your partner.*

PROMPT 3: "I might struggle to [build a tree house] because . . ."

[skillful]

Q *Which would you like to be skillful at doing: drawing or playing soccer? Why?* [Click ❹ to reveal the prompt.] *Turn to your partner.*

PROMPT 4: "I would like to be skillful at [drawing] because . . ."

In this lesson, the students:

- Learn and use the words *opportunity, generally,* and *decline*
- Review synonyms and words with multiple meanings
- Build their speaking and listening skills
- Listen respectfully to the thinking of others and share their own

Words Taught

opportunity (p. 18)
An *opportunity* is a "chance to do something."

generally (p. 23)
Generally means "usually or almost always."

decline (p. 28)
Decline means "get smaller or worse."

INTRODUCE AND USE *OPPORTUNITY*

1 ## Introduce and Define *Opportunity* and Review Synonyms

Show pages 18–19 of *Polar Bears* and review that this part of the book tells about what polar bears eat. Read page 18 aloud, emphasizing the word *opportunity*.

Explain that an *opportunity* is a "chance to do something" and that *opportunity* and *chance* are synonyms. Point out that polar bears usually hunt seals. Once in a great while, they get the opportunity, or chance, to hunt walruses and beluga whales—but this opportunity is rare.

Display word card 142 (◖ WA4) and have the students say the word *opportunity*.

2 ## Discuss Fun and Interesting Opportunities

Give a few examples of fun or interesting opportunities you or the students have had recently.

> **You might say:**
> "Last night I had the opportunity, or chance, to see a movie with my best friend. Last summer I had the opportunity to visit Mexico. This year our class had an opportunity to go on a field trip to the space museum. We also had an opportunity to go to the book fair last week."

Materials

- *Polar Bears*
- Word card 142 (WA4)
- Word card 143 (WA5)
- Word card 144 (WA6)

Teacher Note

If you started a synonym chart, add the words *opportunity* and *chance* to it.

Ask:

 Q *When have you had an opportunity to do something fun or interesting?* [Click **1** on WA4 to reveal the prompt.] *Turn to your partner.*

> opportunity
>
> **PROMPT 1:** I had the **opportunity** to _____
> when . . .
>
> **1**

PROMPT 1: "I had the opportunity to [jump on a giant trampoline] when . . ."

After partners have talked, have a few volunteers use the prompt to share their thinking with the class.

Follow up by discussing as a class:

Q *What is a fun opportunity you would like to have?*

Point to the word *opportunity* and review the pronunciation and meaning of the word.

INTRODUCE AND USE *GENERALLY*

3 Introduce and Define *Generally*

Show pages 22–23 and review that this part of the book tells how polar bears swim fast. Read the first four sentences on page 23 aloud, emphasizing the word *generally*.

Explain that *generally* is the next word the students will learn. Tell the students that *generally* means "usually or almost always" and that *generally* and *usually* are synonyms. Explain that polar bears can swim six miles per hour, which is much faster than they generally, or usually, walk.

Display word card 143 ( WA5) and have the students say the word *generally*.

🌐 ELL Note

The Spanish cognate of *generally* is *generalmente*.

Teacher Note

If you started a synonym chart, add the words *generally* and *usually* to it.

4 Discuss Things We Generally Do

Give examples of things you generally do:

> **You might say:**
>
> "In the mornings, I generally, or usually, eat toast and drink coffee before leaving the house. On the weekends, my family and I generally go hiking if the weather is nice. During reading time, we generally gather on the rug in the class library."

Ask:

 Q *What is something you generally do in the morning before school?* [Click ❶ on WA5 to reveal the first prompt.] *Turn to your partner.*

PROMPT 1: "In the morning, I generally . . ."

After partners have talked, have one or two volunteers use the prompt to share their thinking with the class.

Follow up by asking:

 Q *What is something you generally do after school?* [Click ❷ to reveal the next prompt.] *Turn to your partner.*

PROMPT 2: "After school, I generally . . ."

After partners have talked, have one or two volunteers use the prompt to share their thinking with the class.

Point to the word *generally* and review the pronunciation and meaning of the word.

INTRODUCE AND USE *DECLINE*

5 Introduce and Define *Decline*

Show pages 28–29 and explain that this part of the book has more facts about polar bears. Ask the students to listen carefully as you read facts about the population of polar bears, or the number of polar bears still living, in the Arctic. Then read the second paragraph on page 28 aloud, emphasizing the word *decline*.

Tell the students that the last word they will learn today is *decline* and that *decline* means "get smaller or worse." When there is a decline in something, it gets smaller or worse. Explain that the author is concerned because in some parts of the Arctic, the number of polar bears is declining, or getting smaller. The author fears that the population of polar bears may decline even more in the future because global warming is causing the Arctic ice to melt, making it difficult for polar bears to find food.

Display word card 144 (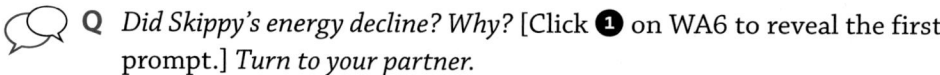 WA6) and have the students say the word *decline*.

6 Play "Did It Decline?"

Tell the students that they will play a game called "Did It Decline?" Explain that you will describe something and partners will discuss whether or not the thing you described declined and why they think so.

Begin by saying:

- *Our dog, Skippy, is 12 years old. When he was young, he played fetch for hours. Now his energy is much lower and he gets tired after a short time.*

Q *Did Skippy's energy decline? Why?* [Click ❶ on WA6 to reveal the first prompt.] *Turn to your partner.*

PROMPT 1: "Skippy's energy [did/did not] decline because . . ."

After partners have talked, have a few volunteers use the prompt to share their thinking with the class.

Using the same procedure, discuss one or both of the following:

- *When we arrived in Hawaii for vacation, the temperature was a pleasant 80 degrees. A day or two later, the temperature fell by 20 degrees and it rained. Fortunately, the temperature went back up and the rain stopped.*

Q *Did the temperature decline during the vacation in Hawaii? Why?* [Click ❷ to reveal the next prompt.] *Turn to your partner.*

PROMPT 2: "The temperature [did/did not] decline because . . ."

- *During the summer, about 100 to 150 people visit our community pool each day. On the Fourth of July, however, that number rises to 200 to 250. After the holiday, the numbers go back down.*

Q *Does the number of people at the pool decline on the Fourth of July? Why?* [Click ❸ to reveal the prompt.] *Turn to your partner.*

PROMPT 3: "The number of people [does/does not] decline on the Fourth of July because . . ."

Point to the word *decline* and review the pronunciation and meaning of the word.

MORE STRATEGY PRACTICE

Discuss Another Meaning of *Decline*

Review that words can have more than one meaning and that the meanings are often very different. Write the word *decline* where everyone can see it, and explain that the word *decline* has two very different meanings. Review that *decline* can mean "get smaller or worse." Then tell the students that *decline* can also mean "politely turn something down or refuse something."

Remind the students that when they read or hear a word that has more than one meaning—like *decline*—they can usually figure out the correct meaning by thinking about how the word is used. Explain that you will read a sentence that uses the word *decline*. The students will decide whether *decline* means "get smaller or worse" or "politely turn something down or refuse something."

Then read the following sentence aloud twice:

- *Jenna declines the invitation to Paul's party this weekend because she is going camping with her family.*

Ask:

Q *In the sentence, does* decline *mean "get smaller or worse" or "politely turn something down or refuse something"? Why do you think that?*

Show the prompt and read it aloud.

PROMPT: "I think *decline* means ['politely turn something down or refuse something'] because . . ."

Have one or two volunteers use the prompt to share their thinking with the class. Using the same procedure, discuss the following sentence:

- *The population of fish declined after the lake froze over.*

<table>
<tr><td>

Day 4

</td><td>

Review *Opportunity, Generally,* and *Decline*

</td></tr>
</table>

Materials

- Daily review cards (WA7)
- Daily review activity (WA8)
- Copy of this week's family letter (BLM1) for each student
- (Optional) Copy of the "Week 24 Crossword Puzzle" (BLM3) for each student

In this lesson, the students:

- Review and practice using the words *opportunity, generally,* and *decline* from Day 3
- Build their speaking and listening skills
- Give reasons for their thinking

Words Reviewed

opportunity
An *opportunity* is a "chance to do something."

generally
Generally means "usually or almost always."

decline
Decline means "get smaller or worse."

REVIEW THE WORDS

1 Briefly Review the Words

Display the daily review cards (WA7). Review the pronunciation and meaning of each word.

Ask:

 Q *Does the temperature decline at night? Why?* [Click ❶ on WA7 to reveal the first prompt.] *Turn to your partner.*

WA7

> | opportunity | generally | decline |
>
> **PROMPT 1:** The temperature [does/does not] **decline** at night because . . .
>
> ❶ ②

PROMPT 1: "The temperature [does/does not] decline at night because . . ."

After partners have talked, have a few volunteers use the prompt to share their thinking with the class.

Using the same procedure, discuss:

 Q *Do you generally accept opportunities to go over to your friends' houses? Why?* [Click ❷ to reveal the next prompt.] *Turn to your partner.*

PROMPT 2: "I [do/do not] generally accept opportunities to go over to friends' houses because . . ."

PRACTICE USING THE WORDS

2 Play "Find Another Word"

Tell the students that partners will play the game "Find Another Word." Remind the students that you will show a sentence with one or more words underlined. You will read each sentence aloud, and partners will decide which vocabulary word can replace the underlined part of the sentence.

Display the daily review activity (◖ WA8) and begin playing the game:

1. Click ❶ to reveal the first sentence. Point to the sentence and read it aloud, emphasizing the underlined words.

   ▪ Sentence 1: *Dwight is excited for band recital because he has been given the <u>chance</u> to perform a flute solo.*

2. Give the students a few moments to think about the sentence and the underlined word. Then point to the three word choices and ask:

 Q *Which vocabulary word could replace the underlined word? Why?* [Click ❶ again and point to the prompt.] *Turn to your partner.*

PROMPT 1: "I think the word [*opportunity*] could replace *chance* because . . ."

   After partners have talked, have a few volunteers use the prompt to share their thinking with the class.

3. Conclude the discussion by clicking ❶ a third time to highlight the correct vocabulary word and reveal the sentence with the correct word in place.

Teacher Note

You might explain that the students may need to change the form of the word to complete the sentence by adding an ending such as *-s*, *-ing*, or *-ed*.

Teacher Note

Each sentence in the ongoing review activity (WA8) has a corresponding number: the first sentence is ❶; the second sentence is ❷; and the third sentence is ❸. To play the game, click the corresponding number four times:

▪ The first click reveals the sentence.

▪ The second click reveals the prompt.

▪ The third click highlights the correct answer and reveals the sentence with the correct answer in place.

▪ The fourth click clears the screen.

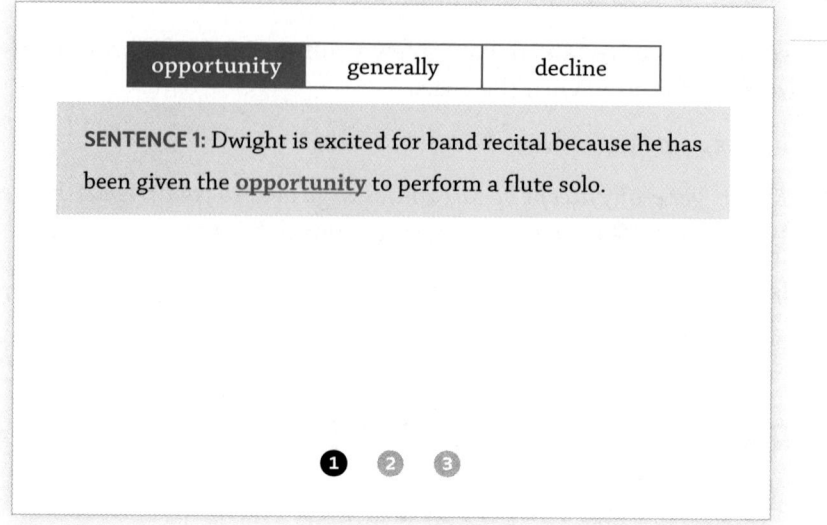

| opportunity | generally | decline |

SENTENCE 1: Dwight is excited for band recital because he has been given the <u>opportunity</u> to perform a flute solo.

❶ ② ③

Teacher Note

Send home with each student a copy of this week's family letter (BLM1). Encourage the students to talk about this week's words with their families.

Teacher Note

To provide the students with additional review of words taught during Weeks 23 and 24, you might distribute a copy of the "Week 24 Crossword Puzzle" (BLM3) to each student.

4. Click ❶ to clear the screen.

Use the same procedure to discuss the following sentences:

- Sentence 2: *The squirrel population in Helen's backyard <u>became less</u> after she got her new dog, Sadie.*

PROMPT 2: "I think the word [*declined*] could replace *became less* because . . ."

- Sentence 3: *On weeknights, Wesley's family <u>usually</u> eats dinner together and talks about their day.*

PROMPT 3: "I think the word [*generally*] could replace *usually* because . . ."

In this lesson, the students:

- Review words learned earlier
- Build their speaking and listening skills
- Listen respectfully to the thinking of others and share their own

Words Reviewed

avoid
Avoid means "keep away from."

customary
Customary means "usual or normal or happening regularly."

disrupt
Disrupt means "disturb or interrupt something that is happening."

texture
Texture is "how a material feels—for example, rough or smooth."

trample
Trample means "damage or crush by walking or stepping on something heavily."

REVIEW THE WORDS

1 Briefly Review the Words

Display the ongoing review cards (WA9). Review the pronunciation and meaning of each word.

PRACTICE USING THE WORDS

2 Play "What's the Missing Word?"

Tell the students that they will play the game "What's the Missing Word?" Review that you will read some sentences aloud and that a word will be missing from each sentence. Explain that the partners will decide which vocabulary word could replace the missing word and explain why they think so.

Display the ongoing review activity (WA10) and begin playing the game:

1. Point to the words *avoid, customary, disrupt, texture,* and *trample.* Then click ❶ to reveal the first sentence and read it aloud. Point out that a word is missing.

   - Sentence 1: *The velvet chair has a very soft _____ .*

Materials

- Ongoing review cards (WA9)
- Ongoing review activity (WA10)
- "Class Vocabulary Assessment Record" sheet (CA1)
- Class set of the "Individual Vocabulary Assessment: Word Check 6" answer sheet (IA1)
- Class set of the "Individual Vocabulary Assessment Student Record" sheet (SR1)
- "Individual Vocabulary Assessment Class Record" sheet (CR1)
- (Optional) Class set of the "Student Self-assessment" response sheet (SA1)

Teacher Note

Each sentence on the ongoing review activity (WA10) has a corresponding number: the first sentence is ❶; the second sentence is ❷; the third sentence is ❸; and so on. To play the game, click the corresponding number four times:

- The first click reveals the sentence.
- The second click reveals the prompt.
- The third click reveals the correct answer.
- The fourth click clears the screen.

Teacher Note

You might explain that the students may need to change the form of the word to complete the sentence by adding an ending such as *-s, -es,* or *-ing.*

2. Give the students a few moments to think about the sentence. Then ask:

> **Q** *What's the missing word? Why do you think so?* [Click ❶ again and read the prompt aloud.] *Turn to your partner.*

PROMPT: "I think [*texture*] is the missing word because . . ."

After partners have talked, have a few volunteers use the prompt to share their thinking with the class.

3. Conclude the discussion of this sentence by clicking ❶ a third time to highlight the correct vocabulary word and reveal the correct word in place. Read the sentence again with the word *texture* at the end.

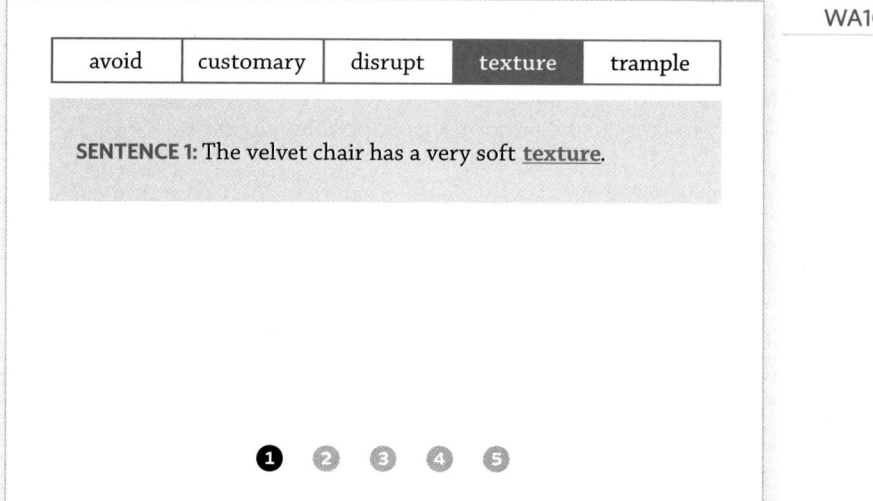

WA10

| avoid | customary | disrupt | texture | trample |

SENTENCE 1: The velvet chair has a very soft <u>texture</u>.

❶ ② ③ ④ ⑤

4. Click ❶ to clear the screen.

Repeat the procedure to discuss the following sentences:

- Sentence 2: *The park ranger told the hikers to _____ poison oak.* (avoid)

- Sentence 3: *It is _____ to shake hands with someone when you first meet.* (customary)

- Sentence 4: *The puppy _____ the blocks and knocks them all over.* (tramples)

- Sentence 5: *It's important not to _____ birds in their nests.* (disrupt)

Assessment Notes

CLASS VOCABULARY ASSESSMENT NOTE

Observe the students and ask yourself:

- Are the students able to complete the sentences using the vocabulary words?
- Can they explain why they finished the sentences the way they did?
- Are they using the vocabulary words in their speech and writing?

Record your observations on the "Class Assessment Record" sheet (CA1); see page 197 of the *Assessment Resource Book*.

Use the following suggestions to support struggling students:

- If **only a few students** understand a word's meaning, reteach the word using the vocabulary lesson in which it was first taught as a model.
- If **about half of the students** understand a word's meaning, provide further practice by inviting the students to tell or write stories in which they use the word.

INDIVIDUAL VOCABULARY ASSESSMENT NOTE

Before continuing with the week 25 lesson, take this opportunity to assess individual students' understanding of words taught in Weeks 21–24 by using the "Individual Vocabulary Assessment: Word Check 6" answer sheet (IA1) on page 201 of the *Assessment Resource Book*. For instructions on administering this assessment, see "Completing the Individual Vocabulary Assessment" on page 198 of the *Assessment Resource Book*.

STUDENT SELF-ASSESSMENT NOTE

In addition to or in place of the Individual Vocabulary Assessment, you might have each student evaluate her understanding of words taught in Weeks 21–24 using the "Student Self-assessment" response sheet (SA1). For instructions on administering this assessment, see "Completing the Student Self-assessment" on page 202 of the *Assessment Resource Book*.

Week 25

RESOURCES

Articles

- "Banning Tag" (see page 530–531)
- "Smile—You've Got Homework!" (see page 532–533)
- "Homework—Who Needs It?" (see page 534–535)

More Strategy Practice

- "Discuss Another Meaning of *Unwind*"

 More ELL Support

- "Draw a Picture of Unwinding"

 ## Online Resources

Visit the CCC Learning Hub (ccclearninghub.org) to find your online resources for this week.

Whiteboard Activities

- WA1–WA9

Reproducibles

- Week 25 family letter (BLM1)
- (Optional) "Week 25 Word Cards" (BLM2)

OVERVIEW

Words Taught	Words Reviewed
ban	deadly
permit	flashy
valuable	graceful
task	intense
unwind	opportunity
stressful	

Word-learning Strategies

- Recognizing antonyms (review)
- Using the suffix *-ful* to determine word meanings (review)
- Recognizing words with multiple meanings (review)

Vocabulary Focus

- Students learn and use six words from or about the articles.
- Students review antonyms.
- Students review the suffix *-ful* and words with multiple meanings.
- Students review words learned earlier.
- Students build their speaking and listening skills.

Social Development Focus

- Students develop the skill of giving reasons for their opinions.
- Students listen respectfully to the thinking of others and share their own.

⏱ DO AHEAD

✓ (Optional) Prior to Day 3, review the more strategy practice activity "Discuss Another Meaning of *Unwind*" on page 523.

✓ Prior to Day 4, visit the CCC Learning Hub (ccclearninghub.org) to access and print this week's family letter (BLM1). Make enough copies to send one letter home with each student.

✓ (Optional) Visit the CCC Learning Hub (ccclearninghub.org) to access and print "Week 25 Word Cards" (BLM2). These cards can be used to provide your students with more opportunities to review the words.

In this lesson, the students:

- Learn and use the words *ban, permit,* and *valuable*
- Review antonyms
- Build their speaking and listening skills
- Give reasons for their opinions

Words Taught

ban (p. 530)
Ban means "forbid something or prevent someone from doing something."

permit
Permit means "allow something to happen or let someone do something."

valuable (p. 533)
Valuable means "very important or useful in some way."

Materials

- "Banning Tag" (page 530–531)
- "Smile—You've Got Homework!" (page 532–533)
- Word cards 145–146 (WA1)
- Word card 147 (WA2)

INTRODUCE AND USE *BAN* AND *PERMIT*

1 Introduce and Define *Ban*

Remind the students that they read the article "Banning Tag," and review that the article is about the pros and cons of banning the game of tag in schools. Tell the students that the first word they will learn today is *ban* and explain that *ban* means "forbid something or prevent someone from doing something." Review that some schools are banning tag. They are forbidding or preventing students from playing the game because it is too dangerous.

Reveal word card 145 on word cards 145–146 (◖ WA1) and have the students say the word *ban*.

Explain that some things are banned, or forbidden, at school and in the classroom. Give a few examples, and explain why each is banned.

> **You might say:**
>
> "Knives and other weapons are banned, or forbidden, at school and in the classroom because they are dangerous. Fighting is banned also. In our classroom, running is banned, or not allowed, because someone might trip and get hurt when running."

Teacher Note

You might remind the students that they learned the word *forbid* earlier and that it means "order someone not to do something."

Ask:

 Q *What else is banned at our school or in our classroom? Why is it banned?* [Click ❶ on WA1 to reveal the first prompt.] *Turn to your partner.*

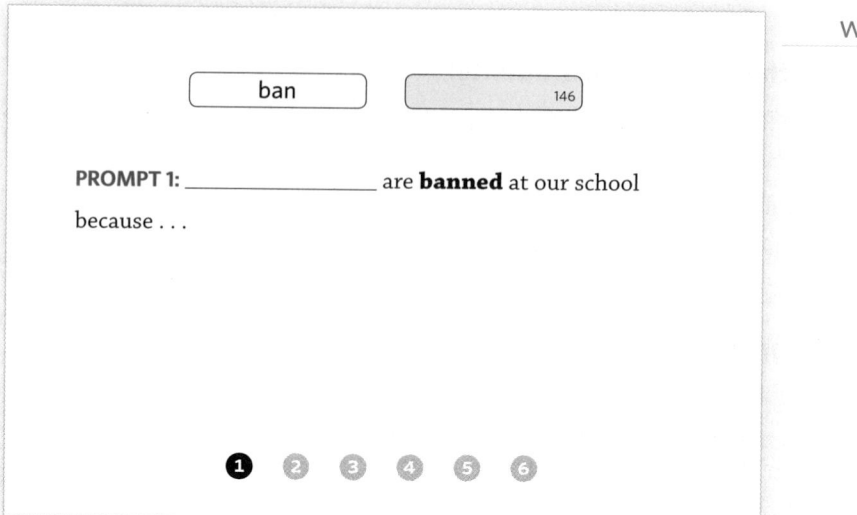

WA1

| ban | 146 |

PROMPT 1: _____ are **banned** at our school because . . .

❶ ② ③ ④ ⑤ ⑥

PROMPT 1: "[Skateboards] are banned at our school because . . ."

After partners have talked, have a few volunteers use the prompt to share their thinking with the class.

2 Introduce and Use *Permit* and Review Antonyms

Reveal word card 146 on WA1 and tell the students that *permit* is the next word they will learn today. Explain that *ban* and *permit* are *antonyms*, or "words that have opposite meanings."

Ask:

Q *If* ban *and* permit *are antonyms, and* ban *means "forbid something or prevent someone from doing something," what do you think the word* permit *means?*

Click ❷ on WA1 to reveal the prompt and have a few volunteers use the prompt to share their thinking with the class.

PROMPT 2: "I think *permit* means . . ."

If necessary, explain that *permit* means "allow something to happen or let someone do something." Remind the students that, according to the article, some parents and students think tag should be permitted, or allowed, in school. Tell the students that as you read the section called "The Other Side" from the article "Banning Tag," you want them to listen for the reasons people think tag should be permitted in school. Then read "The Other Side" aloud.

Briefly discuss as a class:

Q *Why do some parents and students think tag should be permitted, or allowed, in school?* [Click ❸ to reveal the prompt.]

 **ELL Note**

The Spanish cognate of *permit* is *permitir.*

Teacher Note

If you started an antonym chart, add *ban* and *permit* to it.

PROMPT 3: "They think tag should be permitted because . . ."

Have a few volunteers use the prompt to share their thinking with the class.

3 Play "Banned or Permitted?"

Tell the students that partners will play a game called "Banned or Permitted?" Explain that you will describe something and partners will discuss whether it should be banned or permitted and why they think so.

Begin by saying:

- *Food and drinks on a school bus*

Use "Think, Pair, Share" to discuss:

 Q *Food and drinks on a school bus: banned or permitted? Why?* [Pause; click ❹ to reveal the prompt.] *Turn to your partner.*

PROMPT 4: "Food and drinks should be [banned/permitted] on a school bus because . . ."

After partners have talked, have a few volunteers use the prompt to share their thinking with the class.

Using the same procedure, discuss one or both of the following:

- *Loud music in the school library*

 Q *Loud music in the school library: banned or permitted? Why?* [Pause; click ❺ to reveal the prompt.] *Turn to your partner.*

PROMPT 5: "Loud music should be [banned/permitted] in the library because . . ."

- *Students using cell phones in class*

 Q *Students using cell phones in class: banned or permitted? Why?* [Pause; click ❻ to reveal the prompt.] *Turn to your partner.*

PROMPT 6: "Students using cell phones in class should be [banned/permitted] because . . ."

Point to the words *ban* and *permit* and review the pronunciation and meaning of the words.

INTRODUCE AND USE *VALUABLE*

4 Introduce and Define *Valuable*

Remind the students that they read two essays about homework and that the essay in favor of homework is called "Smile—You've Got Homework!" Review that, according to the essay, having students memorize facts for homework frees up class time for teachers to do other things. Read the following sentences aloud, emphasizing the word *valuable*: "Students need to memorize math facts, how words are spelled, historical dates, and other information. But memorizing information—like practicing skills—takes up valuable class time. Having students memorize facts for homework gives teachers more time during the school day for actual teaching."

Tell the students that *valuable* is the last word they will learn today, and explain that *valuable* means "very important or useful in some way." Explain that class time is valuable, or very important and useful, to both teachers and students. If students memorize things such as math facts for homework, valuable class time is freed up for teachers to teach important reading, writing, and math skills.

Display word card 147 (⚫ WA2) and have the students say the word *valuable*.

5 Play "Valuable or Not Valuable?"

Tell the students that they will play a game called "Valuable or Not Valuable?" Explain that you will describe ways that the students might spend their time after school. The students will decide if they think what you describe is a valuable, or important and useful, way to spend time after school, and why they think so.

Begin by saying:

- *Talking on the phone with your best friend*

Ask:

 Q *Is talking on the phone with your best friend a valuable way to spend your time after school? Why or why not?* [Click ❶ on WA2 to reveal the prompt.] *Turn to your partner.*

PROMPT 1: "Talking on the phone with my best friend [would/would not] be a valuable way to spend time after school because . . ."

After partners have talked, have a few volunteers use the prompt to share their thinking with the class.

Using the same procedure, discuss one or more of the following:

- *Going on a walk with my family*

 Q *Is going on a walk with your family a valuable way to spend your time after school? Why or why not?* [Click ❷ to reveal the prompt.] *Turn to your partner.*

PROMPT 2: "Going on a walk with my family [would/would not] be a valuable way to spend time after school because . . ."

- *Taking a nap*

 Q *Is taking a nap a valuable way to spend your time after school? Why or why not?* [Click ❸ to reveal the prompt.] *Turn to your partner.*

PROMPT 3: "Taking a nap [would/would not] be a valuable way to spend time after school because . . ."

- *Studying for a test*

 Q *Is studying for a test a valuable way to spend your time after school? Why or why not?* [Click **4** to reveal the prompt.] *Turn to your partner.*

PROMPT 4: "Studying for a test [would/would not] be a valuable way to spend time after school because . . ."

Point to the word *valuable* and review the pronunciation and meaning of the word.

Review *Ban, Permit, and Valuable* | Day 2

In this lesson, the students:

- Review and practice using the words *ban, permit,* and *valuable* from Day 1
- Build their speaking and listening skills
- Listen respectfully to the thinking of others and share their own

Materials

- Daily review cards (WA3)

Words Reviewed

ban
Ban means "forbid something or prevent someone from doing something."

permit
Permit means "allow something to happen or let someone do something."

valuable
Valuable means "very important or useful in some way."

REVIEW THE WORDS

1 Briefly Review the Words

Display the daily review cards (WA3). Review the pronunciation and meaning of each word.

Ask:

 Q *Which of the words might you use when talking to our school principal? How might you use the word?* [Click **1** on WA3 to reveal the first prompt.] *Turn to your partner.*

ban	permit	valuable

PROMPT 1: I would use the word _____.

I might say . . .

1 ② ③ ④

PROMPT 1: "I would use the word [*permit*]. I might say . . ."

After partners have talked, have a few volunteers use the prompt to share their thinking with the class.

PRACTICE USING THE WORDS

2 Play "Make a Choice"

Explain that partners will use the words to play the game "Make a Choice." Point to the word *ban* and tell the students that they will play the first round of the game with this word. Explain that you will describe two things and ask them to decide which one they think should be banned and tell why they think so. Explain that partners may not always agree and that is fine. What is important is that they explain their thinking.

Ask:

 Q *Which of these should be banned: running in the halls or running on the playground? Why?* [Click ② to reveal the prompt.] *Turn to your partner.*

PROMPT 2: "I think [running in the halls] should be banned because . . ."

After partners have talked, have one or two volunteers use the prompt to share their thinking with the class.

Using the same procedure, discuss:

[valuable]

 Q *Which of these is a more valuable use of your time after school: reading a book or watching TV? Why?* [Click ③ to reveal the prompt.] *Turn to your partner.*

PROMPT 3: "I think [reading a book] is more valuable because . . ."

 **ELL Note**

Rather than have the students choose between two things, you might have them discuss each thing individually by first asking "Should running in the halls be banned? Why?" and then asking "Should running on the playground be banned? Why?"

[permit]

 Q *Which of these do you think third-graders should be permitted to do: vote for president of the United States or vote for school president? Why?* [Click ❹ to reveal the prompt.] *Turn to your partner.*

PROMPT 4: "I think third-graders should be permitted to [vote for president of the United States] because . . ."

Introduce *Task, Unwind, and Stressful* — Day 3

In this lesson, the students:

- Learn and use the words *task, unwind,* and *stressful*
- Review synonyms and the suffix *-ful*
- Review words with multiple meanings
- Build their speaking and listening skills
- Give reasons for their opinions

Words Taught

task (p. 533)
A *task* is a "job, chore, or other particular thing you have to do."

unwind (p. 534)
Unwind means "relax."

stressful
Stressful means "causing worry or tension."

INTRODUCE AND USE *TASK*

1 Introduce and Define *Task*

Remind the students that they heard and talked about the essay "Smile—You've Got Homework!" and that the essay discusses the benefits of doing homework. Review that, according to the article, one benefit is that homework helps students learn to organize and plan their time. Read the following sentences from the section "Organization and Planning" aloud, emphasizing the words *tasks* and *task*: "Homework also helps kids learn how to prioritize tasks—or decide which tasks must be done and in what order—and how to plan for how long each task should take."

Materials

- "Smile—You've Got Homework!" (page 532–533)
- "Homework—Who Needs It?" (page 534–535)
- Word card 148 (WA4)
- Word card 149 (WA5)
- Word card 150 (WA6)
- (Optional) *Making Meaning Student Response Book*

Teacher Note

You might have the students bring their *Student Response Books* to the rug and turn to page 58 to follow along as you read from the article.

Tell the students that *task* is the first word they will learn today and that a *task* is a "job, chore, or other particular thing you have to do." Explain that homework is a task, or particular thing, that students must sometimes do for school. It is a job that needs to be done.

Display word card 148 (WA4) and have the students say the word *task*.

2 Discuss Tasks

Explain that all of us have tasks, or jobs or chores or other particular things that we must do. Sometimes tasks are pleasant; sometimes they are unpleasant. But in all cases, a task is something you are responsible for getting done. Give some examples of tasks you have.

> **You might say:**
>
> "One task, or job, I have at home that I really enjoy is taking care of the garden. I have other tasks at home, such as washing dishes and cleaning the house, that I don't enjoy as much as gardening—but they are particular things I have to do. I also have many tasks, or things I have to get done, as a teacher. Every weekend, I have the task of planning my lessons for the upcoming school week. Another task I have is cleaning up the classroom at the end of each day."

Ask:

Q *What is a task you have at home? What is a job, chore, or other thing that you have to get done?* [Click ❶ on WA4 to reveal the prompt.] *Turn to your partner.*

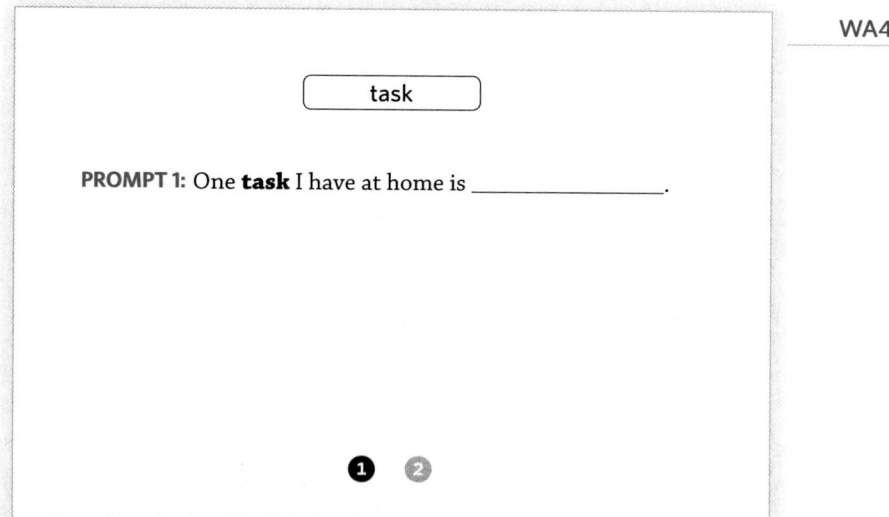

WA4

task

PROMPT 1: One **task** I have at home is _____.

❶ ❷

PROMPT 1: "One task I have at home is [giving my dog Rolf a bath when he gets really dirty]."

After partners have talked, have a few volunteers use the prompt to share their thinking with the class.

Discuss as a class:

Q *What tasks do you have at school? What jobs, chores, or other things do you have to get done?* [Click ❷ to reveal the prompt.]

PROMPT 2: "One task I have at school is [writing stories, poems, and other things]."

Have a few volunteers use the prompt to share their thinking with the class.

Point to the word *task* and review the pronunciation and meaning of the word.

INTRODUCE AND USE *UNWIND*

3 ### Introduce and Define *Unwind* and Review Synonyms

Remind the students that they read an essay that argued against homework called "Homework—Who Needs It?" Review that one argument the article makes against homework is that kids need free time after school—not more work. Read the following sentence from "Let Kids Be Kids" aloud, emphasizing the word *unwind*: "When children get home from school, they need time to unwind."

Tell the students that *unwind* is the next word they will learn today and that *unwind* means "relax." Explain that *unwind* and *relax* are synonyms. Review that, according to the essay, students need time to unwind, or relax, after a full and busy day of school.

Display word card 149 (🌙 WA5) and have the students say the word *unwind*.

Discuss as a class:

Q *Do you think it is important to unwind? Why?*

Click ❶ on WA5 to reveal the first prompt and have a few volunteers use the prompt to share their thinking with the class.

PROMPT 1: "It [is/is not] important to unwind because . . ."

4 ## Discuss Unwinding

Explain that there are many things people do to unwind, or relax. Give some examples of things you do to unwind.

> **You might say:**
>
> "One thing I do to unwind, or relax, after a long day is curl up on the couch and read a book. On Sunday nights, I like to unwind by watching a movie with my family. My daughter likes to unwind by listening to music and writing in her journal."

Teacher Note

If you started a synonym chart, add the words *unwind* and *relax* to it.

Ask:

 Q *What are some things you do to unwind?* [Click **2** on WA5 to reveal the prompt.] *Turn to your partner.*

PROMPT 2: "To unwind, I [play basketball with my brother]."

After partners have talked, have a few volunteers use the prompt to share their thinking with the class.

Point to the word *unwind* and review the pronunciation and meaning of the word.

INTRODUCE AND USE *STRESSFUL*

5 Introduce and Define *Stressful*

Remind the students that another argument the essay "Homework—Who Needs It?" makes is that homework is a burden for moms and dads, as well as for kids. Read the following sentences from "Let Families Be Families" aloud, emphasizing the word *stress*: "Homework can be confusing or difficult, and parents don't always have time to help. This means that kids must sometimes struggle through hard homework assignments on their own—and moms and dads are left feeling guilty for not helping. This is stress that busy families don't need."

Tell the students that the last word they will learn today is *stressful*, which is a form of the word *stress*. Explain that *stressful* means "causing worry or tension." Explain that homework is stressful for students and families—it causes worry and tension—because homework can be difficult and not all parents have the time to help their kids. Display word card 150 (WA6) and have the students say the word *stressful*.

Point to the suffix *-ful* in *stressful* and review that *-ful* is a suffix that means "full of." Explain that if you add the suffix *-ful* to the word *stress*, which means "worry or tension," you make the word *stressful*, which means "full of stress, or worry or tension."

6 Discuss Stressful Situations

Explain that a stressful situation is a situation that causes you to feel worried or tense. Give some examples of situations that are stressful for you or for people you know.

> **You might say:**
>
> "Being late for an appointment is stressful for me. I feel worried and tense because I like to be prompt and don't like to keep other people waiting. I also find that driving in heavy traffic is stressful. My shoulders get tense and I get grouchy and nervous when I'm stuck in traffic. I also find going to parties is a little stressful for me because I'm basically a shy person and meeting new people can make me feel tense."

Teacher Note

You might remind the students that they discussed the suffix *-ful* when they learned the words *doubtful* ("full of doubt or uncertainty"), *joyful* ("full of joy"), *sorrowful* ("full of sorrow or very sad"), and *graceful* ("full of grace or full of smoothness and beauty of movement").

Use "Think, Pair, Share" to discuss:

 Q *When have you been in a stressful situation, or a situation that caused you to feel worried or tense? Why was the situation stressful?* [Pause; click ❶ on WA6 to reveal the prompt.] *Turn to your partner.*

PROMPT 1: "[Losing my backpack] was stressful because . . ."

After partners have talked, have a few volunteers use the prompt to share their thinking with the class.

Point to the word *stressful* and review the pronunciation and meaning of the word.

MORE STRATEGY PRACTICE

Discuss Another Meaning of *Unwind*

Remind the students that words often have more than one meaning and sometimes the meanings are very different. Write the word *unwind* where everyone can see it, pronounce it, and review that *unwind* means "relax."

Ask and discuss as a class:

Q *What else do you know about the word* unwind?

If necessary, follow up by asking:

Q *What do we mean when we say we need to unwind a hose or a ball of yarn?*

PROMPT: "*Unwind* also means . . ." or "If you unwind a hose or a ball of yarn, you . . ."

Have a few volunteers use the prompt to share their thinking with the class.

Explain that *unwind* can also mean to "undo something that is wound up by turning it in the opposite direction."

Day 4 | Review *Task, Unwind,* and *Stressful*

Materials

- Daily review cards (WA7)
- Copy of this week's family letter (BLM1) for each student

In this lesson, the students:

- Review and practice using the words *task*, *unwind*, and *stressful* from Day 3
- Build their speaking and listening skills
- Share their partners' thinking with the class

Words Reviewed

task
A *task* is a "job, chore, or other particular thing you have to do."

unwind
Unwind means "relax."

stressful
Stressful means "causing worry or tension."

REVIEW THE WORDS

1 Briefly Review the Words

Display the daily review cards (WA7). Review the pronunciation and meaning of each word.

Ask:

Q *Which of the words you learned yesterday do you think is particularly interesting? Why?* [Click ❶ on WA7 to reveal the first prompt.] *Turn to your partner.*

WA7

| task | unwind | stressful |

PROMPT 1: I think _____ is particularly interesting because . . .

❶ ② ③ ④ ⑤

PROMPT 1: "I think [*stressful*] is particularly interesting because . . ."

After partners have talked, have a few volunteers use the prompt to share their thinking with the class.

PRACTICE USING THE WORDS

2 Answer Questions About the Words

Point to the words *unwind* and *stressful* and review the pronunciation and meaning of each word. Ask:

 Q *What do you do to unwind after a stressful day? Why?* [Click ❷ to reveal the prompt.] *Turn to your partner.*

PROMPT 2: "To unwind after a stressful day, I . . ."

After partners have talked, have a few volunteers use the prompt to share their thinking with the class.

Using the same procedure, discuss:

[task/stressful]

 Q *What task do you think is stressful? Why?* [Click ❸ to reveal the next prompt.] *Turn to your partner.*

PROMPT 3: "I think the task of [watching my baby sister] is stressful because . . ."

[unwind]

 Q *Would cleaning your room help you unwind? Why?* [Click ❹ to reveal the prompt.] *Turn to your partner.*

PROMPT 4: "Cleaning my room [would/would not] help me unwind because . . ."

[stressful]

 Q *Would losing your bike be stressful? Why?* [Click ❺ to reveal the prompt.] *Turn to your partner.*

PROMPT 5: "Losing my bike [would/would not] be stressful because . . ."

🌐 MORE ELL SUPPORT

Draw a Picture of Unwinding

Tell the students that they will draw a picture of themselves doing something to unwind. Remind the students that *unwind* means "relax."

Discuss:

Q *What do you do to unwind? What does it look like?*

Q *Where are you unwinding? What does that look like?*

Teacher Note

Send home with each student a copy of this week's family letter (BLM1). Encourage the students to talk about this week's words with their families.

Have the students draw pictures of themselves unwinding. For example, a student might draw a picture of himself playing at the park. Ask the students to share and discuss their drawings in pairs. Encourage them to use the following prompt:

PROMPT: "I drew [myself playing at the park with my friends]. There are [trees and a playground]."

Have a few volunteers share and discuss their drawings with the group.

Day 5 | Ongoing Review

Materials

- Ongoing review cards (WA8)
- Ongoing review activity (WA9)

In this lesson, the students:

- Review words learned earlier
- Build their speaking and listening skills
- Listen respectfully to the thinking of others and share their own

Words Reviewed

deadly
Deadly means "dangerous and likely to cause death."

flashy
Flashy means "very big, bright, or expensive." Something that is flashy catches your attention.

graceful
Graceful means "moving in a smooth and beautiful way."

intense
Intense means "very great or strong."

opportunity
An *opportunity* is a "chance to do something."

REVIEW THE WORDS

1 Briefly Review the Words

Display the ongoing review cards (◖ WA8) and review the pronunciation and meaning of each word.

PRACTICE USING THE WORDS

2 Play "Finish the Story"

Tell the students that partners will play the game "Finish the Story." Review that you will tell a story, leaving off the last word. Explain that partners will finish the story by deciding which of the ongoing review words makes the best ending for it.

Display the ongoing review activity (WA9) and begin playing the game:

1. Click ❶ to reveal the first story. Point to the story and read it aloud twice, slowly and clearly. Point out that the ending is missing.

   - Story 1: *Juanita received a jewelry kit for her birthday. She told her mom, "I'm going to make you a sparkling necklace that everyone will admire. It will be _____."*

2. Give the students a few moments to think about the story. Then point to the word choices and read each word aloud. Ask:

   Q *Which vocabulary word makes the best ending for the story? Why?* [Click ❶ again and point to the prompt.] *Turn to your partner.*

   PROMPT: "I think the word [*flashy*] makes the best ending because . . ."

   After partners have talked, have one or two volunteers use the prompt to share their thinking with the class.

3. Conclude the discussion by clicking ❶ a third time to highlight the correct vocabulary word and reveal the story with the correct word in place.

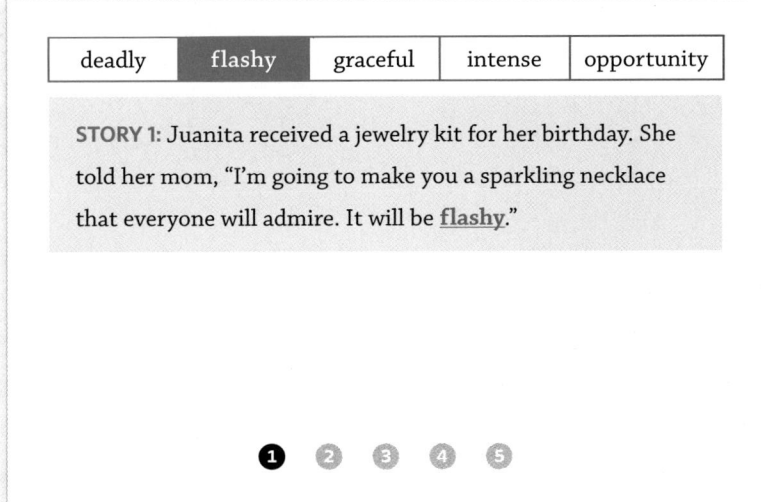

WA9

4. Click ❶ to clear the screen.

Teacher Note

Each story on the ongoing review activity (WA9) has a corresponding number: the first story is ❶; the second story is ❷; the third story is ❸; and so on. To play the game, click the corresponding number four times:

- The first click reveals the story.
- The second click reveals the prompt.
- The third click highlights the correct answer and reveals the story with the answer in place.
- The fourth click clears the screen.

Use the same procedure to discuss the following stories:

- Story 2: *"I dance smoothly and beautifully. I move like a swan," the dancer bragged. "I am ever so _____."* (graceful)

- Story 3: *Jun jumped off his bike and landed right next to a giant spider. He carefully took a step back and whispered, "Uh oh. I hope this spider isn't _____."* (deadly)

- Story 4: *After gym class, Magda and Sasha huffed and puffed as they tried to catch their breath. They told the gym teacher, "That workout was _____."* (intense)

- Story 5: *Mr. Kerr asked Omar to read his story at the school assembly. Omar was nervous at first, but Mr. Kerr coaxed him into it by saying, "Omar, you are an excellent writer so you shouldn't be afraid. You don't want to miss this _____."* (opportunity)

Teacher Note

You might remind the students that they learned the word *coax* earlier and that it means "persuade someone to do something by talking to the person gently and kindly."

Banning TAG

Imagine that you are being chased. You run as fast as you can, but you are not quick enough. You feel hands on your back, touching you. You trip, fall down, skinning your knee. Not again! You are tired of always being "it."

Has this ever happened to you? If it has, you know that it does not feel very good. Some principals, teachers, and parents are worried that playing tag at recess is too dangerous. They argue that kids run into one another, fall down, and get hurt playing tag. They say that sometimes tag leads to hitting, pushing, and bullying. In response to these concerns, schools all over the country are banning the game of tag during recess.

The Other Side

Some parents and kids think schools should not ban tag. A third-grader from the state of Washington even started a petition to get his principal to change the ban and let the kids play tag again at recess. There are a lot of good things about the game. It is easy to get started because you do not need anything to play except some friends. Also, while you run around, you are getting exercise and having fun at the same time. Many people are upset that recess has to be ruined for everyone just because a few children play too rough. After all, the game of tag has been around for hundreds of years.

Different Types of Tag

There are many different versions of tag. You probably know how to play some of them. One of the most popular versions of tag is "freeze tag," where instead of being "it" when you are caught, you have to stand still until another player touches you. There is also "tunnel tag," which is like freeze tag except that your teammate must crawl through your legs before you can play again.

"Monster tag" starts with one person chasing all the others. As each player is tagged, he or she joins hands with "it" to help chase the others. In the end, there is a long chain of players who are all "it," working together. With all the hands and feet, the chain reminds some people of a monster! That is how this kind of tag got its name.

Other Games

If your school does not allow tag at recess, there are lots of other games you can play instead! If you have a ball, you can organize a game of kickball or four square. With a piece of chalk and a few pebbles, you can play hopscotch. You can probably think of many more fun things to do during recess.

Whatever you are allowed to do at recess, it is important that you play fair and are gentle with others. When everyone feels safe, everyone can have fun!

Smile—You've Got Homework!

"Homework." Now there's a word that can put a frown on your face! Many kids don't like doing it. Busy teachers don't always have time to plan it or grade it. Many exhausted parents have to remind their children to do it. If homework causes so much unhappiness, then why do teachers assign it? One simple reason: Homework helps kids learn. A 2006 study showed that children who do homework do better on class tests. That's one benefit of homework. Here are some others.

Practice Makes Perfect

As any kindergarten teacher will tell you, students need to practice saying their ABCs in order to learn them. In fact, practice is necessary to learn most of what is taught in school. Unfortunately, there is not enough time in the school day for students to practice all that they learn. That's what homework is for. Homework provides the practice time that students need.

Homework also helps a teacher teach more effectively. Reviewing homework assignments helps the teacher know what the students understand and what they don't. With this information, teachers can decide whether to reteach a lesson or move on.

Homework helps students practice what they are learning in school.

Memorizing Facts

Like it or not, memorization is an important part of learning in school. Students need to memorize math facts, how words are spelled, historical dates, and other information. But memorizing information—like practicing skills—takes up valuable class time. Having students memorize facts for homework gives teachers more time during the school day for actual teaching. In addition, students don't always need a teacher's help to memorize information. Why waste the teacher's time with this type of schoolwork?

Organization and Planning

Homework can help kids learn how to organize and plan their time. Students with homework must set aside time to get it done. Other activities, like spending time with friends or watching TV, may have to wait until homework is done.

Homework also helps kids learn how to prioritize tasks—or decide which tasks must be done and in what order—and how to plan for how long each task should take. Skills like these are very important to academic success.

School and Home

Homework gives parents a chance to become more involved in their children's school lives. Parents can help with homework while talking with their kids about what they are learning. Parents can also make homework more fun and interesting, and they can help their children see the importance of the work they are doing.

So smile when you hear the word "homework." It's good for you!

Homework provides an opportunity for parents and kids to work together.

Homework— Who Needs It?

Is homework good for kids? Do kids learn more if they do homework? Teachers, students, and parents have been debating these questions for years. Many studies have looked at the impact of homework on student learning, but there is no clear evidence that homework helps students learn more. In fact, one 2012 study found no significant relationship between time spent on homework and grades. That's one argument against homework, but it's not the only one. Let's take a look at some others.

Let Kids Be Kids

Students spend about seven hours a day in school. Most of that time they are thinking, listening, reading, and writing—pretty exhausting stuff! Kids have little time during the school day to relax or spend time with friends. When children get home from school, they need time to unwind. They do not need to do more schoolwork! Most adults don't come home from a full day at work and do even more work for their job. So why should kids?

Kids need time to be kids after school.

Let Families Be Families

Homework is a burden for kids, but it can be a burden for moms and dads, too. After a long day, parents are tired. The last thing they want to do is to keep reminding their reluctant children, "Do your homework!" Homework can be confusing or difficult, and parents don't always have time to help. This means that kids must sometimes struggle through hard homework assignments on their own—and moms and dads are left feeling guilty for not helping. This is stress that busy families don't need.

Families need time to do enjoyable things together. Many children and their parents say goodbye in the morning and often don't see each other again until after five o'clock. That leaves only a few hours for family time before going to bed. It's important for families to spend the little time they have together talking, reading, and doing things they all enjoy.

Who Likes Homework?

If you ask students if they like homework, many will probably say they do not. Because students associate homework with school, negative feelings about homework can turn into negative feelings about school—and disliking school makes learning more difficult.

Is homework worth the stress, family conflict, and loss of interest in learning that it seems to cause? The answer is no.

Homework can cause stress for the whole family.

RESOURCES

Read-aloud

- *Lifetimes* by David L. Rice, illustrated by Michael S. Maydak

Extension

- "Explore Related Words: *Considerate* and *Consider*"

More ELL Support

- "Discuss Being Considerate"

Assessment Resource Book

- Week 26 vocabulary assessment

☁ Online Resources

Visit the CCC Learning Hub (ccclearninghub.org) to find your online resources for this week.

Whiteboard Activities

- WA1–WA10

Assessment Form

- "Class Vocabulary Assessment Record" sheet (CA1)

Reproducibles

- Week 26 family letter (BLM1)
- (Optional) "Week 26 Word Cards" (BLM2)
- (Optional) "Week 26 Crossword Puzzle" (BLM3)

OVERVIEW

Words Taught	Words Reviewed
collaborate	adapt
aggressive	forbid
evacuate	struggle
distress	task
unaggressive	unwind
considerate	

Word-learning Strategies

- Recognizing synonyms (review)
- Recognizing antonyms (review)
- Using the prefix *un-* to determine word meanings (review)

Vocabulary Focus

- Students learn and use six words about the book.
- Students review synonyms and antonyms.
- Students review the prefix *un-*.
- Students review words learned earlier.
- Students build their speaking and listening skills.

Social Development Focus

- Students give reasons for their ideas.
- Students listen respectfully to the thinking of others and share their own.

⏱ DO AHEAD

✓ Prior to Day 4, visit the CCC Learning Hub (ccclearninghub.org) to access and print this week's family letter (BLM1). Make enough copies to send one letter home with each student.

✓ Prior to Day 5, make a copy of the "Class Vocabulary Assessment Record" sheet (CA1); see page 205 of the *Assessment Resource Book*.

✓ (Optional) Visit the CCC Learning Hub (ccclearninghub.org) to access and print the following materials: "Week 26 Word Cards" (BLM2) and "Week 26 Crossword Puzzle" (BLM3). These materials can be used to provide your students with more opportunities to review the words.

In this lesson, the students:

- Learn and use the words *collaborate*, *aggressive*, and *evacuate*
- Review synonyms
- Build their speaking and listening skills
- Give reasons for their ideas

Words Taught

collaborate
Collaborate means "work with others to make or do something."

aggressive
Aggressive means "threatening or ready and eager to fight or attack others." Aggressive animals or people are frightening because they can be mean, dangerous, or violent.

evacuate
Evacuate means "leave a place and go somewhere safer."

INTRODUCE AND USE *COLLABORATE*

1 ## Introduce and Define *Collaborate* and Review Synonyms

Briefly review "A lifetime for an army ant is about three years" in *Lifetimes*.

Show page 6 and begin reading aloud, stopping after: "If the river is very wide, they form large 'ant balls' and float to the other side."

Explain that the first word the students will learn today is *collaborate*, and that *collaborate* means "work with others to make or do something." Explain that *collaborate* and *cooperate* are synonyms.

Explain that army ants collaborate, or work together, in amazing ways. They march together like soldiers and use their bodies to form an ant bridge and ant balls that float across a river.

Display word card 151 ( WA1) and have the students say the word *collaborate*.

Materials

- "A lifetime for an army ant is about three years" in *Lifetimes* (page 6)
- Word card 151 (WA1)
- Word card 152 (WA2)
- Word card 153 (WA3)

🌐 **ELL Note**
The Spanish cognate of *collaborate* is *colaborar*.

Teacher Note
If you started a synonym chart, add *collaborate* and *cooperate* to it.

2 Talk About Collaborating

Explain that the students often collaborate, or work together, to learn and do things, and give a few examples.

> **You might say:**
>
> "As a class, we collaborated to put on a play. This week you collaborated with partners to write stories. You also collaborated in groups of four to learn about the solar system. On the playground, you collaborate when you jump rope with others and play basketball."

Ask:

 Q *When else have you collaborated in class or on the playground? With whom did you collaborate? [Click ❶ on WA1 to reveal the prompt.] Turn to your partner.*

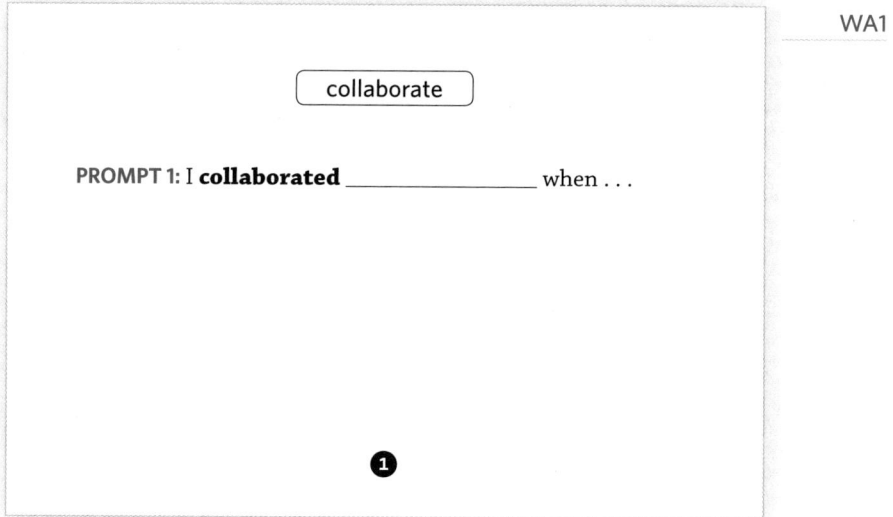

WA1

collaborate

PROMPT 1: I **collaborated** _____ when . . .

❶

PROMPT 1: "I collaborated [with Ian and Michelle] when . . ."

After partners have talked, have one or two volunteers use the prompt to share their thinking with the class.

Point to the word *collaborate* and review the pronunciation and meaning of the word.

INTRODUCE AND USE *AGGRESSIVE*

3 Introduce and Define *Aggressive*

Read the rest of page 6 of *Lifetimes* aloud.

Tell the students that the next word they will learn is *aggressive*, and explain that *aggressive* means "threatening or ready and eager to fight or attack others." Explain that aggressive animals or people are frightening because they can be mean, dangerous, or violent.

Explain that army ants are very aggressive creatures. They will attack and eat an animal as large and ferocious as a tiger. When army ants attack, people leave their homes because they feel that their lives are in danger. Display word card 152 ( WA2) and have the students say the word *aggressive*.

Explain that animals other than army ants can be aggressive, especially if they are hungry or are being threatened themselves. Ask and discuss as a class:

Q *What other animals are aggressive? Why do you think that?*

Click ❶ on word card 152 (WA2) to reveal the first prompt and have a few volunteers use the prompt to share their thinking with the class.

PROMPT 1: "A [shark] is aggressive because . . ."

4 Play "Which Is Aggressive?"

Explain that partners will play "Which Is Aggressive?" You will describe two animals, and partners will decide which animal is aggressive and why they think so.

Ask:

 Q *Which of these is aggressive: an alligator snapping at a turtle or a sleeping alligator? Why do you think that?* [Click ❷ on WA2 to reveal the prompt.] *Turn to your partner.*

PROMPT 2: "I think [an alligator snapping at a turtle] is aggressive because . . ."

After partners have talked, have one or two volunteers use the prompt to share their thinking with the class.

Discuss the following using the same procedure:

- *A puppy chasing its tail or a guard dog growling and jumping at people*
- *A lion chasing a zebra or a tiger drinking water from a creek*

Point to the word *aggressive* and review the pronunciation and meaning of the word.

🌐 **ELL Note**

The Spanish cognate of *aggressive* is *agresivo/a*.

Teacher Note

If the students struggle to name aggressive animals, ask questions such as "What animals attack other animals and people?" and "What animals would you be afraid of if they were angry or hungry?"

INTRODUCE AND USE *EVACUATE*

5 Introduce and Define *Evacuate*

Explain that the last word the students will learn today is *evacuate*, and that *evacuate* means "leave a place and go somewhere safer." Review that when army ants come through, people have to evacuate their homes, or leave their homes to go someplace safer until the ants are gone.

Display word card 153 (WA3) and have the students say the word *evacuate*.

6 Talk About Evacuating

Explain that people evacuate their houses for other reasons, such as when the house is on fire or is threatened by a fire.

Use "Think, Pair, Share" to discuss:

Q *Why else might people evacuate their houses?* [Pause; then click ❶ on WA3 to reveal the prompt.] *Turn to your partner.*

PROMPT 1: "People might evacuate their houses because . . ."

After partners have talked, have a few volunteers use the prompt to share their thinking with the class.

Explain that when we have fire drills, we practice evacuating the school building.

As a class, discuss:

Q *Where do we go when we evacuate the school building during a fire drill? Why?*

Click ❷ on WA3 to reveal the next prompt and have a few volunteers use the prompt to share their thinking with the class.

PROMPT 2: "When we evacuate the school, we go [outside to the playground] because . . ."

Point to the word *evacuate* and review the pronunciation and meaning of the word.

ELL Note

The Spanish cognate of *evacuate* is *evacuar*.

Teacher Note

Support struggling students by suggesting one or two other reasons, such as because of a flood or tornado. Then ask the question again.

In this lesson, the students:

- Review and practice using the words *collaborate*, *aggressive*, and *evacuate* from Day 1

- Build their speaking and listening skills

- Listen respectfully to the thinking of others and share their own

Words Reviewed

collaborate
Collaborate means "work with others to make or do something."

aggressive
Aggressive means "threatening or ready and eager to fight or attack others." Aggressive animals or people are frightening because they can be mean, dangerous, or violent.

evacuate
Evacuate means "leave a place and go somewhere safer."

REVIEW THE WORDS

1 Briefly Review the Words

Display the daily review cards (🔊 WA4). Review the pronunciation and meaning of each word.

Use "Think, Pair, Share" to discuss:

 Q *If you were writing a story about a fierce creature that was threatening your home, which of the words would you use? How would you use the word?* [Pause; click ❶ on WA4 to reveal the prompt.] *Turn to your partner.*

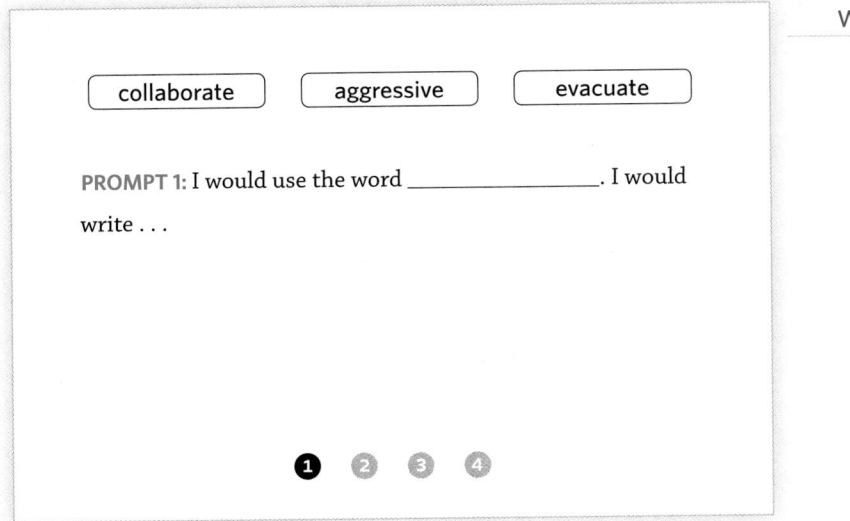

WA4

| collaborate | aggressive | evacuate |

PROMPT 1: I would use the word _____. I would write . . .

❶ ❷ ❸ ❹

Materials

- Daily review cards (WA4)

Teacher Note

You might remind the students that they learned the word *fierce* and that *fierce* means "dangerous or violent."

PROMPT 1: "I would use the word [*aggressive*]. I would write . . ."

After partners have talked, have a few volunteers use the prompt to share their thinking with the class.

PRACTICE USING THE WORDS

2 Answer Questions About Olive

Explain that partners will use the words to answer questions about Olive.

Point to the word *collaborate* and ask:

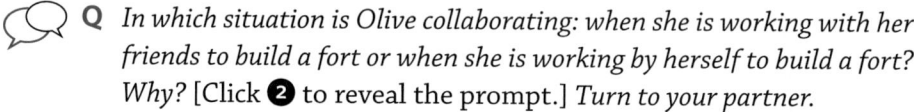 **Q** *In which situation is Olive collaborating: when she is working with her friends to build a fort or when she is working by herself to build a fort? Why?* [Click ❷ to reveal the prompt.] *Turn to your partner.*

PROMPT 2: "Olive is collaborating when she [is working with her friends to build a fort] because . . ."

After partners have talked, have one or two volunteers use the prompt to share their thinking with the class.

Discuss the following, using the same procedure:

[aggressive]

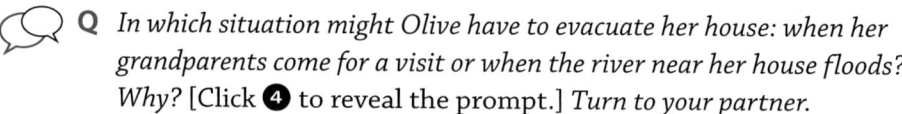 **Q** *In which situation is Olive being aggressive: when she is bullying a boy on the playground or when she is helping a little boy on the playground? Why?* [Click ❸ to reveal the prompt.] *Turn to your partner.*

PROMPT 3: "Olive is being aggressive when she [is bullying the boy] because . . ."

[evacuate]

Q *In which situation might Olive have to evacuate her house: when her grandparents come for a visit or when the river near her house floods? Why?* [Click ❹ to reveal the prompt.] *Turn to your partner.*

PROMPT 4: "Olive might have to evacuate her home [when the river near her house floods] because . . ."

In this lesson, the students:

- Learn and use the words *distress, unaggressive,* and *considerate*
- Review antonyms and synonyms
- Review the prefix *un-*
- Build their speaking and listening skills
- Give reasons for their ideas

Words Taught

distress
Distress is a "feeling of deep sadness, worry, or pain."

unaggressive
Unaggressive means "not aggressive, or not threatening or ready and eager to fight or attack others."

considerate
Considerate means "thoughtful of the feelings and needs of others."

Materials

- "A lifetime for an elephant is about 65 years" in *Lifetimes* (page 19)
- Word card 154 (WA5)
- Word card 155 (WA6)
- Word card 156 (WA7)

INTRODUCE AND USE *DISTRESS*

1 ## Introduce and Define *Distress*

Briefly review "A lifetime for an elephant is about 65 years" in *Lifetimes*.

Show page 19 and begin reading, stopping after: "Elephants are among the few animals that weep tears when they are very, very sad."

Tell the students that the first word they will learn today is *distress* and that *distress* is a "feeling of deep sadness, worry, or pain." Explain that when an elephant's baby or friend dies, an elephant shows its distress, or deep sadness, by moaning and crying. Like people, elephants weep tears when they feel distress.

Display word card 154 (WA5) and have the students say the word *distress*.

② Play "Is Olive Feeling Distress?"

Explain that you will describe something that has happened to Olive, and partners will discuss whether they think Olive is feeling distress, and why.

Begin by saying:

- *Olive has to take her puppy to the veterinary hospital for an operation.*

Ask:

 Q *Is Olive feeling distress? Why do you think that?* [Click ❶ on WA5 to reveal the prompt.] *Turn to your partner.*

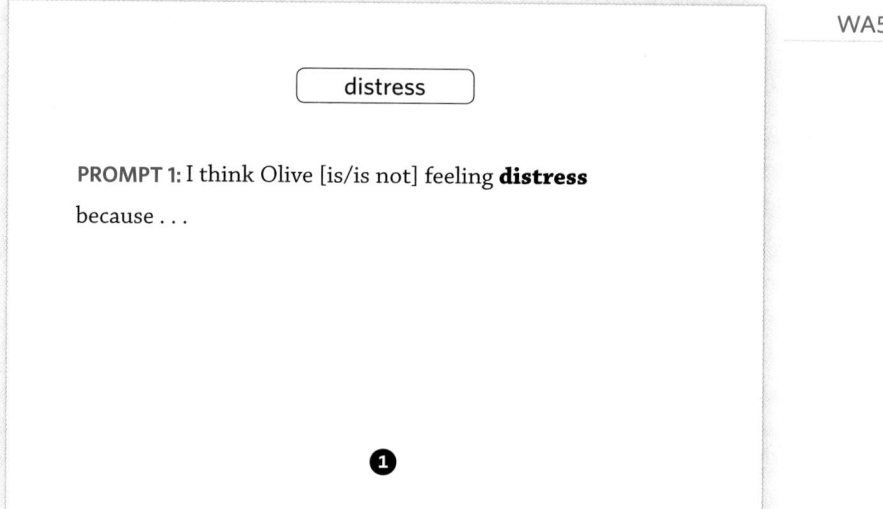

WA5

```
┌─────────────┐
│  distress   │
└─────────────┘

PROMPT 1: I think Olive [is/is not] feeling distress
because . . .

                    ❶
```

PROMPT 1: "I think Olive [is/is not] feeling distress because . . ."

After partners have talked, have a few volunteers use the prompt to share their thinking with the class.

Discuss the following using the same procedure:

- *Olive's family is going out for ice cream.*
- *Olive falls out of a tree and scrapes her arm.*

Point to the word *distress* and review the pronunciation and meaning of the word.

INTRODUCE AND USE *UNAGGRESSIVE*

③ Introduce and Define *Unaggressive,* and Review Antonyms and the Suffix *un-*

Read this sentence on page 19 of *Lifetimes* aloud: "Although elephants are the largest animals on land, they don't kill or bother other animals."

Tell the students that the next word they will learn is *unaggressive*, and explain that *unaggressive* and *aggressive* are antonyms. Explain that *unaggressive* means "not aggressive, or not threatening or ready and eager to fight or attack others." Explain that, unlike army ants, elephants are for the most part unaggressive animals. They do not threaten or harm other animals.

Display word card 155 (WA6) and have the students say the word *unaggressive*. Point out the prefix *un-* in *unaggressive*, and review that *un-* means "not."

4 Play "Aggressive or Unaggressive?"

Explain that partners will play "Aggressive or Unaggressive?" You will describe how an animal or person is acting, and partners will decide whether the animal or person is aggressive or unaggressive, and why.

Begin by saying:

- *A cat is hiding under a table.*

Ask:

Q *Is the cat aggressive or unaggressive? Why do you think that?* [Click ❶ on WA6 to reveal the prompt.] *Turn to your partner.*

PROMPT 1: "I think the [cat] is [aggressive/unaggressive] because . . ."

After partners have talked, have a few volunteers use the prompt to share their thinking with the class.

Discuss the following using the same procedure:

- *A snake is hissing and striking at a hiker.*
- *A woman is pushing people out of her way so she can be first in line.*
- *A child is waiting patiently for his turn on the slide.*

Point to the word *unaggressive* and review the pronunciation and meaning of the word.

INTRODUCE AND USE
CONSIDERATE

5 Introduce and Define *Considerate* and Review Synonyms

Read the last three sentences on page 19 aloud: "When ponds and streams dry up, elephants use their trunks to dig down to water. When they finish drinking, they let other animals drink. Without water these animals would die."

Tell the students that *considerate* is the last word they will learn today. Explain that *considerate* means "thoughtful of the feelings and needs of others" and that *considerate*, *thoughtful*, and *kind* are synonyms. Explain that when elephants let other animals drink, they are being considerate, or thoughtful or kind.

Display word card 156 (WA7) and have the students say the word *considerate*.

6 Review the Activity "What Might You Say or Do?"

Explain that you will describe a situation and partners will discuss what they would say or do to be considerate, or thoughtful or kind.

Begin by saying:

- *You are watching a baby panda in its cage at the zoo. It is very crowded around the panda cage, and a child behind you can't see.*

Ask:

 Q *What might you say or do to be considerate?* [Click ❶ on WA7 to reveal the prompt.] *Turn to your partner.*

PROMPT 1: "To be considerate, I would . . ."

After partners have talked, have a few volunteers use the prompt to share their thinking with the class.

Discuss the following situations using the same procedure:

- *You are playing a game on your computer at home. Your sister tells you that she needs to do some research online for a school project.*

- *You are in the school cafeteria eating lunch. Across the table, you see a boy who is upset because he left his lunch at home.*

Point to the word *considerate* and review the pronunciation and meaning of the word.

EXTENSION

Explore Related Words: *Considerate* and *Consider*

Write the word *considerate* where everyone can see it, and review that *considerate* means "thoughtful of the feelings and needs of others."

Tell the students that knowing the meaning of *considerate* can help them figure out the meanings of other words that are related to *considerate*. Write these sentences where everyone can see them:

> Donny's best friend Lana can't go to his birthday party so he will consider changing the date of his party.

Ask:

Q *What word in the sentence is related to* considerate? *Why do you say that?*

If necessary, point out that *consider* is related to *considerate*, and that you can see the word *consider* (*c-o-n-s-i-d-e-r*) in *considerate*. Then ask:

Q *Based on what you know about the word* considerate *and clues in the sentence, what do you think the word* consider *means?*

If necessary, explain that *consider* means "think carefully about something," and point out that Donny considers, or thinks carefully, about changing the date of his party because his best friend Lana can't go.

 ## MORE ELL SUPPORT

Discuss Being Considerate

Write the word *considerate* where everyone can see it, and remind the students that *considerate* means "thoughtful of the feelings and needs of others." Ask the students to think about a time they were considerate. Then ask:

Q *When were you considerate?*

Q *Why do you think you were considerate?*

Have the students use the prompts to share their thinking with a partner:

PROMPT: "I was considerate when . . ." and "I think I was considerate because . . ."

Have volunteers use the prompt to share their thinking with the group.

Materials

- Daily review cards (WA8)
- Copy of this week's family letter (BLM1) for each student
- (Optional) Copy of the "Week 26 Crossword Puzzle" (BLM3) for each student

In this lesson, the students:

- Review and practice using the words *distress, unaggressive,* and *considerate* from Day 3
- Build their speaking and listening skills
- Listen respectfully to the thinking of others and share their own

Words Reviewed

distress
Distress is a "feeling of deep sadness, worry, or pain."

unaggressive
Unaggressive means "not aggressive, or not threatening or ready and eager to fight or attack others."

considerate
Considerate means "thoughtful of the feelings and needs of others."

REVIEW THE WORDS

1 Briefly Review the Words

Display the daily review cards (◖ WA8). Review the pronunciation and meaning of each word.

Point to the word *considerate* and ask:

 Q *Would you want someone who is considerate as a friend? Why?* [Click **❶** on WA8 to reveal the prompt.] *Turn to your partner.*

WA8

| distress | unaggressive | considerate |

PROMPT 1: I [would/would not] want someone who is **considerate** as a friend because . . .

❶ ❷ ❸ ❹ ❺

PROMPT 1: "I [would/would not] want someone who is considerate as a friend because . . ."

After partners have talked, have one or two volunteers use the prompt to share their thinking with the class.

Discuss the remaining words using the same procedure:

[unaggressive]

 Q *Would you want an unaggressive dog as a pet? Why?* [Click ❷ to reveal the prompt.] *Turn to your partner.*

PROMPT 2: "I [would/would not] want an unaggressive dog as a pet because . . ."

[distress]

 Q *Would you feel distress if someone you loved were sad? Why?* [Click ❸ to reveal the prompt.] *Turn to your partner.*

PROMPT 3: "I [would/would not] feel distress if someone I loved were sad because . . ."

PRACTICE USING THE WORDS

2 Play "Which Word Goes With?"

Explain that partners will play "Which Word Goes With?" You will write a word where everyone can see it and partners will discuss which vocabulary word goes with the word you wrote and why.

Begin by writing:

- *family*

Ask:

 Q *Which vocabulary word goes with the word* family? *Why?* [Click ❹ to reveal the prompt.] *Turn to your partner.*

PROMPT 4: "I think [*considerate*] goes with *family* because . . ."

After partners have talked, have a few volunteers use the prompt to share their thinking with the class.

Using the same procedure, discuss:

- *playground*

 Q *Which vocabulary word goes with the word* playground? *Why?* [Click ❺ to reveal the prompt.] *Turn to your partner.*

PROMPT 5: "I think [*unaggressive*] goes with *playground* because . . ."

Teacher Note

If the students have trouble making associations or make associations to only one of the words, call for attention and ask questions such as [*distress*] "How might the word *distress* go with *family*?" and "Why might someone in your family feel distress?" [*unaggressive*] "How might the word *unaggressive* go with *family*?" and "Why would you want the members of your family to be unaggressive?" [*considerate*] "How might the word *considerate* go with *family*?" and "What might you do to be considerate of the people in your family?"

Teacher Note

Send home with each student a copy of this week's family letter (BLM1). Encourage the students to talk about this week's words with their families.

Teacher Note

To provide students with additional review of words taught during Weeks 25 and 26, you might distribute a copy of the "Week 26 Crossword Puzzle" (BLM3) to each student.

Materials

- Ongoing review cards (WA9)
- Ongoing review activity (WA10)
- "Class Vocabulary Assessment Record" sheet (CA1)

Teacher Note

You might explain that the students may need to change the form of the word to complete the sentence by adding an ending such as -s, -ing, or -ed.

Teacher Note

Each sentence in the ongoing review activity (WA10) has a corresponding number: the first story is **1**; the second story is **2**; the third story is **3**; and so on. To play the game, click the corresponding number four times:

- The first click reveals the story.
- The second click reveals the prompt.
- The third click highlights the correct answer and reveals the sentence with the correct answer in place.
- The fourth click clears the screen.

In this lesson, the students:

- Review words learned earlier
- Build their speaking and listening skills
- Give reasons for their ideas

Words Taught

adapt
Adapt means "change to fit new situations or conditions." People adapt to new situations or conditions by changing their behavior or ideas.

forbid
Forbid means "order someone not to do something."

struggle
Struggle means "try very hard to do something."

task
A *task* is a "job, chore, or other particular thing you have to do."

unwind
Unwind means "relax."

REVIEW THE WORDS

1 Briefly Review the Words

Display the ongoing review cards ((WA9). Review the pronunciation and meaning of each word.

PRACTICE USING THE WORDS

2 Play "Find Another Word"

Tell the students that partners will play the game "Find Another Word." Remind the students that you will show a story with one or more words underlined. You will read each story aloud, and partners will decide which vocabulary word can replace the underlined part of the story.

Display the ongoing review activity ((WA10) and begin playing the game:

1. Click **1** to reveal the first story. Point to the story and read it aloud, emphasizing the underlined words.

   - Story 1: *When Leonard moved from the city to the country, it took him awhile to <u>change his behavior to fit in</u>.*

2. Give the students a few moments to think about the story and the underlined word. Then point to the five word choices and ask:

   Q *Which vocabulary word could replace the underlined words? Why?* [Click ❶ again and point to the prompt.] *Turn to your partner.*

PROMPT 1: "I think the word [*adapt*] could replace *change his behavior to fit in* because . . ."

After partners have talked, have a few volunteers use the prompt to share their thinking with the class.

3. Conclude the discussion by clicking ❶ a third time to highlight the correct vocabulary word and reveal the story with the correct word in place.

WA10

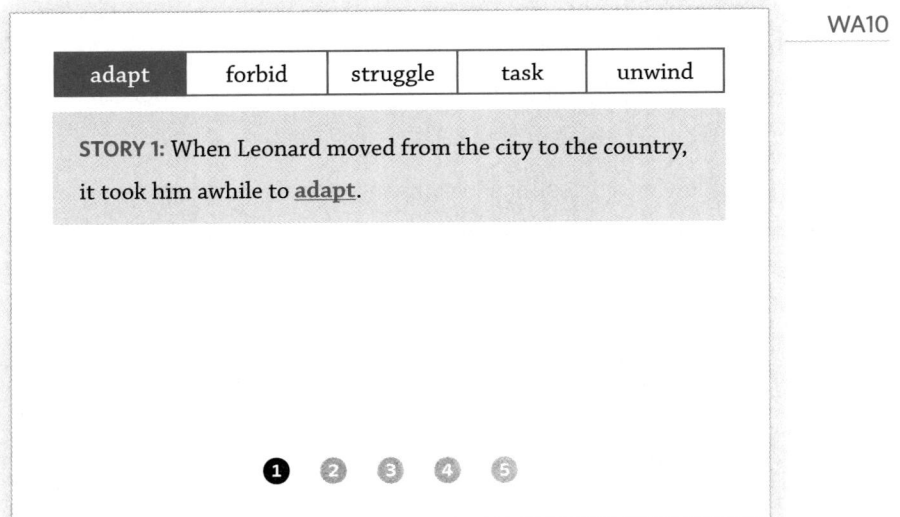

4. Click ❶ to clear the screen.

Use the same procedure to discuss the following sentences:

- Story 2: *Kendall and her dad are setting up for the family barbecue and Kendall has the <u>job</u> of setting the table. She must put plates, utensils, and napkins on the table.*

PROMPT 2: "I think [*task*] could replace *job* because . . ."

- Story 3: *At Frank's soccer tournament his team played three games in one day! He was exhausted when he got home and lay on the couch to <u>relax</u>.*

PROMPT 3: "I think [*unwind*] could replace *relax* because . . ."

- Story 4: *Nadia and her brother went on a hike up a volcano. After one hour, the trail became very steep. Nadia <u>tried very hard</u> to make it to the top and overcame the challenge.*

PROMPT 4: "I think [*struggled*] could replace *tried very hard* because . . ."

Teacher Note
You might point out that the students learned the word *challenge* earlier and that a *challenge* is "something that is hard to do or requires a lot of work or effort."

Teacher Note

You might point out that the students learned the word *permit* earlier and that *permit* means "allow something to happen or let someone do something."

- Story 5: *The principal decided to <u>order students not to bring</u> food and drinks in the gymnasium because people were slipping on spills and hurting themselves. Now, food is permitted only in the cafeteria.*

PROMPT 5: "I think [*forbid*] could replace *order students not to bring* because . . ."

CLASS VOCABULARY ASSESSMENT NOTE

Observe the students and ask yourself:

- Are the students able to choose the correct words to replace the underlined words?
- Can they explain why they completed the sentence the way they did?
- Do they use the words in their writing?

Record your observations on the "Class Vocabulary Assessment Record" sheet (CA1); see page 205 of the *Assessment Resource Book*.

Use the following suggestions to support struggling students:

- If **only a few students** understand a word's meaning, reteach the word using the vocabulary lesson in which it was first taught as a model.
- If **about half of the students** understand a word's meaning, provide further practice by reviewing the word's meaning and then asking a question that requires the student to talk about the word in terms of his own experiences. For example, ask questions such as "When have you struggled to do something? Why did you struggle to do it?" or "When have you had to adapt to a new situation? How did you adapt?"

RESOURCES

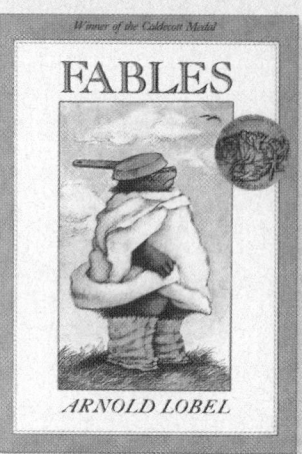

Read-aloud
- *Fables* by Arnold Lobel

Extensions
- "Discuss the Suffix *-ly*"
- "Discuss the Compound Word *Headstrong*"

🌐 More ELL Support
- "Discuss Being Headstrong"

 ## Online Resources

Visit the CCC Learning Hub (ccclearninghub.org) to find your online resources for this week.

Whiteboard Activities
- WA1–WA10

Reproducibles
- Week 27 family letter (BLM1)
- (Optional) "Week 27 Word Cards" (BLM2)

OVERVIEW

Words Taught	Words Reviewed
diligent	aggressive
frank	considerate
self-confident	evacuate
headstrong	skillful
overwhelmed	stressful
contentment	

Word-learning Strategy

- Recognizing synonyms (review)

Vocabulary Focus

- Students learn and use six words from or about the stories.
- Students review synonyms.
- Students review words learned earlier.
- Students build their speaking and listening skills.

Social Development Focus

- Students develop the skill of giving reasons for their ideas.
- Students listen respectfully to the thinking of others and share their own.
- Students work in a responsible way.

① DO AHEAD

✓ Prior to Day 4, visit the CCC Learning Hub (ccclearninghub.org) to access and print this week's family letter (BLM1). Make enough copies to send one letter home with each student.

✓ (Optional) Visit the CCC Learning Hub (ccclearninghub.org) to access and print "Week 27 Word Cards" (BLM2). These cards can be used to provide your students with more opportunities to review the words.

Day 1 — Introduce *Diligent, Frank,* and *Self-confident*

Materials

- "The Camel Dances" in *Fables* (pages 22–23)
- Word card 157 (WA1)
- Word card 158 (WA2)
- Word card 159 (WA3)

In this lesson, the students:

- Learn and use the words *diligent, frank,* and *self-confident*
- Review synonyms
- Build their speaking and listening skills
- Listen respectfully to the thinking of others and share their own

Words Taught

diligent
Diligent means "hard-working." When you are diligent, you work steadily or carefully on something because it is important to you.

frank (p. 22)
When you are frank, you say what you think, openly and honestly.

self-confident
Self-confident means "sure of yourself." If you are self-confident, you are confident or sure you can do something.

INTRODUCE AND USE *DILIGENT*

1 Introduce and Define *Diligent*

Briefly review "The Camel Dances" in *Fables*. Show pages 22–23, and read the first three paragraphs on page 22 aloud, stopping after: "Her feet were blistered, and her body ached with fatigue, but not once did she think of stopping."

Tell the students that the first word they will learn today is *diligent*, and explain that *diligent* means "hard-working." Explain that when you are diligent, you work steadily or carefully on something because it is important to you.

Display word card 157 (WA1) and have the students say the word *diligent*.

Explain that the Camel is diligent, or hard-working, because she has her heart set on being a ballet dancer. Explain that as you reread part of the fable, you want the students to listen for what the Camel does that shows she is diligent. Reread the first three paragraphs on page 22 aloud. Then ask and discuss as a class:

Q *What does the Camel do that shows she is diligent?*

Click ❶ on word card 157 (WA1) and have a few volunteers use the prompt to share their thinking with the class.

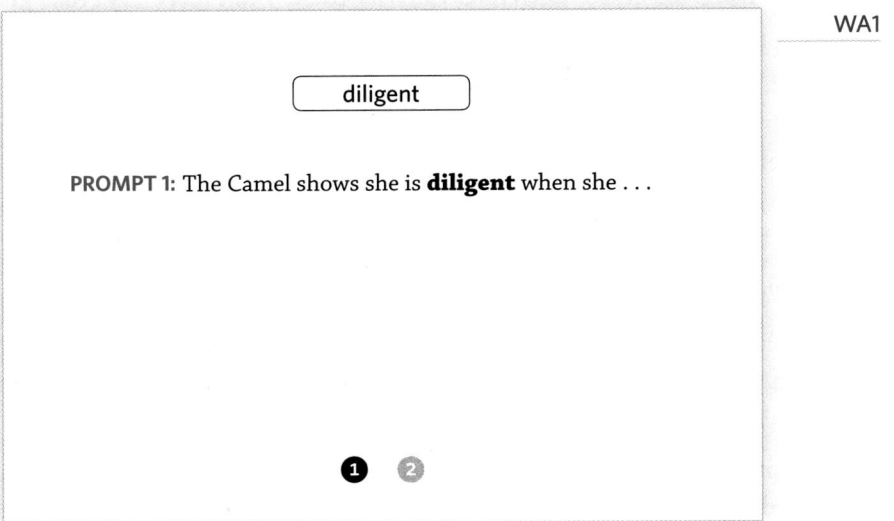

PROMPT 1: "The Camel shows she is diligent when she . . ."

If necessary, explain that carefully practicing the five positions hundreds of times and working steadily for months under the hot desert sun show that the Camel is diligent.

2 Discuss Times We Have Been Diligent

Give a couple of examples of times you have been diligent or noticed others being diligent.

> **You might say:**
>
> "I was diligent when I planted my garden this spring. I spent several weekends digging, planting, fertilizing, and watering. I worked really hard because I wanted the garden to be beautiful. I noticed that Mattie and Kevin were diligent when they made their clay elephant. They spent several days on it and worked very hard to make the best clay elephant they could."

Use "Think, Pair, Share" to discuss:

 Q *When have you been diligent? When have you worked hard to do something or make something because it was important to you?* [Pause; click ❷ on WA1 to reveal the prompt.] *Turn to your partner.*

PROMPT 2: "I was diligent when . . ."

After partners have talked, have one or two volunteers use the prompt to share their thinking with the class.

Point to the word *diligent* and review the pronunciation and meaning of the word.

Teacher Note

Support struggling students by asking questions such as "When have you worked hard on something at home or at school?" "When have you worked on something that took you a few hours or days to finish?" and "When have you practiced something over and over?"

INTRODUCE AND USE *FRANK*

3 Introduce and Define *Frank* and Review Synonyms

Remind the students that the Camel dances for a group of friends and critics, and they do not like her dancing. Read aloud the paragraph that begins, "'I must tell you frankly,' said a member of the audience," emphasizing the word *frankly*.

Tell the students that *frank* is the next word they will learn, and explain that when you are frank, you say what you think, openly and honestly. Explain that *frank*, *truthful*, and *honest* are synonyms.

🌐 **ELL Note**

The Spanish cognate of *frank* is *franco/a*.

Explain that when the critic tells the Camel that she is lumpy, humpy, baggy, and bumpy, he is being frank, or open and honest, about what he thinks, even though it may hurt the Camel's feelings.

Teacher Note

If you started a synonym chart, add the words *frank*, *truthful*, and *honest* to it.

Display word card 158 (WA2) and have the students say the word *frank*.

4 Discuss Whether People Are Frank

Explain that you will tell a story about a person saying something and partners will discuss whether or not the person was frank, or open and honest, and why they think so.

Begin by saying:

- *Svetlana was eating lunch at her friend's house. She didn't like the sandwich she was served, but she said, "Mmmm, this sandwich is delicious."*

Ask:

Q *Was Svetlana being frank? Why?* [Click **1** on WA2 to reveal the prompt.] *Turn to your partner.*

PROMPT 1: "[Svetlana] [was/was not] being frank because . . ."

After partners have talked, have a few volunteers use the prompt to share their thinking with the class.

Using the same procedure, discuss one or more of the following:

- *Dupree watched as his friend Tyler drew a picture of an elephant. He said to Tyler, "Your picture is pretty good, but it would be even better if you made the ears larger and added tusks."*

- *Marianne's friends wanted to play with their dolls. She told them, "I don't want to play with dolls. I'd rather ride bikes."*

Point to the word *frank* and review the pronunciation and meaning of the word.

INTRODUCE AND USE
SELF-CONFIDENT

5 Introduce and Define *Self-confident*

Remind the students that even though friends and critics do not like the Camel's dancing, she does not stop. Read the last two paragraphs on page 22 aloud.

Tell the students that the last word they will learn today is *self-confident*, and explain that *self-confident* means "sure of yourself." Explain that if you are self-confident, you are confident or sure you can do something. Explain that no matter what her friends and critics say, the Camel is self-confident. She is sure she is a splendid dancer.

Display word card 159 (WA3) and have the students say the word *self-confident*.

6 Discuss Times We Have Been Self-confident

Give examples of times you feel or have felt self-confident.

> **You might say:**
>
> "I feel self-confident when I play tennis because I practice regularly and I feel confident that I will play well. I felt self-confident when I took a test in my Spanish class the other evening. I had studied hard and was sure I would do well."

Use "Think, Pair, Share" to discuss:

Q *When have you felt self-confident? When have you felt confident or sure that you could do something?* [Pause; click ❶ on WA3 to reveal the first prompt.] *Turn to your partner.*

PROMPT 1: "I felt self-confident when . . ."

After partners have talked, have one or two volunteers use the prompt to share their thinking with the class.

Follow up by asking:

Q *Why did you feel self-confident when you [read your story to the class]?*

Click ❷ on WA3 to reveal the next prompt, and have a few volunteers use the prompt to share their thinking with the class.

PROMPT 2: "I felt self-confident because . . ."

Teacher Note

Support struggling students by asking questions such as "When have you felt confident doing something at school?" and "When have you felt confident playing a sport or game?"

7 Play "Is Olive Self-confident?"

Tell the students that partners will play "Is Olive Self-confident?" You will describe something that our friend Olive does, and partners will discuss whether or not she is self-confident and why they think so.

Begin by saying:

- *Olive really likes thinking about numbers. On her own, she does lots of number puzzles. She tells her mom, "I'm good at math."*

Ask:

 Q *Is Olive self-confident? Why do you think so?* [Click ❸ to reveal the prompt.] *Turn to your partner.*

PROMPT 3: "I think Olive [is/is not] self-confident because . . ."

After partners have talked, have a few volunteers use the prompt to share their thinking with the class.

Using the same procedure, discuss one or more of the following:

- *Olive doesn't like to take spelling tests because she is worried she will spell a word wrong. Before a spelling test, she is always very nervous.*

- *Olive likes to make friends. Whenever she doesn't know someone, she introduces herself. She is sure that she can make new friends.*

Point to the word *self-confident* and review the pronunciation and meaning of the word.

EXTENSION
Discuss the Suffix *-ly*

Review that a *suffix* is a "letter or group of letters that is added to the end of a word to make a new word." Explain that the suffix *-ly* means "in a certain way" or "how." Explain that *-ly* can be added to *diligent, frank,* and *self-confident* to form these words:

- *diligently*, which means "in a diligent, or hard-working, way"
- *frankly*, which means "in a frank, or open and honest, way"
- *self-confidently*, which means "in a self-confident way or a way that shows you are sure of yourself"

Have the students discuss these questions:

Q *If you wanted to write a good story, would you work diligently on it? Why?*

Q *Is it always a good idea to speak frankly? Why?*

Q *If you have practiced diligently for a soccer game, are you likely to play self-confidently? Why?*

In this lesson, the students:

- Review and practice using the words *diligent, frank,* and *self-confident* from Day 1
- Build their speaking and listening skills
- Work in a responsible way

Materials

- Daily review cards (WA4)
- Daily review activity (WA5)

Words Taught

diligent
Diligent means "hard-working." When you are diligent, you work steadily or carefully on something because it is important to you.

frank
When you are frank, you say what you think, openly and honestly.

self-confident
Self-confident means "sure of yourself." If you are self-confident, you are confident or sure you can do something.

REVIEW THE WORDS

1 Briefly Review the Words

Display the daily review cards (WA4). Review the pronunciation and meaning of each word.

Point to the word *diligent*, and ask:

Q *Would you like to be described as diligent? Why?* [Click ❶ on WA4 to reveal the first prompt.] *Turn to your partner.*

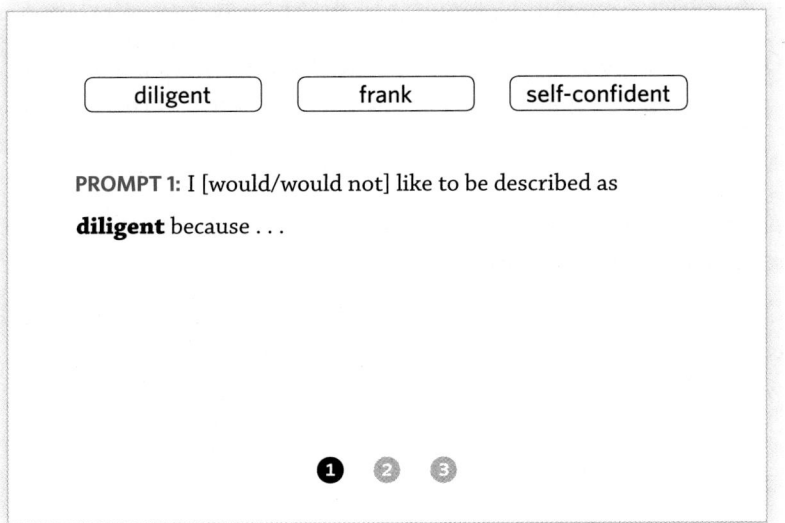

WA4

| diligent | frank | self-confident |

PROMPT 1: I [would/would not] like to be described as **diligent** because . . .

❶ ❷ ❸

PROMPT 1: "I [would/would not] like to be described as diligent because . . ."

After partners have talked, have a few volunteers use the prompt to share their thinking with the class.

Discuss *frank* and *self-confident* using the same procedure.

Q *Would you like to be described as frank? Why?* [Click ❷ to reveal the next prompt.] *Turn to your partner.*

PROMPT 2: "I [would/would not] like to be described as frank because . . ."

Q *Would you like to be described as self-confident? Why?* [Click ❸ to reveal the first prompt.] *Turn to your partner.*

PROMPT 3: "I [would/would not] like to be described as self-confident because . . ."

PRACTICE USING THE WORDS

2 Play "Find Another Word"

Tell the students that partners will play the game "Find Another Word." Remind the students that you will show a sentence with one or more words underlined. You will read each sentence aloud, and partners will decide which vocabulary word can replace the underlined part of the sentence.

Display the daily review activity (◖ WA5) and begin playing the game:

1. Click ❶ to reveal the first sentence. Point to the sentence and read it aloud, emphasizing the underlined word.

   ▪ Sentence 1: *Lucas was being <u>honest</u> when Lila asked for his opinion of her story.*

2. Give the students a few moments to think about the sentence and the underlined word. Then point to the three word choices and ask:

   Q *Which vocabulary word could replace the underlined word? Why?* [Click ❶ again and point to the prompt.] *Turn to your partner.*

PROMPT 1: "I think the word [*frank*] could replace *honest* because . . ."

After partners have talked, have a few volunteers use the prompt to share their thinking with the class.

3. Conclude the discussion by clicking ❶ a third time to highlight the correct vocabulary word and reveal the sentence with the correct word in place.

Teacher Note

You might explain that the students may need to change the form of the word to complete the sentence by adding an ending such as *-s*, *-ing*, or *-ed*.

Teacher Note

Each sentence in the ongoing review activity (WA5) has a corresponding number: the first sentence is ❶; the second sentence is ❷; and the third sentence is ❸. To play the game, click the corresponding number four times:

▪ The first click reveals the sentence.

▪ The second click reveals the prompt.

▪ The third click highlights the correct answer and reveals the sentence with the correct answer in place.

▪ The fourth click clears the screen.

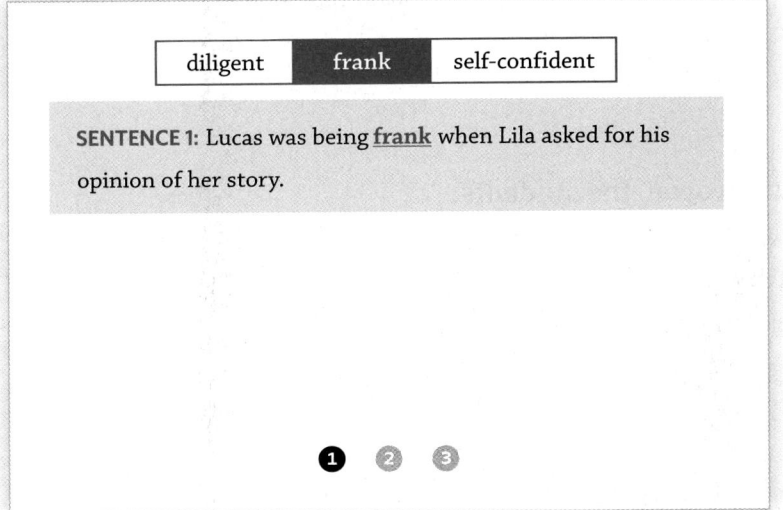

| diligent | frank | self-confident |

SENTENCE 1: Lucas was being <u>frank</u> when Lila asked for his opinion of her story.

1 **2** **3**

4. Click **1** to clear the screen.

Use the same procedure to discuss the following sentences:

- Sentence 2: *When you are <u>sure of yourself</u>, you feel certain you will do well.*

Q *Which vocabulary word could replace the underlined phrase? Why?* [Click **2** again and point to the prompt.] *Turn to your partner.*

PROMPT 2: "I think the word [*self-confident*] could replace *sure of yourself* because . . ."

- Sentence 3: *Mr. Ahmed is a <u>hard-working</u> athlete. He runs five miles every morning.*

Q *Which vocabulary word could replace the underlined word? Why?* [Click **3** again and point to the prompt.] *Turn to your partner.*

PROMPT 3: "I think the word [*diligent*] could replace *hard-working* because . . ."

Materials

- "The Mouse at the Seashore" in *Fables* (pages 40–41)
- Word card 160 (WA6)
- Word card 161 (WA7)
- Word card 162 (WA8)

In this lesson, the students:

- Learn and use the words *headstrong, overwhelmed,* and *contentment*
- Review synonyms
- Build their speaking and listening skills
- Share their partners' thinking with the class
- Give reasons for their ideas

Words Taught

headstrong
Headstrong means "determined to do what you want no matter what anyone says."

overwhelmed (p. 40)
If you are overwhelmed by a feeling, you feel it very strongly—so strongly that you forget everything else.

contentment (p. 40)
Contentment is a "feeling of satisfaction and happiness." People feel contentment when they are doing something they enjoy.

INTRODUCE AND USE *HEADSTRONG*

1 Introduce and Define *Headstrong* and Review Synonyms

Briefly review "The Mouse at the Seashore" in *Fables*. Show pages 40–41, and read the first three paragraphs on page 40 aloud.

Tell the students that the first word they will learn today is *headstrong*, and explain that *headstrong* means "determined to do what you want no matter what anyone says." Explain that *headstrong, obstinate,* and *stubborn* are synonyms.

Explain that the Mouse is headstrong—he is determined to go to the seashore no matter what his mother and father say. He says, "Nothing can make me change my mind."

Display word card 160 (WA6) and have the students say the word *headstrong*.

Teacher Note

You might remind the students that they learned the word *obstinate* earlier. If you started a synonym chart, add the words *headstrong, obstinate,* and *stubborn* to it.

2 Play "Is Olive Headstrong?"

Explain that partners will play "Is Olive Headstrong?" You will describe something Olive does, and partners will discuss whether or not she is headstrong and why they think so.

Begin by saying:

- *Olive wants to play in the rain. Her sister tells her that she will get soaked, but Olive doesn't listen. She runs outside and begins splashing through puddles.*

Ask:

 Q *Is Olive headstrong? Why do you think that?* [Click ❶ on WA6 to reveal the prompt.] *Turn to your partner.*

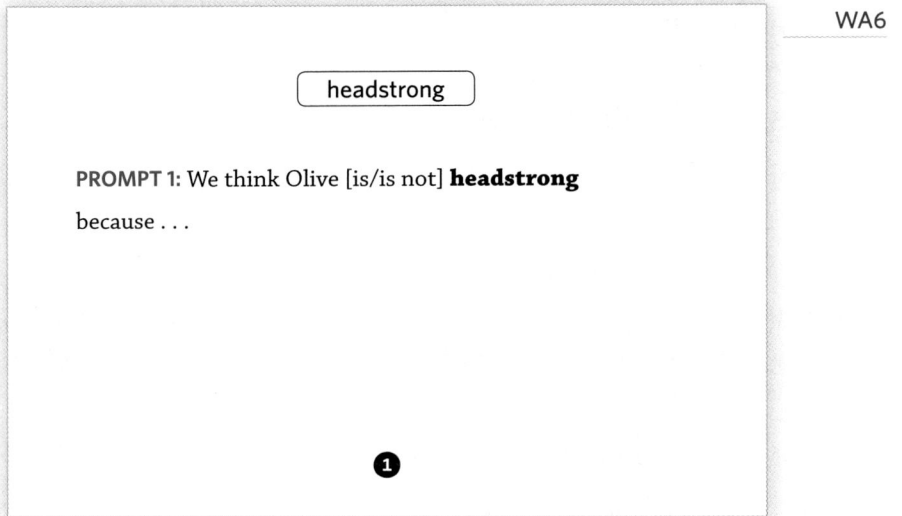

WA6

headstrong

PROMPT 1: We think Olive [is/is not] **headstrong** because . . .

❶

PROMPT 1: "We think Olive [is/is not] headstrong because . . ."

After partners have talked, have a few volunteers use the prompt to share their thinking with the class.

Using the same procedure, discuss one or more of the following:

- *Olive's older brother tells Olive that she is too little to camp out with him. He says, "You'll get scared, Olive, so you can't come." Olive says, "Okay. I won't go," and she stays home.*

- *Olive and her friends are hiking. Olive wants to hike all the way to the lake, but her friends don't want to. "The lake is too far away," they tell Olive, "and it's getting dark." Olive ignores her friends and hikes on by herself.*

Point to the word *headstrong* and review the pronunciation and meaning of the word.

INTRODUCE AND USE
OVERWHELMED

3 Introduce and Define *Overwhelmed*

Review that the Mouse encounters dangers along the way, but he finally reaches the seashore. Read the last paragraph on page 40 aloud, emphasizing the word *overwhelmed*.

Explain that if you are overwhelmed by a feeling, you feel it very strongly—so strongly that you forget everything else. Explain that the Mouse is overwhelmed by a feeling of deep peace at the seashore. He forgets about his fears and the dangers of the trip and feels only peace and happiness.

Display word card 161 (◖ WA7) and have the students say the word *overwhelmed*.

4 Discuss Feeling Overwhelmed

Explain that you can be overwhelmed by many different feelings, such as happiness, sadness, anger, and surprise.

Use "Think, Pair, Share" to discuss:

 Q *When have you been overwhelmed by a feeling of happiness? When have you felt so happy that you forgot everything else?* [Pause; click ❶ on WA7 to reveal the first prompt.] *Turn to your partner.*

PROMPT 1: "I was overwhelmed by happiness when . . ."

After partners have talked, have a few volunteers use the prompt to share their thinking with the class.

Then ask and discuss as a class:

Q *If a person were overwhelmed by a feeling of deep sadness, what might that person do or say?*

Click ❷ to reveal the next prompt and have one or two volunteers use the prompt to share their thinking with the class.

PROMPT 2: "If a person were overwhelmed by sadness, the person might . . ."

Point to the word *overwhelmed* and review the pronunciation and meaning of the word.

Teacher Note

Support struggling students by asking questions such as "When has something happened to you at home or at school that made you very, very happy?" and "When have you been so happy that you shouted with joy and jumped up and down?"

INTRODUCE AND USE
CONTENTMENT

5 Introduce and Define *Contentment*

Reread the following sentence aloud, emphasizing the word *contentment*: "He was overwhelmed by a feeling of deep peace and contentment."

Explain that *contentment* is a "feeling of satisfaction and happiness." Explain that the Mouse feels contentment, or satisfaction and happiness, because he has done what he set out to do—reach the sea—and looking at the sea makes him happy.

Display word card 162 (WA8) and have the students say the word *contentment*.

6 Discuss Times We Feel Contentment

Explain that people feel contentment, or satisfaction and happiness, when they are doing something they enjoy. Give an example of when you feel contentment.

> **You might say:**
>
> "I feel contentment when I'm curled up with a good book in the evening. It makes me happy to have some time to myself after a busy day, and I love reading a good story. I also feel contentment after I have eaten a good meal. I really enjoy food, and eating a delicious meal leaves me satisfied and happy."

Explain that partners will discuss when they feel contentment, and then a few students will share their partners' thinking.

Use "Think, Pair, Share" to discuss:

Q *When do you feel contentment? When do you feel satisfaction and happiness?* [Pause; click **1** on WA8 to reveal the first prompt.] *Turn to your partner.*

PROMPT 1: "I feel contentment when . . ."

After partners have talked, click **2** on WA8 to reveal the next prompt. Have one or two volunteers use the prompt to share their partners' thinking with the class.

PROMPT 2: "[Paulo] feels contentment when . . ."

Point to the word *contentment* and review the pronunciation and meaning of the word.

 **ELL Note**

The Spanish cognate of *contentment* is *contento/a*.

Teacher Note

You might explain that *satisfaction* is "feeling satisfied, or pleased, because you have done something well or something has turned out the way you wanted."

Teacher Note

Support struggling students by asking questions such as, "When do you feel happy or satisfied at home or at school?" and "What do you do alone or with friends that makes you feel happy and satisfied?"

Discuss Being Headstrong

Remind the students that they learned the word *headstrong*, and review that if you are headstrong, you are determined to do what you want no matter what anyone says. Review that the Mouse in the fable "The Mouse at the Seashore" is headstrong—he is determined to go to the seashore no matter what his mother and father say. Ask the students to think about a time they were headstrong. Then ask:

Q *When were you headstrong?*

Q *Why do you think you were headstrong?*

Have the students use the prompts to share their thinking with a partner.

PROMPTS: "I was headstrong when . . ." and "I think I was headstrong because . . ."

Have a few volunteers use the prompts to share their thinking with the group.

Day 4

Review *Headstrong, Overwhelmed,* and *Contentment*

Materials

- Daily review cards (WA9)
- Copy of this week's family letter (BLM1) for each student

In this lesson, the students:

- Review and practice using the words *headstrong, overwhelmed,* and *contentment* from Day 3
- Build their speaking and listening skills
- Listen respectfully to the thinking of others and share their own

Words Reviewed

headstrong
Headstrong means "determined to do what you want no matter what anyone says."

overwhelmed
If you are overwhelmed by a feeling, you feel it very strongly—so strongly that you forget everything else.

contentment
Contentment is "a feeling of satisfaction and happiness." People feel contentment when they are doing something they enjoy.

REVIEW THE WORDS

1 Briefly Review the Words

Display the daily review cards (WA9). Review the pronunciation and meaning of each word.

Use "Think, Pair, Share" to discuss:

Q *Which of these words might you use when you talk with your family or friends? How might you use the word?* [Pause; click ❶ on WA9 to reveal the first prompt.] *Turn to your partner.*

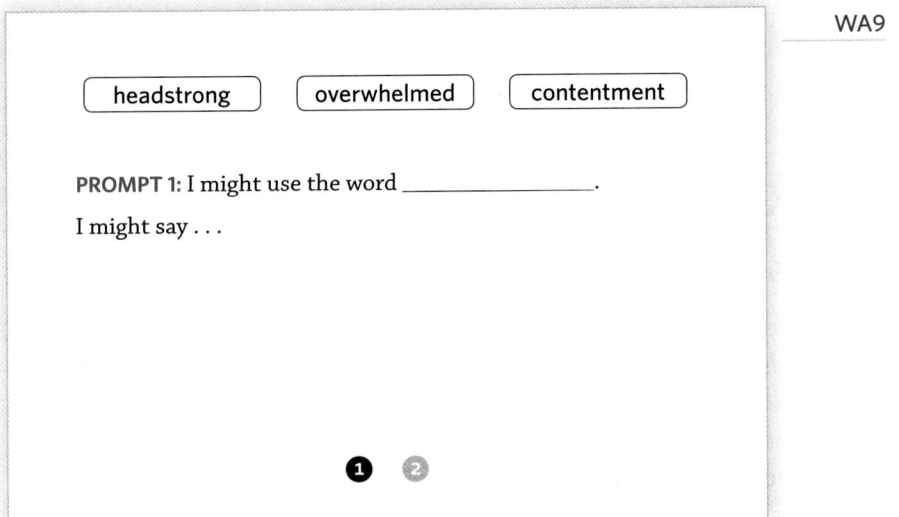

WA9

PROMPT 1: "I might use the word [*headstrong*]. I might say . . ."

After partners have talked, have a few volunteers use the prompt to share their thinking with the class.

PRACTICE USING THE WORDS

2 Play "Which Word Am I?"

Explain that partners will play "Which Word Am I?" Review that you will give a clue about one of the words and partners will figure out the word.

Begin by saying:

- *I'm the feeling you get when you are having fun with your friends.*

Ask:

Q *What word am I? Why do you think that?* [Click ❷ on WA9 to reveal the prompt.] *Turn to your partner.*

PROMPT 2: "I think the word is [*contentment*] because . . ."

After partners have talked, have one or two volunteers share their thinking with the class.

Using the same procedure, discuss one or more of the following:

- *I'm how you feel when you are so scared you can't think or move.* (overwhelmed)

- *I'm how you would describe someone who is stubborn and doesn't listen to good advice.* (headstrong)

- *I'm how you feel when you are very, very sad and nothing can make you feel better.* (overwhelmed)

- *I'm the feeling of happiness and satisfaction you get when you are doing something you enjoy.* (contentment)

- *I'm how you describe someone who does something even though all of her friends tell her not to do it.* (headstrong)

Teacher Note

Send home with each student a copy of this week's family letter (BLM1). Encourage the students to talk about this week's words with their families.

Teacher Note

You might remind the students that earlier they learned the compound word *heartbreaking*, which means "very sad or upsetting."

EXTENSION

Discuss the Compound Word *Headstrong*

Write the word *headstrong* where everyone can see it, and explain that *headstrong* is a compound word. Review that a *compound word* is a "word made up of two or more shorter words," and remind the students that if they see a compound word in their reading and are not sure what it means, they can usually figure out the meaning by identifying the shorter words and thinking about what each word means.

Ask and discuss as a class:

Q *What shorter words make up the word* headstrong?

Have a few volunteers use the prompt to share their thinking.

PROMPT: "[*Head*] and [*strong*] make up the word *headstrong*."

If necessary, point out that the words *head* and *strong* make up the word *headstrong*. Explain that someone who is headstrong has a strong belief or idea in his mind (head), and no one is going to change his thinking.

In this lesson, the students:

- Review words learned earlier
- Build their speaking and listening skills
- Work in a responsible way

Materials

- Ongoing review cards (WA10)

Words Reviewed

aggressive
Aggressive means "threatening or ready and eager to fight or attack others." Aggressive animals or people are frightening because they can be mean, dangerous, or violent.

considerate
Considerate means "thoughtful of the feelings and needs of others."

evacuate
Evacuate means "leave a place and go somewhere safer."

skillful
Skillful means "good at doing something."

stressful
Stressful means "causing worry or tension."

REVIEW THE WORDS

1 Briefly Review the Words

Display the ongoing review cards (WA10) and review the pronunciation and meaning of each word.

PRACTICE USING THE WORDS

2 Play "Does That Make Sense?"

Tell the students that partners will play a game called "Does That Make Sense?" Remind the students that you will read a sentence that includes one of the vocabulary words. Partners will decide whether the word makes sense in the sentence and explain why they think so.

Read the following sentence aloud twice:

- *Harold is always considerate of his sister while she does her homework. He talks loudly on the phone and watches television in the same room.*

Ask:

 Q *Does the word* considerate *make sense in the sentence? Why do you think that?* [Click ❶ on WA10 to reveal the first prompt.] *Turn to your partner.*

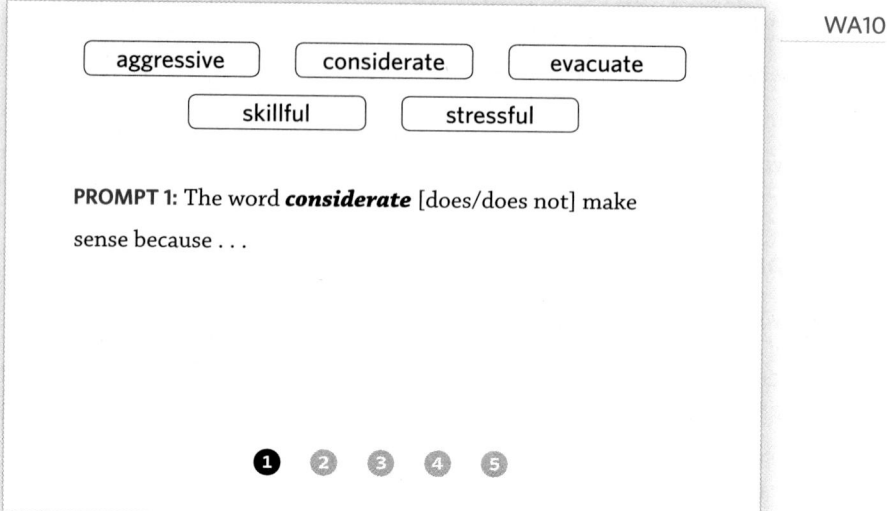
Teacher Note

If the students struggle to answer the questions, call for their attention. Reread the story aloud, and explain that *considerate* does not make sense in the story because talking loudly and having the TV on in the same room would make it difficult to do homework. Harold is not being considerate of his sister.

PROMPT 1: "The word *considerate* [does/does not] make sense because . . ."

After partners have talked, have a few volunteers use the prompt to share their thinking with the class.

Use the same procedure to discuss the following sentences:

[evacuate]

- *The residents of the burning building were evacuated by firefighters.*

 Q *Does the word* evacuated *make sense in the sentence? Why do you think that?* [Click ❷ to reveal the prompt.] *Turn to your partner.*

PROMPT 2: "The word *evacuated* [does/does not] make sense because . . ."

[aggressive]

- *The class bunny, Mr. Bunny, is very aggressive. He is cute and cuddly and loves munching on carrots.*

 Q *Does the word* aggressive *make sense in the sentence? Why do you think that?* [Click ❸ to reveal the prompt.] *Turn to your partner.*

PROMPT 3: "The word *aggressive* [does/does not] make sense because . . ."

[stressful]

- *Aliyah had a very stressful day. She missed her bus, was late for work, and lost her keys.*

 Q *Does the word* stressful *make sense in the sentence? Why do you think that?* [Click ❹ to reveal the prompt.] *Turn to your partner.*

PROMPT 4: "The word *stressful* [does/does not] make sense because . . ."

[skillful]

- *Donny is skillful at baking cookies. He always adds too much flour, burns the bottoms, and makes them too big.*

 Q *Does the word* skillful *make sense in the sentence? Why do you think that?* [Click ❺ to reveal the prompt.] *Turn to your partner.*

PROMPT 5: "The word *skillful* [does/does not] make sense because . . ."

RESOURCES

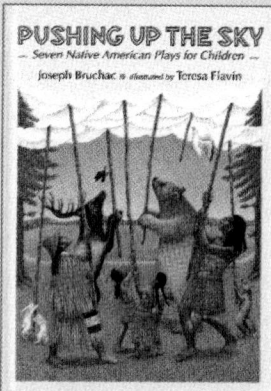

Read-aloud

- "Possum's Tail" from *Pushing Up the Sky: Seven Native American Plays for Children* by Joseph Bruchac, illustrated by Teresa Flavin

More Strategy Practice

- "Discuss Another Meaning of *Brainstorm*"

Extensions

- "Explore the Prefix *dis-*"
- "Explore the Suffix *-y*"

Assessment Resource Book

- Week 28 vocabulary assessments

 Online Resources

Visit the CCC Learning Hub (ccclearninghub.org) to find your online resources for this week.

Whiteboard Activities

- WA1–WA11

Assessment Forms

- "Class Vocabulary Assessment Record" sheet (CA1)
- "Individual Vocabulary Assessment: Word Check 7" answer sheet (IA1)
- "Individual Vocabulary Assessment Student Record" sheet (SR1)

- "Individual Vocabulary Assessment Class Record" sheet (CR1)
- (Optional) "Student Self-assessment" response sheet (SA1)

Reproducibles

- Week 28 family letter (BLM1)
- (Optional) "Week 28 Word Cards" (BLM2)
- (Optional) "Week 28 Crossword Puzzle" (BLM3)

OVERVIEW

Words Taught	Words Reviewed
well-organized	diligent
disorganized	frank
boast	headstrong
silky	overwhelmed
improvise	self-confident
brainstorm	

Word-learning Strategies

- Recognizing antonyms and synonyms (review)
- Recognizing words with multiple meanings (review)
- Recognizing idioms (review)

Vocabulary Focus

- Students learn and use six words from or about the play.
- Students review antonyms and synonyms.
- Students review recognizing words with multiple meanings.
- Students review recognizing idioms.
- Students review words learned earlier.
- Students build their speaking and listening skills.

Social Development Focus

- Students develop the skill of giving reasons for their ideas.
- Students develop the skill of asking clarifying questions.
- Students listen respectfully to the thinking of others and share their own.
- Students work in a responsible way.

⏲ DO AHEAD

✓ Prior to Day 1, identify an area in the classroom that is well-organized, such as your desk, the classroom library, or the computer center. You will use this area to discuss the word *well-organized*.

✓ Prior to Day 3, collect one or more silk items such as a scarf, pillowcase, handkerchief, napkin, or shirt to discuss the word *silky*.

✓ (Optional) Prior to Day 3, review the more strategy practice activity "Discuss Another Meaning of *Brainstorm*" on page 590.

✓ Prior to Day 4, visit the CCC Learning Hub (ccclearninghub.org) to access and print this week's family letter (BLM1). Make enough copies to send one letter home with each student.

✓ Prior to Day 5, make a copy of the "Class Vocabulary Assessment Record" sheet (CA1); see page 206 of the *Assessment Resource Book*.

✓ Prior to Day 5, make a class set of the "Individual Vocabulary Assessment: Word Check 7" answer sheet (IA1); see page 210 of the *Assessment Resource Book*. Make enough copies for each student to have one; set aside a reference copy for yourself.

✓ (Optional) Prior to Day 5, make a master copy of the "Student Self-assessment" response sheet (SA1); see page 213 of the *Assessment Resource Book*. Write the words you have chosen to be assessed on the master copy. Then make enough copies for each student to have one.

✓ (Optional) Visit the CCC Learning Hub (ccclearninghub.org) to access and print the following materials: "Week 28 Word Cards" (BLM2) and "Week 28 Crossword Puzzle" (BLM3). These materials can be used to provide your students with more opportunities to review the words.

In this lesson, the students:

- Learn and use the words *well-organized, disorganized,* and *boast*
- Review antonyms and synonyms
- Build their speaking and listening skills
- Give reasons for their ideas

Words Taught

well-organized (p. 37)
If something is well-organized, it is planned or arranged (put together) in a neat or orderly way.

disorganized
If something is disorganized, it is not planned or arranged (put together) in a neat or orderly way. It is messy or confusing.

boast
Boast means "brag." When people boast, they talk about themselves or something they have with too much pride or pleasure.

INTRODUCE AND USE *WELL-ORGANIZED*

1 Introduce and Define *Well-organized*

Show page 37 of *Pushing Up the Sky* and review that the play "Possum's Tail" is based on a Native American tale told by the Cherokee people. Explain that this introduction to the play gives background information about the Cherokee people. Read the first paragraph aloud, emphasizing the word *well-organized.*

Explain that if something is well-organized, it is planned or arranged (put together) in a neat or orderly way. When the author says that the Cherokee villages were well-organized, he means that the villages were made up of houses that were planned and built in a neat and orderly way.

Display word card 163 (❤ WA1) and have the students say the word *well-organized.*

Materials

- "Possum's Tail"
- Word card 163 (WA1)
- Word card 164 (WA2)
- Word card 165 (WA3)

Teacher Note

You might explain that *well-organized* is a hyphenated word and that a *hyphenated word* is a "word made up of two or more shorter words connected by a hyphen (a small dash)." The hyphenated word *well-organized* is made up of the words *well* and *organized.* Something that is well-organized is organized, or planned or arranged, well.

2 Discuss Well-organized Places and Events

Direct the students' attention to the well-organized classroom area you identified earlier and point out why the area is well-organized.

> **You might say:**
>
> "Our classroom library is well-organized, or arranged in a neat and orderly way. The books are neatly stored in book boxes on shelves. The book boxes are also arranged by genre, or type. The fiction books are in the red boxes and the non-fiction books are in the green boxes. There is a 'check-in' box for returning books. There are beanbags in each corner of the library to sit in while you are reading."

Discuss as a class:

Q *What other area in our classroom is well-organized? Why do you say it is well-organized?*

Click ❶ on word card 163 (WA1) to reveal the first prompt. Have a few volunteers use the prompt to share their thinking with the class.

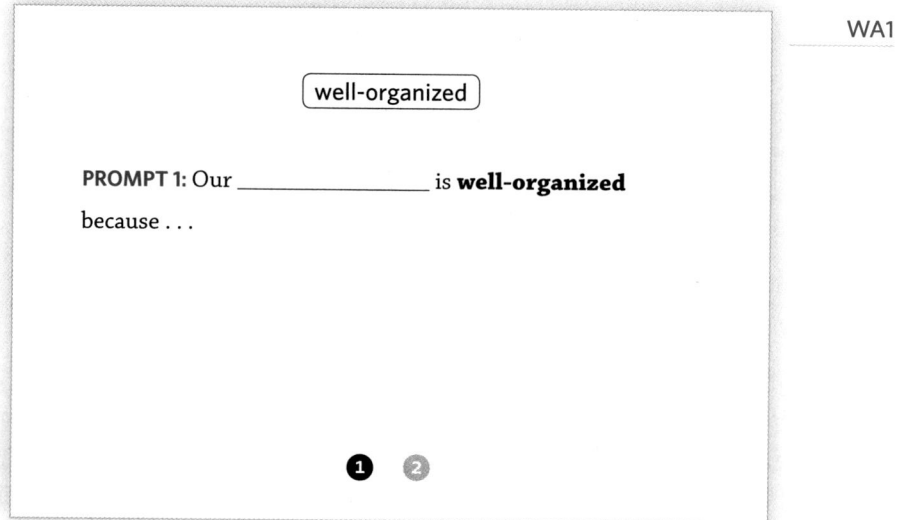

WA1

well-organized

PROMPT 1: Our _____ is **well-organized** because . . .

❶ ❷

PROMPT 1: "Our [writing center] is well-organized because . . ."

Explain that events such as parties and trips can also be well-organized, or carefully planned so that things go well. Give a couple of examples of well-organized events you have planned or attended.

> **You might say:**
>
> "This year's science fair was well-organized. Every student had space for a display, and there was enough time for everyone to present their projects. I enjoyed it very much. I made sure my sister's surprise birthday party this year was well-organized. First, I reserved a space for a picnic well ahead of time, and I sent out invitations a month before the birthday. Next, I asked each person who was attending to bring a different food or dessert so that there would be lots of different kinds of food. The party went well, and everyone had fun."

Use "Think, Pair, Share" to discuss:

 Q *When have you attended an event that was well-organized? Why do you say it was well-organized?* [Click ❷ on WA1 to reveal the next prompt.] *Turn to your partner.*

PROMPT 2: "[My volleyball tournament] was well-organized because . . ."

After partners have talked, have a few volunteers use the prompt to share their thinking with the class.

Point to the word *well-organized* and review the pronunciation and meaning of the word.

INTRODUCE AND USE
DISORGANIZED

3 ## Introduce and Define *Disorganized* and Review Antonyms

Tell the students that the next word they will learn today is *disorganized*. Display word card 164 ( WA2) and have the students say the word *disorganized*. Explain that *well-organized* and *disorganized* are antonyms, and review that *antonyms* are "words with opposite meanings." Ask:

Q *If* well-organized *means "planned or arranged in a neat or orderly way," and* well-organized *and* disorganized *are antonyms, what do you think* disorganized *means?*

Click ❶ on WA2 to reveal the first prompt. Have one or two volunteers use the prompt to share their thinking with the class.

PROMPT 1: "I think *disorganized* means . . ."

If necessary, explain that if something is disorganized, it is not planned or arranged (put together) in a neat or orderly way. It is messy or confusing.

4 ## Play "Well-organized or Disorganized?"

Tell the students that they will play a game called "Well-organized or Disorganized?" Explain that you will describe a place or event and partners will decide whether the place or event is well-organized or disorganized and why they think so.

Begin by saying:

- *In Rhoda's closet, the clothing is arranged by color. Shirts and pants hang neatly on hangers. Shoes sit in neat rows on shelves, and hats are stacked above the clothes.*

Ask:

Q *Is Rhoda's closet well-organized or disorganized? Why?* [Click ❷ on WA2 to reveal the prompt.] *Turn to your partner.*

PROMPT 2: "Rhoda's closet is [well-organized] because . . ."

After partners have talked, have a few volunteers use the prompt to share their thinking with the class.

Repeat the procedure with one or both of the following scenarios:

- *Mr. Lopez had a yard sale. He put up a big sign on his front lawn that said "Yard Sale! Come one, come all!!" There were tidy stacks and neat rows of items for sale. There were different sections for toys, kitchen utensils, and clothes.*

Q *Is the yard sale well-organized or disorganized? Why?* [Click ❸ to reveal the prompt.] *Turn to your partner.*

PROMPT 3: "The yard sale is [well-organized] because . . ."

- *Mrs. Peterson's kitchen is messy. There are dirty plates everywhere and food all over the counters. The cabinets are open and cluttered.*

Q *Is the kitchen well-organized or disorganized? Why?* [Click ❹ to reveal the prompt.] *Turn to your partner.*

PROMPT 4: "The kitchen is [disorganized] because . . ."

Point to the word *disorganized* and review the pronunciation and meaning of the word.

Teacher Note

You might remind the students that they learned the word *cluttered* earlier and that if a place is cluttered, it is messy. There are things scattered here, there, and everywhere.

Teacher Note

If you started a synonym chart, add the words *boast* and *brag* to it.

5 Introduce and Define *Boast* and Review Synonyms

Explain that the last word the students will learn today is *boast* and that *boast* means "brag." Explain that that *boast* and *brag* are synonyms. When people boast, they talk about themselves or something they have with too much pride or pleasure.

Display word card 165 (WA3) and have the students say the word *boast*.

Remind the students that in Scene 1 of "Possum's Tail" the animals are discussing a meeting they plan to have, and Possum arrives. Tell the students that as you read from Scene 1 you want them to listen for what Possum boasts about. Then read Scene 1 on page 39 aloud, stopping at the end of the page.

Ask:

Q *What is Possum boasting or bragging about? What does he say that is an example of boasting?*

Click ❶ on word card 165 (WA3) to reveal the first prompt. Have one or two volunteers use the prompt to share their thinking with the class.

PROMPT 1: "Possum is boasting about [his tail]. He says . . ."

6 Play "Is Olive Boasting?"

Explain that the students will play "Is Olive Boasting?" You will describe something that the imaginary third-grader Olive is saying. Partners will then decide whether or not she is boasting and why they think so. Begin by reading the following scenario aloud twice:

- *Olive got a new bike for her birthday. She brings it to school and won't stop talking about it to her friends. She says, "My new bike is the greatest bike in the world!"*

Ask:

 Q *Is Olive boasting? Why?* [Click **2** on WA3 to reveal the prompt.] *Turn to your partner.*

PROMPT 2: "I think Olive [is/is not] boasting because . . ."

After partners have talked, have a few volunteers use the prompt to share their thinking with the class.

Using the same procedure, discuss one or both of the following:

- *Olive gets a new haircut on the first day of school. Her friend Billy says it looks nice and she says, "Thanks, Billy! My mother cut it. I think she did a nice job."*

 Q *Is Olive boasting? Why?* [Point to prompt 2.] *Turn to your partner.*

- *After Olive's basketball team wins their game, she yells, "We won! I'm so happy! We won!" Then Olive shakes hands with the players on the team that lost.*

 Q *Is Olive boasting? Why?* [Point to prompt 2.] *Turn to your partner.*

Point to the word *boast* and review the pronunciation and meaning of the word.

EXTENSION

Explore the Prefix *dis-*

Write the word *disorganized* where everyone can see it. Remind the students that if something is disorganized, it is not planned or arranged (put together) in a neat or orderly way. It is messy or confusing. Underline the prefix *dis-* and explain that *dis-* is a prefix. Remind the students that a *prefix* is a "letter or group of letters that is added to the beginning of a word to make a new word." Explain that the prefix *dis-* means "not" or "the opposite of." Point out that when *dis-* is added to the word *organized*, it makes the word *disorganized*, which means "not organized."

Have the students discuss the meaning of other words that use the prefix *dis-*, such as *disagree*, *discomfort*, *disconnect*, *disinterested*, and *disobey*.

Materials

- Daily review cards (WA4)

In this lesson, the students:

- Review and practice using the words *well-organized, disorganized,* and *boast* from Day 1
- Build their speaking and listening skills
- Listen respectfully to the thinking of others and share their own

Words Reviewed

well-organized
If something is well-organized, it is planned or arranged (put together) in a neat or orderly way.

disorganized
If something is disorganized, it is not planned or arranged (put together) in a neat or orderly way. It is messy or confusing.

boast
Boast means "brag." When people boast, they talk about themselves or something they have with too much pride or pleasure.

REVIEW THE WORDS

1 Briefly Review the Words

Display the daily review cards (WA4). Review the pronunciation and meaning of each word.

Ask:

Q *Which of these words do you think is the most interesting? Why?*
[Click ❶ on WA4 to reveal the first prompt.] *Turn to your partner.*

WA4

| well-organized | disorganized | boast |

PROMPT 1: I think the word _____ is the most interesting because . . .

❶ ❷ ❸ ❹

PROMPT 1: "I think the word [*boast*] is the most interesting because . . ."

After partners have talked, have a few volunteers use the prompt to share their thinking with the class.

PRACTICE USING THE WORDS

2 Play "Does That Make Sense?"

Tell the students that partners will play the game "Does That Make Sense?" Review that you will read a sentence that includes one of the vocabulary words. Partners will decide whether the word makes sense in the sentence and explain why they think so.

Point to the word *well-organized* on the daily review cards (WA4) and explain that the first sentence includes the word *well-organized*.

Read the following sentence aloud twice:

- *In a well-organized store, empty boxes are scattered here, there, and everywhere, and the shelves are cluttered.*

Ask:

 Q *Does the word* well-organized *make sense in the sentence? Why do you think that?* [Pause; click **2** on WA4 to reveal the prompt.] *Turn to your partner.*

PROMPT 2: "*Well-organized* [does/does not] make sense because . . ."

After partners have talked, have a few volunteers use the prompt to share their thinking with the class.

Use the same procedure to discuss the following sentences:

[boast]

- *"My house is the biggest, fanciest, most expensive, and most beautiful house on the block," Hanna boasted to her friends.*

 Q *Does the word* boasted *make sense in the sentence? Why do you think that?* [Pause; click **3** to reveal the prompt.] *Turn to your partner.*

PROMPT 3: "*Boasted* [does/does not] make sense because . . ."

[disorganized]

- *The disorganized desk had papers neatly stacked in one corner and pens and pencils in a box in another corner.*

 Q *Does the word* disorganized *make sense in the sentence? Why do you think that?* [Pause; click **4** to reveal the prompt.] *Turn to your partner.*

PROMPT 4: "*Disorganized* [does/does not] make sense because . . ."

Teacher Note

If the students struggle to answer the questions, call for their attention. Reread the sentence aloud, and explain that *well-organized* does not make sense in the sentence because a well-organized store would not have empty boxes lying about or cluttered shelves. Instead, the store would be neat and orderly. Then read the next story and discuss it as a class, rather than in pairs.

Materials

- "Possum's Tail"
- Word card 166 (WA5)
- Word card 167 (WA6)
- Word card 168 (WA7)
- A silk item (collected ahead)

In this lesson, the students:

- Learn and use the words *silky, improvise,* and *brainstorm*
- Review idioms
- Review words with multiple meanings
- Build their speaking and listening skills
- Ask clarifying questions

Words Taught

silky (p. 40)
Silky means "soft and smooth like silk."

improvise (p. 40)
Improvise means "make up and perform something without any preparation." *Improvise* can also mean "make or do something using whatever materials are available."

brainstorm
A *brainstorm* is a "sudden idea."

INTRODUCE AND USE *SILKY*

1 Introduce and Define *Silky*

Show page 40 of "Possum's Tail" and review that in this part of the play Possum tells the other animals that he should speak at the meeting they are planning. Then read aloud Turtle, Otter, and Possum's dialogue on page 40, emphasizing the word *silky*.

Explain that *silky* means "soft and smooth like silk." Explain that Possum brags that his tail is silky, or soft and smooth like silk.

Display word card 166 (WA5) and have the students say the word *silky*.

2 Play "Is It Silky?"

Show and describe the silk item you collected ahead of time. Explain that the item is made out of silk, which is a type of fabric that is very soft. You might pass the item around so that the students can touch it. Explain that people also use the word *silky* to describe things that are not made of silk but that have a soft, smooth feel of silk, like Possum's tail.

Tell the students that they will play a game called "Is It Silky?" You will name an object and partners will decide whether or not they would describe the object as silky and why.

Begin by saying:

- *tree bark*

Ask:

 Q *Is tree bark silky? Why?* [Click ❶ on WA5 to reveal the prompt.] *Turn to your partner.*

PROMPT 1: "[Tree bark] [is/is not] silky because . . ."

After partners have talked, have a few volunteers use the prompt to share their thinking with the class.

Using the same procedure, discuss one or more of the following:

- *cat fur*

Q *Is cat fur silky? Why?* [Point to prompt 1.] *Turn to your partner.*

- *gravel*

Q *Is gravel silky? Why?* [Point to prompt 1.] *Turn to your partner.*

- *a rose petal*

Q *Is a rose petal silky? Why?* [Point to prompt 1.] *Turn to your partner.*

Follow up by discussing as a class:

Q *What is something silky that you own?*

Point to the word *silky* and review the pronunciation and meaning of the word.

INTRODUCE AND USE *IMPROVISE*

3 Introduce and Define *Improvise*

Show page 40 again and review that in this part of the play Possum is boasting, or bragging, about his tail to the other animals. Tell the students that the author of the play provides a piece of stage direction—a suggestion to the actors about what they should do—as Possum is boasting. Then read the following stage direction, emphasizing the word *improvise*: "Possum can continue to improvise while Bear and Rabbit speak, saying 'Isn't it beautiful?' etc."

Tell the students that *improvise* means "make up and perform something without any preparation." Explain that in the stage direction, the author is telling the actor playing Possum that he or she can improvise, or make up other things to say, as Possum continues to boast about his tail. For example, the actor playing Possum might improvise, or make up, other boasts about his tail, such as "Isn't it beautiful? Isn't it lovely? Isn't my tail gorgeous, fabulous, and wonderful?"

 **ELL Note**

The Spanish cognate of *improvise* is *improvisar*.

Display word card 167 (◖ WA6) and have the students say the word *improvise*.

4 Improvise a Scene

Tell the students that actors sometimes improvise a scene, or make up what they say and do in the scene, rather than saying and doing something they have prepared or rehearsed.

Explain that the students are going to be actors and improvise a scene with their partner. Explain that you will describe the scene, and then when you say "Turn to your partner," partners will act out the scene, making up their actions and words on the spot.

Read the following scenario:

- *You and your partner are in a rowboat. There is a leak in the boat and it is quickly filling with water.*

Give the students a few moments to think about the situation. Then say "Turn to your partner" and have partners act out the scene. After a minute or two, signal for the students' attention and discuss:

Q *What did you and your partner do and say when you improvised?*

Click ❶ on word card 167 (WA6) to reveal the first prompt. Have one or two volunteers use the prompt to share their thinking with the class.

PROMPT 1: "When we improvised, we . . ."

Discuss as a class:

Q *Did you enjoy improvising? Why?*

Click ❷ to reveal the next prompt and have a few volunteers use the prompt to share their thinking with the class.

PROMPT 2: "I [did/did not] enjoy improvising because . . ."

5 Discuss Another Meaning of *Improvise*

Tell the students that *improvise* has a second meaning. It can also mean "make or do something using whatever materials are available."

Tell the students that often when we are cooking or making crafts, we do not have the exact ingredients or materials the recipe or instructions call for, so we improvise, or use whatever is available. Give the students a few examples of when you have improvised or seen someone improvise.

> **You might say:**
>
> "Last weekend, I wanted to bake muffins but I was out of eggs. I improvised by using mashed bananas in place of the eggs. The last time we had a rain shower, I was caught outside without an umbrella. I improvised and used a newspaper to keep dry. Yesterday, Helen and Neil asked for a spinner to play a game. I did not have a spinner, so they improvised and used a die instead."

Teacher Note

You might explain that a *scene* is "one particular part of a play or movie."

Teacher Note

If the students struggle to improvise the scene, signal for their attention and ask a volunteer pair to act out the scene (or act out the scene yourself with the help of a volunteer). Afterward, have the students discuss what they saw by asking "What did you see [Bryce and Catherine] do when they improvised?"

Use "Think, Pair, Share" to discuss:

Q *When have you had to improvise while you were making or doing something? What did you do to improvise?* [Pause; click **3** on WA6 to reveal the prompt.] *Turn to your partner.*

PROMPT 3: "I had to improvise when . . ." and "I improvised by . . ."

After partners have talked, have one or two volunteers use the prompt to share their thinking with the class.

Point to the word *improvise* and review the pronunciation and meaning of the word.

Teacher Note

Support struggling students by asking questions such as "When have you had to substitute one item for another when you were working on an art project?" and "When have you wanted to use something, but could not find what you were looking for and used something else instead?"

INTRODUCE AND USE *BRAINSTORM*

6 Introduce and Define *Brainstorm* and Review Idioms

Show page 41 and explain that in this part of "Possum's Tail" Bear and Rabbit discuss ideas to make Possum stop boasting about his tail. Read the conversation between Bear and Rabbit on page 41.

Tell the students that the last word they will learn today is *brainstorm*. Explain that a *brainstorm* is a "sudden idea." Explain that, as Rabbit and Bear are talking, Rabbit has a brainstorm, or sudden idea, about Possum.

Display word card 168 (🌑 WA7) and have the students say the word *brainstorm*.

Explain that *brainstorm* is an example of an idiom, and review that an *idiom* is an "expression or phrase that means something different from what it appears to mean." Explain that when you say you had a brainstorm, you do not mean that there was actually a storm inside your brain. Instead, you mean that you had a sudden idea—an idea that came to you quite suddenly, like a powerful thunderstorm.

Teacher Note

If you started an idiom chart, add *brainstorm* and its definition "sudden idea." You might remind the students that they learned the idioms "have eyes in the back of your head," "have a change of heart," "blow your top," and "throw yourself into something."

7 Discuss Having a Brainstorm

Explain that people often have brainstorms when they are confronting a tough problem or situation and they need a good idea to solve the problem. Give some examples of a time you or someone you know has had a brainstorm.

> **You might say:**
>
> "I have lots and lots of books crowding my shelves at home, and I've been wondering what to do with them. The other day I had a brainstorm—an idea suddenly came to me. I will donate some of my old books to our local library. That way others will be able to read them, and I'll have space for new books on my shelves. Jake had a brainstorm during writing time the other day. He was having trouble thinking of something to write about—and then an idea suddenly came to him. He would write a story about going to a baseball game with his grandfather."

Use "Think, Pair, Share" to discuss:

 Q *When have you or someone you know had a brainstorm?* [Click ❶ on WA7 to reveal the prompt.] *Turn to your partner.*

PROMPT 1: "[My friend Annie] had a brainstorm when . . ."

After partners have talked, have a few volunteers use the prompt to share their thinking with the class.

Explain that some people are full of ideas and have a lot of brainstorms. Ask:

Q *Who do you know who has lots of brainstorms?*

Point to the word *brainstorm* and review the pronunciation and meaning of the word.

MORE STRATEGY PRACTICE

Discuss Another Meaning of *Brainstorm*

Review that words can have more than one meaning and that the meanings are often very different. Explain that the word *brainstorm* has two very different meanings. Review that *brainstorm* can mean a "sudden idea." Then tell the students that *brainstorm* can also mean "think of many different ways of doing something."

Remind the students that when they read or hear a word that has more than one meaning—like *brainstorm*—they can usually figure out the correct meaning by thinking about how the word is used. Explain that you will read a sentence that uses the word *brainstorm*. The students will decide whether *brainstorm* means a "sudden idea" or "think of many different ways of doing something."

Then read the following sentence aloud twice:

- *After Claudine loses her house keys and can't get in her front door, she has a brainstorm to check if the back door is open.*

Ask:

Q *In the sentence, does* brainstorm *mean a "sudden idea" or "think of many different ways of doing something"? Why do you think that?*

Show the prompt and read it aloud.

PROMPT: "I think *brainstorm* means ['a sudden idea'] because . . ."

Have one or two volunteers use the prompt to share their thinking with the class. Using the same procedure, discuss the following sentence:

- *The students brainstorm ideas for the topic of their science presentation.*

In this lesson, the students:

- Review and practice using the words *silky, improvise,* and *brainstorm* from Day 3
- Build their speaking and listening skills
- Work in a responsible way
- Give reasons for their ideas

Words Reviewed

silky
Silky means "soft and smooth like silk."

improvise
Improvise means "make up and perform something without any preparation." *Improvise* can also mean "make or do something using whatever materials are available."

brainstorm
A *brainstorm* is a "sudden idea."

Materials

- Daily review cards (WA8)
- "Tell Me a Story" chart (WA9)
- Copy of this week's family letter (BLM1) for each student
- (Optional) Copy of the "Week 28 Crossword Puzzle" (BLM3) for each student

REVIEW THE WORDS

1 Briefly Review the Words

Display the daily review cards (WA8). Review the pronunciation and meaning of each word.

Ask:

Q *Imagine that you are in the school play but forgot to bring your costume to school on the day of the play. What word would you use to describe how you solved the problem? Why? [Click ❶ on WA8 to reveal the prompt.] Turn to your partner.*

PROMPT 1: "I would use the word [*improvise*]. I would say . . ."

After partners have talked, have a few volunteers use the prompt to share their thinking with the class.

PRACTICE USING THE WORDS

2 Do the Activity "Tell Me a Story"

Explain that partners will do the activity "Tell Me a Story." Remind the students that you will tell them the beginning of a story that includes a vocabulary word. They will use what they know about the word and their imaginations to make up an ending for the story.

Display the "Tell Me a Story" chart (WA9). Point to story 1 and begin by reading the story aloud twice, slowly and clearly. Point to the word *improvise* and explain that you will tell the beginning of a story that includes the word *improvise*.

- Story 1: *After arriving at school, Gary realized he forgot to bring his art project. Before art class, he improvised by . . .*

Ask:

 Q *How might you finish the story? How might Gary improvise?* [Point to prompt 1.] *Turn to your partner.*

PROMPT 1: "Gary improvised by . . ."

After partners have talked, have one or two volunteers use the prompt to share their thinking with the class.

Using the same procedure, discuss:

- Story 2: *Cece wants to throw her brother a fun birthday party, but she's not sure what to do. Then she has a brainstorm. Her brainstorm is to . . .*

Ask:

 Q *How might you finish the story? What brainstorm might Cece have for her brother's birthday party?* [Point to prompt 2 on WA9.] *Turn to your partner.*

PROMPT 2: "Cece's brainstorm is to . . ."

- Story 3: *Louis is looking through his grandparents' attic. In an old trunk, he finds a silky . . .*

Ask:

Q *How might you finish the story? What silky thing might Louis find in his grandparents' attic?* [Point to prompt 3.] *Turn to your partner.*

PROMPT 3: "Louis finds a silky . . ."

Teacher Note

If the students have difficulty thinking of an ending, review the definition of *improvise* and think aloud about an ending. (For example, say "Gary improvised by painting a picture.") Then reread the beginning of the story and repeat the question.

Teacher Note

Send home with each student a copy of this week's family letter (BLM1). Encourage the students to talk about this week's words with their families.

Teacher Note

To provide students with additional review of words taught during Weeks 27 and 28, you might distribute a copy of the "Week 28 Crossword Puzzle" (BLM3) to each student.

EXTENSION

Explore the Suffix -*y*

Remind the students that a *suffix* is a "letter or group of letters that is added to the end of a word to make a new word." Explain that the suffix -*y* means "having the quality of or being like." Explain that when -*y* is added to the word *silk*, which means "a type of smooth fabric," it makes the word *silky*, which means "having the quality of or being like silk, or soft or smooth like silk."

Explain that the suffix -*y* can be added to other words, and have the students discuss the meaning of each of these words: *clingy*, *tangy*, *curly*, *wavy*, *cheesy*, and *flaky*.

Teacher Note

You might point out that when you add the suffix -*y* to *wave*, you drop the letter *e* to spell *wavy*.

Ongoing Review | Day 5

In this lesson, the students:

- Review words learned earlier
- Build their speaking and listening skills
- Work in a responsible way

Words Reviewed

diligent
Diligent means "hard-working." When you are diligent, you work steadily or carefully on something because it is important to you.

frank
When you are frank, you say what you think, openly and honestly.

headstrong
Headstrong means "determined to do what you want no matter what anyone says."

overwhelmed
If you are overwhelmed by a feeling, you feel it very strongly—so strongly that you forget everything else.

self-confident
Self-confident means "sure of yourself." If you are self-confident, you are confident or sure you can do something.

Materials

- Ongoing review cards (WA10)
- Ongoing review activity (WA11)
- "Class Vocabulary Assessment Record" sheet (CA1)
- Class set of the "Individual Vocabulary Assessment: Word Check 7" answer sheet (IA1)
- Class set of the "Individual Vocabulary Assessment Student Record" sheet (SR1)
- "Individual Vocabulary Assessment Class Record" sheet (CR1)
- (Optional) Class set of the "Student Self-assessment" response sheet (SA1)

REVIEW THE WORDS

1 ## Briefly Review the Words

Display the ongoing review cards (◖ WA10). Review the pronunciation and meaning of each word.

PRACTICE USING THE WORDS

2 ## Do the Activity "Describe the Character"

Tell the students that partners will do the activity "Describe the Character." Remind the students that you will read a story aloud, and partners will decide which vocabulary word on the chart best describes the main character of the story and explain why they think so.

Display the ongoing review activity (◖ WA11) and begin the activity:

1. Click **❶** to reveal the first story. Explain that the main character of the story is Benjamin; then point to the story and read it aloud twice, slowly and clearly.

   - *Story 1: Benjamin is sad because he is too sick to go to summer camp. All he can think about is how much fun his friends are having while he is sick in bed. Benjamin becomes sadder and sadder and sadder as he thinks about camp.*

2. Give the students a few moments to think about the story. Then point to the vocabulary words and ask:

   Q *Which vocabulary word best describes Benjamin? Why?* [Click **❶** again and read the prompt aloud.] *Turn to your partner.*

   PROMPT 1: "[*Overwhelmed*] best describes Benjamin because . . ."

   After partners have talked, have a few volunteers use the prompt to share their thinking with the class.

3. Conclude the discussion by clicking **❶** a third time to highlight the correct vocabulary word.

Teacher Note

Each sentence on the weekly review activity (WA11) has a corresponding number: the first story is **❶**; the second story is **❷**; the third story is **❸**; and so on. To play the game, click the corresponding number four times:

- The first click reveals the story.
- The second click reveals the prompt.
- The third click highlights the correct answer.
- The fourth click clears the screen.

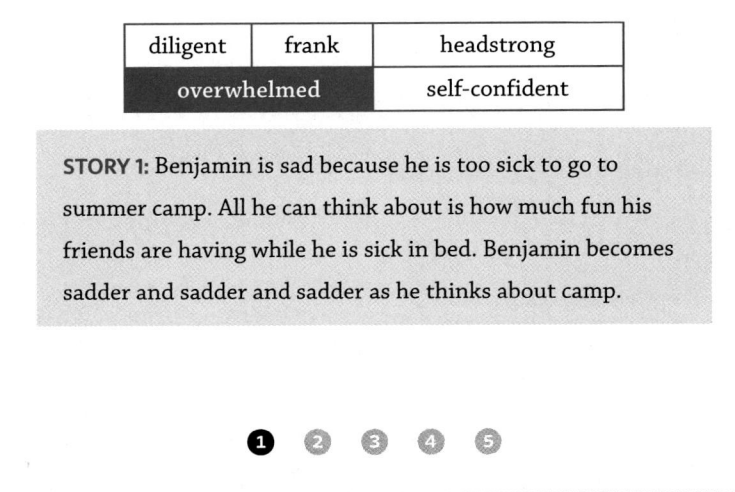

4. Click ❶ to clear the screen.

Using the same procedure, discuss the following stories:

- Story 2: *Heather's neighbor will not let anyone else use the swing at the park. Heather walks up to him and says, "I think you are being unfair. I would appreciate it if you would let other people have turns on the swing."* (frank)

- Story 3: *Liam decides to paint a picture of a boat for his art project. He looks at several photographs of boats before starting and then works on his painting every day for a whole week.* (diligent)

- Story 4: *Nadia is excited about her first track meet. She tells her friends, "I have been running all summer, and I am faster than I was last year. I think I am ready for our first meet."* (self-confident)

- Story 5: *David wants to build a tree house in his backyard. His friends tell him he needs help to do such a big job, but David doesn't listen. He goes ahead and tries to build the tree house on his own.* (headstrong)

Teacher Note

If you are not using an interactive whiteboard, write each story and the words where everyone can see them.

Assessment Notes

CLASS VOCABULARY ASSESSMENT NOTE

Observe the students and ask yourself:

- Do the students' responses indicate that they understand the words' meanings?
- Do they use the vocabulary words correctly to explain their thinking?
- Are they using the words spontaneously and accurately in conversations outside of vocabulary time?

Record your observations on the "Class Vocabulary Assessment Record" sheet (CA1); see page 206 of the *Assessment Resource Book.*

Use the following suggestions to support struggling students:

- If *only a few students* understand a word's meaning, reteach the word using the vocabulary lesson in which it was first taught as a model.
- If *about half of the students* understand a word's meaning, provide further practice in using the word through a game modeled on "Is Olive Gruff?" (see Week 15, Day 1, Step 8). For example, if the students are struggling with the word *frank,* play "Is Olive Frank?" by describing situations in which Olive is or is not being frank.

INDIVIDUAL VOCABULARY ASSESSMENT NOTE

Before continuing with the week 29 lesson, take this opportunity to assess individual students' understanding of words taught in Weeks 25–28 by using the "Individual Vocabulary Assessment: Word Check 7" answer sheet (IA1) on page 210 of the *Assessment Resource Book.* For instructions on administering this assessment, see "Completing the Individual Vocabulary Assessment" on page 207 of the *Assessment Resource Book.*

STUDENT SELF-ASSESSMENT NOTE

In addition to or in place of the Individual Vocabulary Assessment, you might have each student evaluate her understanding of words taught in Weeks 25–28 using the "Student Self-assessment" response sheet (SA1). For instructions on administering this assessment, see "Completing the Student Self-assessment" on page 211 of the *Assessment Resource Book.*

RESOURCES

Read-aloud

- *Keepers* by Jeri Hanel Watts, illustrated by Felicia Marshall

More Strategy Practice

- "Discuss Another Meaning of *Ease*"

Extensions

- "Discuss the Compound Word *Caretaker*"
- "Explore Related Words: *Aroma* and *Aromatic*"

 Online Resources

Visit the CCC Learning Hub (ccclearninghub.org) to find your online resources for this week.

Whiteboard Activities

- WA1–WA12

Reproducibles

- Week 29 family letter (BLM1)
- (Optional) "Week 29 Word Cards" (BLM2)

OVERVIEW

Words Taught	Words Reviewed
ease	boast
clench	brainstorm
display	disorganized
caretaker	improvise
aroma	well-organized
slump	

Word-learning Strategies

- Using context to determine word meanings (review)
- Recognizing words with multiple meanings (review)

Vocabulary Focus

- Students learn and use six words from the story.
- Students review using context to determine word meanings.
- Students review words with multiple meanings.
- Students review words learned earlier.
- Students build their speaking and listening skills.

Social Development Focus

- Students act in fair and caring ways.
- Students listen respectfully to the thinking of others and share their own.

DO AHEAD

✓ (Optional) Prior to Day 1, review the more strategy practice activity "Discuss Another Meaning of *Ease*" on page 605.

✓ Prior to Day 4, visit the CCC Learning Hub (ccclearninghub.org) to access and print this week's family letter (BLM1). Make enough copies to send one letter home with each student.

✓ (Optional) Visit the CCC Learning Hub (ccclearninghub.org) to access and print "Week 29 Word Cards" (BLM2). These cards can be used to provide your students with more opportunities to review the words.

Materials

- *Keepers*
- Word card 169 (WA1)
- "Sentences from *Keepers*" chart (WA2)
- Word card 170 (WA3)
- Word card 171 (WA4)

In this lesson, the students:

- Learn and use the words *ease, clench,* and *display*
- Review using context to determine word meanings
- Review words with multiple meanings
- Act in fair and caring ways

Words Taught

ease (p. 4)
Ease means "move slowly and carefully."

clench (p. 11)
Clench means "hold or squeeze something tightly."

display (p. 17)
Display means "show something or put something where people can easily see it."

INTRODUCE AND USE *EASE*

1 Introduce and Define *Ease*

Briefly review *Keepers*.

Show pages 4–5 of *Keepers* and review that Kenyon's grandmother falls asleep as she is telling him a story. Read the last two sentences on page 4 aloud, emphasizing the word *eased*.

Explain that *ease* means "move slowly and carefully." Display word card 169 (◖ WA1) and ask the students to say the word *ease*.

Ask and discuss as a class:

Q *Why do you think Kenyon eases, or moves slowly and carefully, to the kitchen?*

Click ❶ on word card 169 (WA1) to reveal the first prompt. Have one or two volunteers use the prompt to share their thinking with the class.

ease

PROMPT 1: I think Kenyon **eases** to the kitchen because . . .

❶ **②** **③**

PROMPT 1: "I think Kenyon eases to the kitchen because . . ."

If necessary, explain that Kenyon eases to the kitchen so that he will not disturb his grandmother. If he moves quickly and noisily, she might hear him and awaken.

2 Act Out Easing

Explain that, like Kenyon, people sometimes ease, or move slowly and carefully, because they want to be quiet or do not want to be noticed. Ask a volunteer to act out easing across the room because he does not want to be heard or noticed, and have the class watch carefully. Then ask:

 Q *What did you notice [Raymond] doing when he eased across the room?* [Click **❷** on WA1 to reveal the prompt.] *Turn to your partner.*

PROMPT 2: "When [Raymond] eased across the room, he . . ."

After partners have talked, have one or two volunteers use the prompt to share their thinking with the class.

Explain that people also ease, or move slowly and carefully, because they are tired, sick, or sore and cannot move quickly. Ask a volunteer to act out easing into a chair because she is tired or sore, and have the class watch carefully. Then ask:

 Q *What did you notice [Kay] doing when she eased into the chair?* [Click **❸** to reveal the prompt.] *Turn to your partner.*

PROMPT 3: "When [Kay] eased into the chair, she . . ."

After partners have talked, have a few volunteers use the prompt to share their thinking with the class.

Point to the word *ease* and review the pronunciation and meaning of the word.

INTRODUCE AND USE CLENCH

3 Introduce *Clench* and Review Using Context to Determine Word Meanings

Teacher Note

Alternatively, you may wish to write the context sentences where everyone can see them.

Display the "Sentences from *Keepers*" chart (WA2). Show pages 10–11 of *Keepers* again and remind the students that in this part of the story Kenyon is late getting to the park to play baseball. Read the charted sentences aloud where they appear on page 11, emphasizing the word *clenched*.

Tell the students that the other word they will learn today is *clench*. Point to the word *clenched* on the chart and underline it. Remind them that sometimes you can figure out the meaning of a word by reading the sentence that includes the word, or the sentence before or after, and looking for clues. Explain that as you read these sentences again, you want them to think about what the word *clench* might mean and what words in the sentences are clues to the meaning of *clench*.

Read the sentences aloud. Ask:

Q *Based on what you just heard, what do you think the word* clenched *might mean?* [Point to prompt 1 on WA2.] *Turn to your partner.*

WA2

> ### Sentences from *Keepers*
>
> "It's about time," Mo taunted. "Did you have to help Granny into the sun?"
>
> Kenyon's knuckles burned as he <u>clenched</u> his fists tightly. He didn't like to hear Little Dolly spoken of poorly. So much for another wallop-bat day, he thought.
>
> ---
>
> **PROMPT 1:** I think ***clenched*** might mean . . .
>
> **PROMPT 2:** The clues _____ help me figure out the meaning of the word ***clenched***.

PROMPT 1: "I think *clenched* might mean . . ."

Teacher Note

If the students do not immediately figure out the meaning, tell them.

After partners have talked, have one or two volunteers use the prompt to share their thinking with the class. If necessary, explain that *clench* means "hold or squeeze something tightly." Discuss as a class:

Q *What clues in the sentences help you figure out that* clench *means "hold or squeeze something tightly"?* [Point to prompt 2.] *Turn to your partner.*

PROMPT 2: "The clues ['knuckles burned,' 'fists,' and 'tightly'] help me figure out the meaning of the word *clenched*."

After partners have talked, have a few volunteers use the prompt to share their thinking with the class. Circle the context clues on the chart as the students identify them. If necessary, point out that *knuckles burned*, *fists*, and *tightly* are all clues that help us figure out that *clench* means "hold or squeeze something tightly." Explain that people sometimes clench, or squeeze, their fists when they are angry. Kenyon clenches his fists because Mo taunts (teases) him about his grandmother.

Act out how Kenyon might have clenched his fists, or point to the picture of Kenyon's clenched fist on page 10. Then have the students clench their fists.

Display word card 170 (◑ WA3) and have the students say the word *clench*.

4 Act Out and Discuss Clenching

Explain that you will act out clenching the book *Keepers* and you want the students to watch carefully and notice what you do. Then act out clenching *Keepers* by holding it tightly with both hands. Ask and discuss as a class:

Q *What did you see me do when I clenched the book?*

Click ❶ on word card 170 (WA3) to reveal the first prompt. Have a few volunteers use the prompt to share their thinking with the class.

PROMPT 1: "When you clenched the book, you . . ."

Ask the students to listen carefully as you describe some clenching that our imaginary friend Olive did. Then read the following story aloud:

- *Olive's mother asked her to go to the grocery store and buy eggs and bread. Her mother handed her a five-dollar bill. Olive clenched the bill in her hand as she walked to the store.*

Ask:

Q *Why do you think Olive clenched the five-dollar bill?* [Click ❷ on WA3 to reveal the prompt.] *Turn to your partner.*

PROMPT 2: "I think Olive clenched the bill because . . ."

After partners have talked, have a few volunteers use the prompt to share their thinking with the class.

Point to the word *clench* and review the pronunciation and meaning of the word.

🌐 ELL Note

You might use a piece of paper to represent a five-dollar bill and act out the scenario or have a volunteer act it out.

INTRODUCE AND USE *DISPLAY*

5 Introduce and Define *Display*

Show pages 16–17 and review that Kenyon goes to the bakery when he is trying to figure out what to get his grandmother for her birthday. Read the first paragraph on page 17 aloud, emphasizing the word *display*.

Explain that *display* means "show something or put something where people can easily see it." Point to the display case in the picture on pages 16–17 and explain that most bakeries have a glass case like this where they can display, or show, the delicious sweets they have for sale. Such a case is called a "display case."

Display word card 171 (WA4) and have the students say the word *display*.

6 Discuss Things That Are Displayed in the Classroom

Explain that teachers often display things in the classroom, or put things in places where students and visitors can easily see them, and point out a couple of things you have displayed (for example, the students' artwork or writing, the students' photographs, the letters of the alphabet, a sign or poster, a school map, or spelling or vocabulary words).

Explain that you would like the students to look around the classroom and notice other things that are displayed. Then partners will discuss what they noticed.

Give the students a few moments to look around the classroom. Then ask:

 Q *What is something that is displayed in our classroom? Why do you think it is displayed?* [Click ❶ on WA4 to reveal the first prompt.] *Turn to your partner.*

PROMPT 1: "[Our museum stories] are displayed. I think they're displayed because . . ."

After partners have talked, have one or two volunteers use the prompt to share their thinking with the class.

Then ask and discuss as a class:

Q *If you want to display a story or drawing you are proud of at home, where might you display it? Why?*

Click ❷ to reveal the next prompt, and have a few volunteers use the prompt to share their thinking with the class.

PROMPT 2: "I might display it [in my bedroom] because . . ."

Point to the word *display* and review the pronunciation and meaning of the word.

MORE STRATEGY PRACTICE

Discuss Another Meaning of *Ease*

Write the word *ease* where everyone can see it and explain that *ease* has more than one meaning. Review that *ease* means "move slowly and carefully." Then explain that *ease* can also mean "relieve or lessen something or make something less painful, difficult, or upsetting." For example, people sometimes take an aspirin or other medication to ease, or relieve, a headache. Children sometimes sleep with a night-light on to ease, or lessen, their fear of the dark.

Remind the students that if they hear or read a word that has more than one meaning, they can usually figure out the correct meaning by thinking about how the word is used. Explain that you will read a story that includes the word *ease*. Partners will decide whether *ease* means "move slowly and carefully" or "relieve or lessen something" in the story and explain why they think so.

Teacher Note

You might write the two meanings on the board.

Read the following aloud:

- *Jaden was nervous. He was about to perform in the class play, and he was afraid he wouldn't do well. "You've practiced your part every day for a month," said Jaden's teacher to ease his worries. "Just do your best. That's what is important."*

Ask:

Q *In the story, does* ease *mean "move slowly and carefully" or "relieve or lessen something"? Why do you think that? Turn to your partner.*

PROMPT: "I think *ease* means ['relieve or lessen something'] because . . ."

Have a few volunteers use the prompt to share their thinking with the class.

In the same way, discuss:

- *The old woman was feeling tired and weak. "I need a rest," she said to herself. She walked slowly across the living room and eased into her favorite chair.*

Materials

- Daily review cards (WA5)

In this lesson, the students:

- Review and practice using the words *ease, clench,* and *display* from Day 1
- Build their speaking and listening skills
- Listen respectfully to the thinking of others and share their own

Words Reviewed

ease
Ease means "move slowly and carefully."

clench
Clench means "hold or squeeze something tightly."

display
Display means "show something or put something where people can easily see it."

REVIEW THE WORDS

1 Briefly Review the Words

Display the daily review cards (WA5). Review the pronunciation and meaning of each word.

Use "Think, Pair, Share" to discuss:

 Q *Which of this week's words do you think was the most interesting to talk about? Why?* [Pause; click ❶ on WA5 to reveal the first prompt.] *Turn to your partner.*

WA5

ease	clench	display

PROMPT 1: I think _____ was the most interesting to talk about because . . .

❶ ❷ ❸ ❹

PROMPT 1: "I think [clench] was the most interesting to talk about because . . ."

After partners have talked, have a few volunteers use the prompt to share their thinking with the class.

PRACTICE USING THE WORDS

2 Discuss "Would You?" Questions

Explain that you will ask some questions that partners will discuss.

Point to the word *ease* and ask:

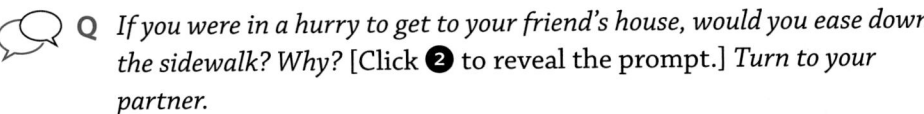 **Q** *If you were in a hurry to get to your friend's house, would you ease down the sidewalk? Why?* [Click ❷ to reveal the prompt.] *Turn to your partner.*

PROMPT 2: "I [would/would not] ease down the sidewalk because . . ."

After partners have talked, have one or two volunteers use the prompt to share their thinking with the class.

Using the same procedure, discuss the following questions:

[clench]

Q *If you were holding a paper cup filled with water, would you clench the cup? Why?* [Click ❸ to reveal the prompt.] *Turn to your partner.*

PROMPT 3: "I [would/would not] clench the paper cup because . . ."

[display]

Q *If you made a clay sculpture you were not proud of, would you display it? Why?* [Click ❹ to reveal the prompt.] *Turn to your partner.*

PROMPT 4: "I [would/would not] display the clay sculpture because . . ."

Day 3

Introduce *Caretaker, Aroma,* and *Slump*

Materials

- *Keepers*
- Word card 172 (WA6)
- Word card 173 (WA7)
- Word card 174 (WA8)

In this lesson, the students:

- Learn and use the words *caretaker, aroma,* and *slump*
- Act in fair and caring ways

Words Taught

caretaker (p. 19)
A *caretaker* is a "person whose job is to take care of a property (building or land) for the owner."

aroma (p. 20)
An *aroma* is a "pleasant smell."

slump (p. 24)
Slump means "fall or sit down suddenly and heavily."

INTRODUCE AND USE *CARETAKER*

1 Introduce and Define *Caretaker*

Show pages 18–19 of *Keepers* and review that Kenyon talks to people in town to get ideas for Little Dolly's birthday gift. Read the text on page 19 aloud, emphasizing the word *caretaker*.

Tell the students that a *caretaker* is a "person whose job is to take care of a property (building or land) for the owner." Explain that the caretaker at the soldier's cemetery takes care of the cemetery for the owner, doing things like watering and mowing the grass and decorating the cemetery with flags on holidays.

Display word card 172 ( WA6) and have the students say the word *caretaker*.

2 Discuss Caretakers

Explain that the school has caretakers, or people who take care of the classrooms, hallways, library, cafeteria, playground, and other areas inside and around the school. Use "Think, Pair, Share" to discuss:

Q *What do our caretakers do to take care of the school?* [Pause; click ❶ on WA6 to reveal the first prompt.] *Turn to your partner.*

Teacher Note

If the students know the school custodian or other caretakers, you might name the caretakers and ask the students what they have seen the caretakers do to take care of the school. Alternatively, you might invite a caretaker to talk with the students about what he or she does to take care of the school.

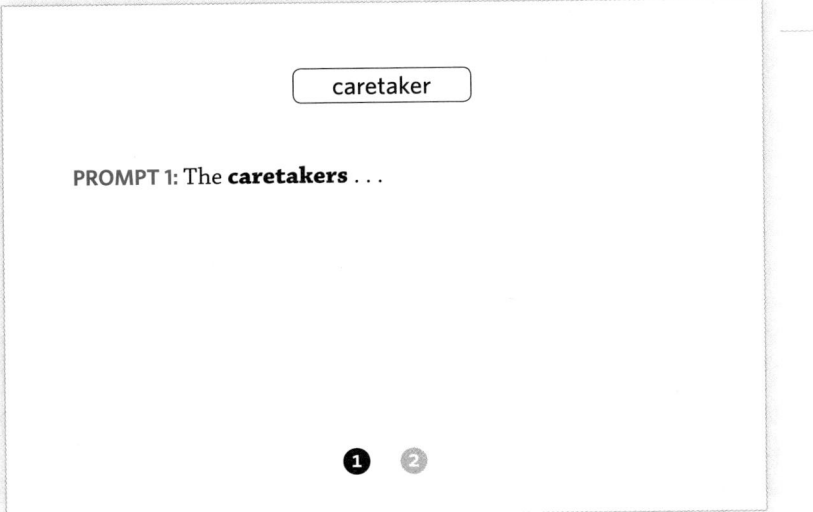

caretaker

PROMPT 1: The **caretakers** . . .

1 **2**

PROMPT 1: "The caretakers . . ."

After partners have talked, have a few volunteers use the prompt to share their thinking with the class.

Ask and discuss as a class:

Q *What might we do to help the caretakers take care of our school?*

Click **2** to reveal the next prompt and have a few volunteers use the prompt to share their thinking with the class.

PROMPT 2: "We might help the caretakers by . . ."

Point to the word *caretaker* and review the pronunciation and meaning of the word.

INTRODUCE AND USE *AROMA*

3 Introduce and Define *Aroma*

Show pages 20–21 and review that when Kenyon is in town, he sees a baseball glove in a store window. Read page 20 aloud, emphasizing the word *aroma*.

Explain that an *aroma* is a "pleasant smell." Explain that Kenyon loves not only the feel of the baseball glove but also its aroma, or pleasant smell. Because of the aroma and the feel of the glove, Kenyon buys it.

Display word card 173 (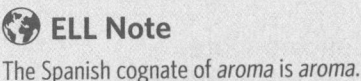 WA7) and have the students say the word *aroma*.

🌐 **ELL Note**

The Spanish cognate of *aroma* is *aroma*.

4 Discuss Aromas the Students Like

Give examples of aromas you like.

> **You might say:**
>
> "I like the aroma of a rose. Roses have a wonderful smell. Lots of foods have pleasant aromas. I like the aroma of bread baking in the oven. I like the aroma of popcorn, too. My grandmother wears a perfume that has a wonderful aroma."

Use "Think, Pair, Share" to discuss:

Q *What is an aroma you like?* [Pause; click **❶** on WA7 to reveal the first prompt.] *Turn to your partner.*

PROMPT 1: "I like the aroma of [my dad's enchiladas]."

After partners have talked, have one or two volunteers use the prompt to share their thinking with the class.

Point to the word *aroma* and review the pronunciation and meaning of the word.

INTRODUCE AND USE *SLUMP*

5 Introduce and Define *Slump*

Show pages 24–25 and review that Kenyon feels bad after he spends his money on a baseball glove. Read the first four paragraphs on page 24 aloud, emphasizing the word *slumped* and stopping after: "Kenyon slumped onto his bed. 'I'm not sick. I'm just stupid.'"

Tell the students that *slump* means "fall or sit down suddenly and heavily." Explain that Kenyon slumps, or falls suddenly and heavily, onto his bed because he is angry with himself for spending Little Dolly's birthday money on a baseball glove.

Display word card 174 (WA8) and have the students say the word *slump*.

6 Act Out and Discuss Slumping

Explain that people might slump if they are feeling angry and frustrated, like Kenyon, or if they are feeling very tired or weak. Ask a volunteer to act out slumping into a chair because she is very tired, and ask the class to watch carefully and notice what the volunteer does.

Then ask:

 Q *What did you notice [Kendra] do when she slumped into the chair?* [Click ❶ on WA8 to reveal the prompt.] *Turn to your partner.*

PROMPT 1: "When [Kendra] slumped, she . . ."

After partners have talked, have a few volunteers use the prompt to share their thinking with the class.

Ask and discuss as a class:

Q *If you were feeling really tired at home, where might you slump? Why?*

Click ❷ on WA8 to reveal the next prompt and have one or two volunteers use the prompt to share their thinking with the class.

PROMPT 2: "If I were feeling really tired, I might slump [onto the couch] because . . ."

Point to the word *slump* and review the pronunciation and meaning of the word.

EXTENSIONS

Discuss the Compound Word *Caretaker*

Write the word *caretaker* where everyone can see it. Remind the students that a *caretaker* is a "person whose job is to take care of a property (building or land) for the owner." Explain that *caretaker* is a compound word, and that a *compound word* is a "word made up of two or more shorter words."

Tell the students that if you come upon a compound word in your reading and are not sure what it means, you can sometimes figure out the meaning by identifying the shorter words that make up the compound word and thinking about what each word means. Point to the words *care* and *take* in *caretaker* and explain that these are the shorter words that make up *caretaker*. Explain that if you put together the meanings of *care* and *take*, you can figure out that a *caretaker* is a person who takes care of something.

In the same way, discuss some of these compound words from the story: *ballfield* (page 6), *homework* (page 6), *leftovers* (page 11), *storyteller* (page 13), *shopkeeper* (page 19), and *handmade* (page 30).

Ask the students for other examples of compound words, discuss them, and add them to the chart. Have the students listen and watch for more examples of compound words during the next few days, and add any new examples to the chart.

Explore Related Words: *Aroma* and *Aromatic*

Write the word *aroma* where everyone can see it and review that an *aroma* is a "pleasant smell." Tell the students that knowing the meaning of *aroma* can help them figure out the meaning of a word that is related to *aroma*. Write this sentence where everyone can see it:

- *Mick washes his hands with an aromatic soap, and he always smells wonderful.*

Ask:

Q *What word in the sentence is related to* aroma? *Why do you say that?*

If necessary, point out that *aromatic* is related to *aroma* and that you can see the word *aroma* in *aromatic*. Then ask:

Q *Based on what you know about the word* aroma *and clues in the sentence, what do you think the word* aromatic *means?*

If necessary, explain that *aromatic* means "pleasant to smell," and point out that Mick smells nice because he washes with soap that is aromatic.

Day 4 — Review *Caretaker, Aroma,* and *Slump*

Materials

- Daily review cards (WA9)
- Daily review activity (WA10)
- Copy of this week's family letter (BLM1) for each student

In this lesson, the students:

- Review and practice using the words *caretaker, aroma,* and *slump* from Day 3
- Build their speaking and listening skills
- Listen respectfully to the thinking of others and share their own

Words Reviewed

caretaker
A *caretaker* is a "person whose job is to take care of a property (building or land) for the owner."

aroma
An *aroma* is a "pleasant smell."

slump
Slump means "fall or sit down suddenly and heavily."

REVIEW THE WORDS

1 Briefly Review the Words

Display the daily review cards (WA9). Review the pronunciation and meaning of each word.

Point to the word *caretaker* and ask:

 Q *What is something a caretaker at a zoo might do? Why?* [Click ❶ on WA9 to reveal the first prompt.] *Turn to your partner.*

PROMPT 1: "A caretaker at a zoo might [clean the animals' cages] because . . ."

After partners have talked, have a few volunteers use the prompt to share their thinking with the class.

Discuss the following questions using the same procedure:

[aroma]

 Q *Would there be an aroma in a garbage can? Why?* [Click ❷ to reveal the prompt.] *Turn to your partner.*

PROMPT 2: "There [would/would not] be an aroma in a garbage can because . . ."

[slump]

 Q *Would you be likely or unlikely to slump after running in a race? Why?* [Click ❸ to reveal the prompt.] *Turn to your partner.*

PROMPT 3: "I would be [likely/unlikely] to slump after running a race because . . ."

PRACTICE USING THE WORDS

2 Play "Finish the Story"

Tell the students that they are going to play "Finish the Story." Explain that you are going to read some stories and that you will leave off the last word of each story. Review that partners will decide which word makes the best ending for the story.

Display the daily review activity (WA10) and begin playing the game:

1. Click ❶ to reveal the first story. Point to the story and read it aloud twice, slowly and clearly. Point out that the ending is missing.

   - Story 1: *Julia enjoys cooking tamales. She loves the way they taste and their wonderful _____.*

Teacher Note

You might remind the students that they learned the words *likely* and *unlikely* earlier, and that when something is likely, it probably will happen or is probably true, and when something is unlikely, it probably will not happen or is probably not true.

Teacher Note

Each story on the daily review activity (WA10) has a corresponding number: the first story is ❶; the second story is ❷; and the third story is ❸. To play the game, click the corresponding number four times:

- The first click reveals the story and the word choices.
- The second click reveals the prompt.
- The third click reveals the correct answer.
- The fourth click clears the screen.

2. Give the students a few moments to think about the story. Then ask:

> **Q** *Which word makes the best ending for the story? Why do you think that?* [Pause; click ❶ again and read the prompt aloud.] *Turn to your partner.*

PROMPT: "I think [*aroma*] makes the best ending because . . ."

After partners have talked, have one or two volunteers use the prompt to share their thinking with the class.

3. Conclude the discussion of this story by clicking ❶ a third time to highlight the correct vocabulary word and reveal the story with the correct word in place. Then reread the story with the word *aroma* at the end.

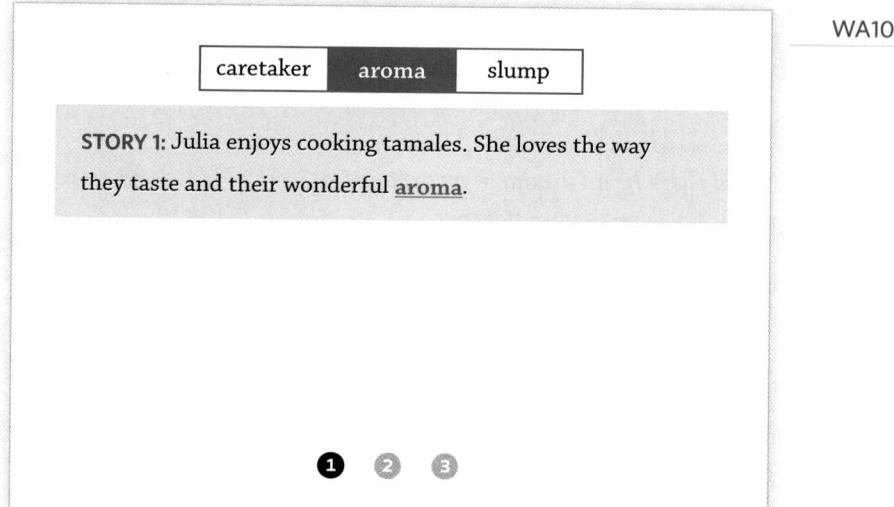

WA10

| caretaker | aroma | slump |

STORY 1: Julia enjoys cooking tamales. She loves the way they taste and their wonderful <u>aroma</u>.

❶ ➋ ➌

4. Click ❶ to clear the screen.

Repeat the procedure to discuss the following stories:

- Story 2: *Khamil noticed a woman fixing a broken window in his apartment building. "Who's that lady?" he asked his father. His father replied, "That's our building's _____."* (caretaker)

- Story 3: *Mrs. Gates was walking in the park. She suddenly felt weak and dizzy, and needed to sit down. She found a park bench and _____ onto it.* (slumped)

Teacher Note

Send home with each student a copy of this week's family letter (BLM1). Encourage the students to talk about this week's words with their families.

In this lesson, the students:

- Review words learned earlier
- Build their speaking and listening skills
- Act in fair and caring ways

Words Reviewed

boast
Boast means "brag." When people boast, they talk about themselves or something they have with too much pride or pleasure.

brainstorm
A *brainstorm* is a "sudden idea."

disorganized
If something is disorganized, it is not planned or arranged (put together) in a neat or orderly way. It is messy or confusing.

improvise
Improvise means "make up and perform something without any preparation." *Improvise* can also mean "make or do something using whatever materials are available."

well-organized
If something is well-organized, it is planned or arranged (put together) in a neat or orderly way.

REVIEW THE WORDS

1 Briefly Review the Words

Display the ongoing review cards (WA11). Review the pronunciation and meaning of each word.

PRACTICE USING THE WORDS

2 Play "Find Another Word"

Tell the students that partners will play the game "Find Another Word." Remind the students that you will show a sentence with one or more words underlined. You will read each sentence aloud, and partners will decide which vocabulary word can replace the underlined part of the sentence.

Materials

- Ongoing review cards (WA11)
- Ongoing review activity (WA12)

Teacher Note

You might explain that the students may need to change the form of the word to complete the sentence by adding an ending such as *-s*, *-ing*, or *-ed*.

Display the ongoing review activity (WA12) and begin playing the game:

1. Click ❶ to reveal the first sentence. Point to the sentence and read it aloud, emphasizing the underlined words.

   - Sentence 1: *The garage was <u>tidy</u>, the boxes labeled, the bikes hung on the wall, and all the tools put away.*

2. Give the students a few moments to think about the sentence and the underlined word. Then point to the three word choices and ask:

   Q *Which vocabulary word could replace the underlined word? Why?* [Click ❶ again and point to the prompt.] *Turn to your partner.*

   PROMPT 1: "I think the word [*well-organized*] could replace *tidy* because . . ."

   After partners have talked, have a few volunteers use the prompt to share their thinking with the class.

3. Conclude the discussion by clicking ❶ a third time to highlight the correct vocabulary word and reveal the sentence with the correct word in place.

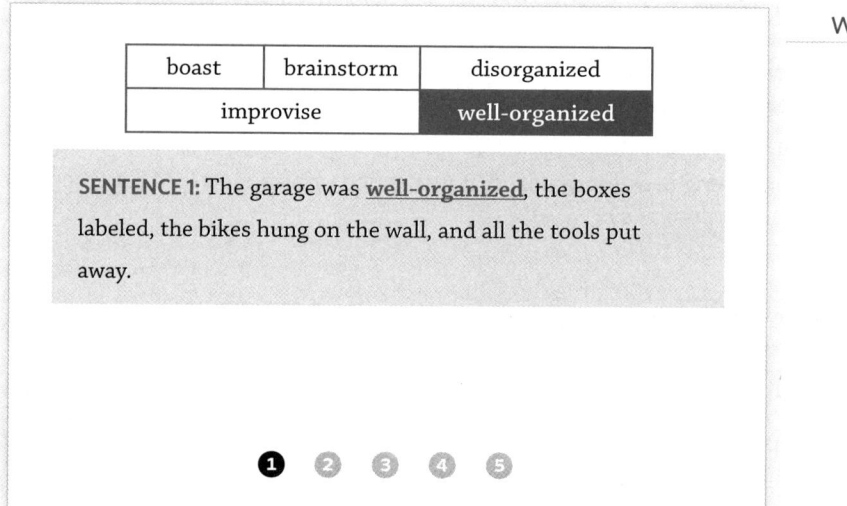

WA12

boast	brainstorm	disorganized
improvise		well-organized

SENTENCE 1: The garage was <u>well-organized</u>, the boxes labeled, the bikes hung on the wall, and all the tools put away.

❶ ❷ ❸ ❹ ❺

4. Click ❶ to clear the screen.

Use the same procedure to discuss the following sentences:

- Sentence 2: *Tyler couldn't decide what to do for his cousin's birthday, but then he had a <u>thought</u> to throw her a surprise party.*

 Q *Which vocabulary word could replace the underlined word? Why?* [Click ❷ again and point to the prompt.] *Turn to your partner.*

PROMPT 2: "I think the word [*brainstorm*] could replace *thought* because . . ."

- Sentence 3: *After Johanna won the spelling bee, she <u>bragged</u> that she was the best speller in the whole world.*

Teacher Note

Each sentence in the ongoing review activity (WA12) has a corresponding number: the first sentence is ❶; the second sentence is ❷; the third sentence is ❸; and so on. To play the game, click the corresponding number four times:

- The first click reveals the sentence.
- The second click reveals the prompt.
- The third click highlights the correct answer and reveals the sentence with the correct answer in place.
- The fourth click clears the screen.

Q *Which vocabulary word could replace the underlined word? Why?*
[Click ❸ again and point to the prompt.] *Turn to your partner.*

PROMPT 3: "I think the word [*boasted*] could replace *bragged* because . . ."

- Sentence 4: *The surprised contest winner <u>made up</u> a very powerful acceptance speech.*

 Q *Which vocabulary word could replace the underlined phrase? Why?*
[Click ❹ again and point to the prompt.] *Turn to your partner.*

PROMPT 4: "I think the word [*improvised*] could replace *made up* because . . ."

- Sentence 5: *The <u>messy</u> bathroom had towels and clothes on the floor, toilet paper rolls all over the place, and toothbrushes in the bathtub!*

 Q *Which vocabulary word could replace the underlined word? Why?*
[Click ❺ again and point to the prompt.] *Turn to your partner.*

PROMPT 5: "I think the word [*disorganized*] could replace *messy* because . . ."

ABOUT WEEK 30

In the week of the *Making Meaning* program that corresponds with this week's vocabulary lessons, the students read self-selected texts, rather than hearing a read-aloud. For that reason, no new words are introduced this week. We suggest that the students spend the week reviewing some of the words they have learned during the year. The review will provide the students with the additional practice they need to make the words they have learned this year a permanent part of their vocabulary. The week will also prepare the students for Word Check 8, an end-of-year vocabulary assessment that focuses on the words reviewed this week.

The students review a set of words each day this week through an activity that varies from day to day. The table on the next page lists the words reviewed and identifies the weeks in which the words were originally taught.

RESOURCES

Assessment Resource Book

- Week 30 vocabulary assessments

 Online Resources

Visit the CCC Learning Hub (ccclearninghub.org) to find your online resources for this week.

Whiteboard Activities

- WA1–WA6

Assessment Forms

- "Class Vocabulary Assessment Record" sheet (CA1)
- "Individual Vocabulary Assessment: Word Check 8" answer sheet (IA1)
- "Individual Vocabulary Assessment Student Record" sheet (SR1)

- "Individual Vocabulary Assessment Class Record" sheet (CR1)
- (Optional) "Student Self-assessment" response sheet (SA1)

Reproducibles

- "'Three Words and a Story' Word Sets" (BLM1)
- Week 30 family letter (BLM2)
- (Optional) "Week 30 Word Cards" (BLM3)

OVERVIEW

Words Reviewed

Day 1 (Weeks 1–5)	**Day 2** (Weeks 6–11)	**Day 3** (Weeks 12–16)	**Day 4** (Weeks 17–21)	**Day 5** (Weeks 22–29)
celebration	cling	adventuresome	abandon	aroma
clatter	magnificent	blow your top	convenient	avoid
debris	quiver	cherish	original	disorganized
recall	reluctant	flabbergasted	prefer	opportunity
ruckus	reunite	gruff	secure	skill
squirm	savory	persist	texture	task
snap	ungrateful	prowl		threatened
swerve	whoosh	urgent		
whoop				

Vocabulary Focus

- Students review words learned earlier.
- Students build their speaking and listening skills.

Social Development Focus

- Students act in fair and caring ways.
- Students listen respectfully to the thinking of others and share their own.

⏱ DO AHEAD

✓ This week the students write stories using one of three sets of review words. Prior to Day 1, prepare enough copies of "'Three Words and a Story' Word Sets" (BLM1) so that each pair of students will have a slip of paper with a set of three words. (Copy or print several copies of the word sets and cut the sets into slips.) Put the slips into a paper bag.

✓ Prior to Day 1, make a copy of the "Class Vocabulary Assessment Record" sheet (CA1); see page 214 of the *Assessment Resource Book*.

✓ Prior to Day 4, visit the CCC Learning Hub (ccclearninghub.org) to access and print this week's family letter (BLM2). Make enough copies to send one letter home with each student.

(continues)

⏱ DO AHEAD *(continued)*

✓ Prior to Day 5, make a class set of the "Individual Vocabulary Assessment: Word Check 8" answer sheet (IA1); see page 218 of the *Assessment Resource Book*. Make enough copies for each student to have one; set aside a reference copy for yourself.

✓ (Optional) Prior to Day 5, make a master copy of the "Student Self-assessment" response sheet (SA1); see page 221 of the *Assessment Resource Book*. Write the words you have chosen to be assessed on the master copy. Then make enough copies for each student to have one.

✓ (Optional) Visit the CCC Learning Hub (ccclearninghub.org) to access and print "Week 30 Word Cards" (BLM3). These cards can be used to provide your students with more opportunities to review the words.

In this activity, the students:

- Review and practice using words learned earlier
- Write a story using three of the words
- Build their speaking and listening skills
- Listen respectfully to the thinking of others and share their own

Words Reviewed

celebration
A *celebration* is a "happy event held to honor a special occasion."

clatter
When things clatter, they bang together or rattle noisily.

debris
Debris is the "scattered pieces of something that has been thrown away, broken, or destroyed."

recall
Recall means "remember."

ruckus
Ruckus means "noisy confusion or excitement." Something unexpected or frightening can cause a ruckus.

snap
Snap means "speak sharply or angrily."

squirm
Squirm means "wiggle, or twist your body from side to side, usually because you are bored or uncomfortable."

swerve
Swerve means "change directions quickly, usually to avoid something."

whoop
Whoop means "shout from excitement."

REVIEW THE WORDS

1 Introduce the Activity

Tell the students that this week they will review and practice using words they learned in previous weeks. Remind them that thinking and talking about the words they have learned helps them remember the words.

Explain that today the students will do an activity called "Three Words and a Story." Display the day 1 review cards (WA1), and explain that these are nine vocabulary words that the students learned earlier in

Materials

- Day 1 review cards (WA1)
- One set of three words for each pair (see "Do Ahead" on page 619)
- A paper bag
- A sheet of paper for each student
- "Class Vocabulary Assessment Record" sheet (CA1)

the year. Show the paper bag and tell the students that in it are slips of paper with three of nine review words written on each slip. Explain that each pair of students will draw a slip of paper from the bag. Partners will talk about what they know about the words, and then each student will write a story that includes the three words. Explain that later, partners will share their stories with each other and with the class.

WA1

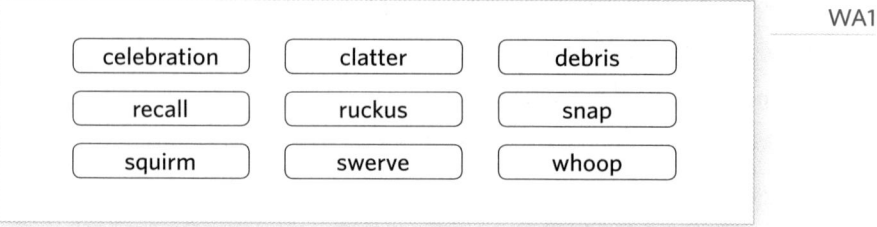

celebration	clatter	debris
recall	ruckus	snap
squirm	swerve	whoop

Have each pair draw a slip from the paper bag. Then ask:

Q *What do you know about the three words on your slip?*

Q *What story might you write using the words?*

Give the students a few moments to think about the questions. Then say "Turn to your partner," and have partners discuss the questions. Tell the students that if they cannot remember the meaning of a word, they can ask you or another pair about the meaning.

PRACTICE USING THE WORDS

2 Write and Share Stories

Distribute a sheet of paper to each student. Then give the students time to plan and write their stories.

Have the students share their stories with their partners. Then have volunteers share their stories with the class. After each reading, discuss the story as a class by asking questions such as:

Q *Which vocabulary words did you hear [Louise] use in the story?*

Q *What was [interesting/funny] about the way [Louise] used the word [clatter]?*

Q *What questions do you want to ask [Louise] about her story?*

Q *What did you like about [Louise's] story?*

Explain that students who did not share with the class today will have an opportunity to share later.

Teacher Note

Circulate as partners share. If the students are having trouble generating ideas, signal for their attention and have a volunteer pair share their story ideas with the class and discuss how they came up with the ideas. If the students continue to struggle, suggest that they pick one of the words, think about a story they might write using that one word, and then think about how they might use the other words in the story. You might model the strategy, using one of the word sets.

Teacher Note

If the students need more time for writing, they might finish their stories during the writing period. They can then share the stories during the week at vocabulary time.

CLASS VOCABULARY ASSESSMENT NOTE

Observe the students and ask yourself:

- Do the students' responses indicate that they understand the words' meanings?

- Are they able to use the words to explain their thinking?

- Are they using the words they have learned this year in their writing and in conversations outside of vocabulary time?

Record your observations on the "Class Vocabulary Assessment Record" sheet (CA1); see page 214 of the *Assessment Resource Book*.

Use the following suggestions to support struggling students:

- If **only a few students** understand a word's meaning, reteach the word using the vocabulary lesson in which it was first taught as a model.

- If **about half of the students** understand a word's meaning, incorporate the word into one or more of the other activities used to review words this week.

Teacher Note
You might use this Class Vocabulary Assessment Note each day this week to evaluate your students' understanding of the words being reviewed.

Materials

- Day 2 review cards (WA2)

In this activity, the students:

- Review and practice using words learned earlier
- Build their speaking and listening skills
- Act in fair and caring ways

Words Reviewed

cling
Cling means "hold onto someone or something very tightly."

magnificent
If something is magnificent, you admire it because of its great beauty or size.

quiver
Quiver means "tremble or shake."

reluctant
If you are reluctant to do something, you do not want to do it.

reunite
Reunite means "come together again after being separated."

savory
Savory means "pleasant to smell or taste."

ungrateful
Ungrateful means "not thankful or not grateful." If you are ungrateful, you do not thank someone who has done something for you or show your appreciation.

whoosh
Whoosh means "move very fast." When something whooshes, it makes a rushing or hissing sound.

REVIEW THE WORDS

1 Briefly Review the Words

Display the day 2 review cards (WA2) and review the pronunciation and meaning of each word.

PRACTICE USING THE WORDS

2 Play "I'm Thinking of a Word"

Tell the students that partners will play the game "I'm Thinking of a Word." Review that you will think aloud about one of the review words; then partners will discuss which word they think it is and explain why they think that. Begin by reading the following clue aloud, slowly and clearly:

- *I'm thinking of a word that tells what you do when you get together with a friend you haven't seen in a long time.*

Ask:

 Q *What word am I thinking of? Why do you think that?* [Click ❶ on WA2 to reveal the prompt.] *Turn to your partner.*

WA2

cling	magnificent	quiver
reluctant	reunite	savory
ungrateful	whoosh

PROMPT 1: _____ is thinking of the word

_____ because . . .

❶ ②

PROMPT 1: "[Mrs. Durn] is thinking of the word [*reunite*] because . . ."

After partners have talked, click ❷ on the day 2 review cards (WA2) to reveal the next prompt. Have one or two volunteers use the prompt to share their thinking with the class.

PROMPT 2: "You are thinking of the word [*reunite*] because . . ."

Use the same procedure to continue playing the game, using the following clues:

- *I'm thinking of a word that tells what you might do if you are caught in a rainstorm without a coat or umbrella.* (quiver)

- *I'm thinking of a word that describes a delicious plate of pasta with yummy sauce and cheese.* (savory)

🌐 **ELL Note**

Choosing from among all the review words may be challenging for the students. If so, you might have them choose between two words or from among three or four words you provide. For example, you might say "I'm thinking of a word that tells what you do when you get together with a friend you haven't seen in a long time. Am I thinking of the word *magnificent* or the word *reunite*? Why?"

- *I'm thinking of a word you might use to describe an amazing sunrise in the mountains.* (magnificent)

- *I'm thinking of a word that tells what you do when you are gripping the rope in a game of tug-of-war.* (cling)

- *I'm thinking of a word that describes how you might feel if you have to go to your brother's soccer game instead of your friend's birthday party.* (reluctant)

- *I'm thinking of a word that tells what a tennis ball does as it flies quickly over the net.* (whoosh)

- *I'm thinking of a word that you might use to describe a person who doesn't say "thank you."* (ungrateful)

Day 3 Does That Make Sense?

Materials

- Day 3 review cards (WA3)

In this activity, the students:

- Review and practice using words learned earlier
- Build their speaking and listening skills
- Listen respectfully to the thinking of others and share their own

Words Reviewed

adventuresome
If you are feeling adventuresome, you are feeling bold and ready for an adventure.

blow your top
"Blow your top" means "get very angry."

cherish
Cherish means "care for something deeply." If you cherish something, you treat it with great care because it is very important to you.

flabbergasted
Flabbergasted means "very surprised, or shocked or astonished."

gruff
Gruff means "unpleasant or rude." If someone is gruff, he or she may seem unfriendly or mean.

persist
Persist means "keep doing something, even though it is difficult." If you persist, you refuse to give up.

prowl
Prowl means "move quietly or secretly, trying not to be seen or heard."

urgent
Urgent means "very important." If something is urgent, it needs to be taken care of immediately.

REVIEW THE WORDS

1 ## Briefly Review the Words

Display the day 3 review cards (WA3) and review the pronunciation and meaning of each word.

PRACTICE USING THE WORDS

2 ## Play "Does That Make Sense?"

Tell the students that partners will play the game "Does That Make Sense?" Explain that you will read a scenario that includes one of the review words. Partners will decide whether or not the word makes sense in the scenario and explain why they think so.

Point to the word *adventuresome* on the day 3 review cards (WA3), and explain that the first scenario includes the word *adventuresome*.

Then read the following scenario aloud twice:

- *Carly is tired and decides to stay home instead of meeting her friends to explore a new hiking trail. Carly is feeling quite adventuresome!*

Ask:

 Q *Does the word* adventuresome *make sense in the scenario? Why do you think that?* [Click ❶ on WA3 to reveal the prompt.] *Turn to your partner.*

WA3

adventuresome	blow your top	cherish
flabbergasted	gruff	persist
prowl	urgent

PROMPT 1: The word _____ [does/does not] make sense because . . .

❶

PROMPT 1: "The word [*adventuresome*] [does/does not] make sense because . . ."

After partners have talked, have a few volunteers use the prompt to share their thinking with the class.

Teacher Note

If the students struggle to answer the questions, signal for their attention. Reread the scenario aloud, and explain that *adventuresome* does not make sense. If Carly is feeling adventuresome she would leave her house and do something fun or exciting—she would not stay home.

Use the same procedure to discuss the following scenarios:

[urgent]

- *Benjamin is bringing drinks to the class party. It is urgent that he arrive early so that he can put the drinks in the refrigerator to stay cold.*

[blow your top]

- *Liliya is very hungry after a long hike. She blows her top when her uncle makes her a scrumptious sandwich with her favorite fixings.*

[prowl]

- *Jorge sees his cat, Midnight, moving slowly and silently as she hunts in the backyard. She is prowling across the yard looking for food.*

[cherish]

- *Ophelia cherishes the new set of paints she got for her birthday. She puts them under her bed and forgets about them.*

[flabbergasted]

- *Karl is waiting for his mom to pick him up from school. He is flabbergasted when his cousin, Lenore, walks through the door because he hasn't seen Lenore in a long, long time.*

[persist]

- *Nadia wants to learn how to juggle. It is very difficult at first, but she persists by practicing nearly every day. Eventually she becomes an excellent juggler!*

[gruff]

- *Danny asks his cousin for help. His gruff cousin, Elise, says, "Of course, Danny. I'll help you in any way I can."*

In this activity, the students:

- Review and practice using words learned earlier
- Build their speaking and listening skills
- Act in fair and caring ways

Words Reviewed

abandon
Abandon means "leave and not return."

convenient
If something is convenient, it is useful because it makes our lives easier or more comfortable.

original
Original means "completely new and different." If something is original, it is not like anything else.

prefer
Prefer means "like better." If you prefer something, you like it better than something else.

secure
Secure means "safe and protected."

texture
Texture is "how a material feels—for example, rough or smooth."

REVIEW THE WORDS

1 Briefly Review the Words

Display the day 4 review cards (WA4) and review the pronunciation and meaning of each word.

PRACTICE USING THE WORDS

2 Play "Find Another Word"

Tell the students that partners will play the game "Find Another Word." Remind the students that you will show several stories with one or more words underlined. You will read each story aloud, and partners will decide which of the vocabulary words could replace the underlined part of the story.

Display the day 4 review activity (WA5) and begin playing the game:

1. Click ❶ to reveal the first story. Point to the story and read it aloud, emphasizing the underlined word.

Materials

- Day 4 review cards (WA4)
- Day 4 review activity (WA5)
- Copy of this week's family letter (BLM2) for each student

Teacher Note

Each story on the day 4 review activity (WA5) has a corresponding number: the first story is ❶; the second story is ❷; the third story is ❸; and so on. To play the game, click the corresponding number four times:

- The first click reveals the story.
- The second click reveals the prompt.
- The third click highlights the correct answer and reveals the story with the answer in place.
- The fourth click clears the screen.

- Story 1: *On their class field trip to the art museum, Mr. Eckman's class sees <u>unique</u> art. It is unlike anything they have seen before.*

2. Give the students a few moments to think about the story and the underlined word. Then point to the five word choices and ask:

   Q *Which vocabulary word could replace the underlined word? Why?* [Click ❶ again to reveal the prompt.] *Turn to your partner.*

   PROMPT: "I think the word [*original*] could replace [*unique*] because . . ."

   After partners have talked, have a few volunteers use the prompt to share their thinking with the class.

3. Conclude the discussion by clicking ❶ a third time to highlight the correct vocabulary word and reveal the story with the correct word in place.

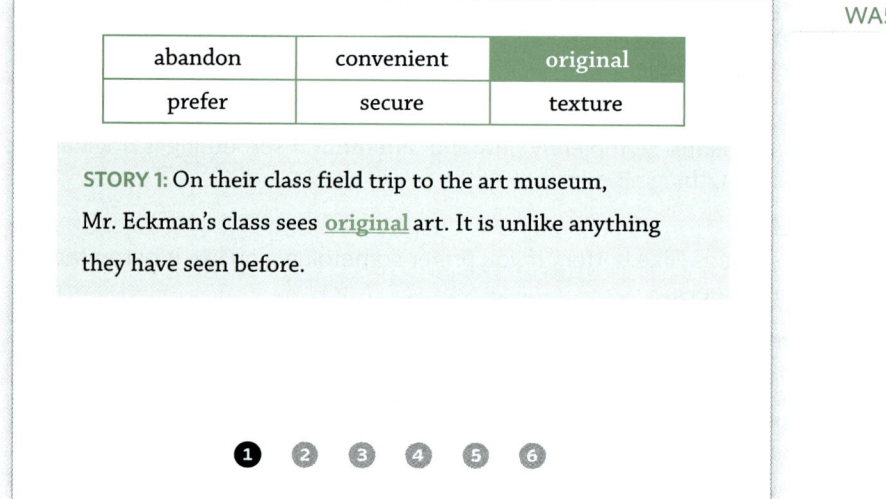

WA5

abandon	convenient	original
prefer	secure	texture

STORY 1: On their class field trip to the art museum, Mr. Eckman's class sees <u>original</u> art. It is unlike anything they have seen before.

❶ ② ③ ④ ⑤ ⑥

4. Click ❶ to clear the screen.

Use the same procedure to discuss the following stories:

- Story 2: *A new library opened a block away from Maria's house. She loves going there and finding new books to read. The library is very <u>useful</u>.* (convenient)

- Story 3: *Lucas feels <u>safe</u> when he goes fishing with his sister and father. He knows that if anything bad happens, they will know what to do.* (secure)

- Story 4: *Peyton took her dog, Lucky, to play fetch at the park. After Lucky jumped in the pond, his fur had a smooth and wet <u>feel</u>.* (texture)

- Story 5: *During the storm, the boat hit a rock. The crew had to <u>leave</u> their boat because it was flooding and sinking slowly.* (abandon)

- Story 6: *Carlton is shopping for some new sneakers. He would <u>like</u> a pair with flashing blue lights instead of a plain white pair.* (prefer)

Teacher Note

You might remind the students that they learned the words *flashy* and *plain* earlier. Review that *flashy* means "very big, bright, or expensive." Something that is flashy catches your attention. Also review that *plain* means "without anything added or without decoration." If something is plain, it is simple, not fancy.

Teacher Note

Send home with each student a copy of this week's family letter (BLM2). Encourage the students to talk about this week's words with their families.

In this activity, the students:

- Review and practice using words learned earlier
- Build their speaking and listening skills
- Listen respectfully to the thinking of others and share their own

Words Reviewed

aroma
An *aroma* is a "pleasant smell."

avoid
Avoid means "keep away from."

disorganized
If something is disorganized, it is not planned or arranged (put together) in a neat or orderly way. It is messy or confusing.

opportunity
An *opportunity* is a "chance to do something."

skill
Skill is the "ability to do something well." A skill comes from training and practice.

task
A *task* is a "job, chore, or other particular thing you have to do."

threatened
If something is threatened, it is in danger or likely to be harmed or destroyed.

REVIEW THE WORDS

1 Briefly Review the Words

Display the day 5 review cards ( WA6) and review the pronunciation and meaning of each word.

PRACTICE USING THE WORDS

2 Play "Make a Choice"

Tell the students that partners will play the game "Make a Choice." Point to the word *skill* on the day 5 review cards (WA6) and explain that partners will play the first round of the game with the word *skill*. Then ask:

 Q *Which of these skills is important to have when baking a cake: good measuring skills or good drawing skills? Why?* [Click ❶ on WA6 to reveal the first prompt.] *Turn to your partner.*

Materials

- Day 5 review cards (WA6)
- Class set of the "Individual Vocabulary Assessment: Word Check 8" answer sheet (IA1)
- Class set of the "Individual Vocabulary Assessment Student Record" sheet (SR1)
- "Individual Vocabulary Assessment Class Record" sheet (CR1)
- (Optional) Class set of the "Student Self-assessment" response sheet (SA1)

🌐 ELL Note

Rather than having the students choose between two scenarios, you might have them discuss each one individually by first asking "Would good measuring skills be important for baking a cake? Why?" and then asking "Would good drawing skills be important for baking a cake? Why?"

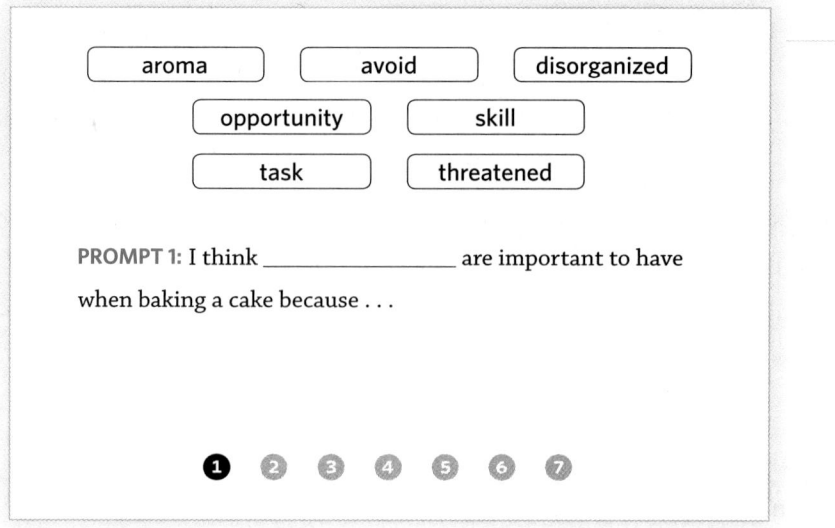

PROMPT 1: I think _____ are important to have when baking a cake because . . .

① ② ③ ④ ⑤ ⑥ ⑦

PROMPT 1: "I think [good measuring skills] are important to have when baking a cake because . . ."

After partners have talked, have one or two volunteers use the prompt to share their thinking with the class.

Use the same procedure to continue playing the game using the following questions:

[avoid]

Q *Which of these would you avoid at night: a dark path with no lights or a well-lit street? Why?* [Click ❷ to reveal the next prompt.] *Turn to your partner.*

PROMPT 2: "I would avoid [a dark path with no lights] at night because . . ."

[opportunity]

Q *Which of these opportunities would you like to have: seeing your favorite musician perform or listening to your sister play the flute? Why?* [Click ❸ to reveal the next prompt.] *Turn to your partner.*

PROMPT 3: "I would like to have the opportunity to [see my favorite musician perform] because . . ."

[aroma]

Q *Which aroma would you prefer: lasagna cooking in the oven or cinnamon bread toasting in the toaster? Why?* [Click ❹ to reveal the prompt.] *Turn to your partner.*

PROMPT 4: "I would prefer the aroma of [cinnamon toast] because . . ."

Teacher Note

You might remind the students that they learned the word *prefer* earlier and that *prefer* means "like better." If you prefer something, you like it better than something else.

[disorganized]

 Q *Which one of these backpacks is disorganized: a backpack packed with pencils, notepads, and books neatly arranged or a backpack packed with trash, candy, and some change lying here and there? Why? [Click* ❺ *to reveal the prompt.] Turn to your partner.*

PROMPT 5: "[A backpack packed with trash, candy, and some change lying here and there] is disorganized because . . ."

[task]

 Q *Which task would you like to have: scrubbing the kitchen floor or planting flowers in a garden? Why? [Click* ❻ *to reveal the prompt.] Turn to your partner.*

PROMPT 6: "I would like to have the task of [planting flowers in the garden] because . . ."

[threatened]

 Q *Which of these people is more likely to feel threatened: a person who steps in a puddle or a person whose house is flooding? Why? [Click* ❼ *to reveal the prompt.] Turn to your partner.*

PROMPT 7: "I think someone [whose house is flooding] is threatened because . . ."

Teacher Note

You might remind the students that they learned the word *likely* earlier and that when something is likely, it probably will happen or is probably true.

 ## Assessment Notes

INDIVIDUAL VOCABULARY ASSESSMENT NOTE

The final Individual Vocabulary Assessment of the year focuses on a representative group of words selected from Weeks 1–29 of the vocabulary lessons. (These words are reviewed through a series of activities in Week 30.) To assess individual students' understanding of the words, use the "Individual Vocabulary Assessment: Word Check 8" answer sheet (IA1). For instructions on administering this assessment, see "Completing the Individual Vocabulary Assessment" on page 215 of the *Assessment Resource Book*. We recommend that you pair this assessment with the Student Self-assessment described below.

STUDENT SELF-ASSESSMENT NOTE

In addition to or in place of the Individual Vocabulary Assessment, you might have each student evaluate his understanding of a group of words you select from Weeks 1–29 using the "Student Self-assessment" response sheet (SA1). For instructions on administering this assessment, see "Completing the Student Self-assessment" on page 219 of the *Assessment Resource Book*.

Appendices

Appendix A

VOCABULARY LESSONS AND *MAKING MEANING*

This table shows each week of the vocabulary lessons, the read-aloud text used during that week, and the week in which that text was taught in the *Making Meaning Teacher's Manual*. We suggest that you teach a week from the *Vocabulary Teaching Guide* one week after you have taught the corresponding week in the *Teacher's Manual*. (For example, teach Vocabulary Week 1 a week after you have taught Unit 1, Week 1 in the *Teacher's Manual*.)

Making Meaning Vocabulary Teaching Guide	Read-aloud Text(s)	Making Meaning Teacher's Manual
Week 1	*Miss Nelson is Missing!*	Unit 1, Week 1
Week 2	*Two Bobbies: A True Story of Hurricane Katrina, Friendship, and Survival*	Unit 1, Week 2
Week 3	"Seal"	Unit 2, Week 1
Week 4	*The Spooky Tail of Prewitt Peacock*	Unit 2, Week 2
Week 5	*Aunt Flossie's Hats (and Crab Cakes Later)*	Unit 2, Week 3
Week 6	*The Paper Bag Princess*	Unit 3, Week 1
Week 7	*Julius, the Baby of the World*	Unit 3, Week 2
Week 8	*Boundless Grace*	Unit 3, Week 3
Week 9	*The Raft*	Unit 3, Week 4
Week 10	*Alexander, Who's Not (Do you hear me? I mean it!) Going to Move*	Unit 3, Week 5
Week 11	*The Girl Who Loved Wild Horses*	Unit 4, Week 1
Week 12	*A Day's Work*	Unit 4, Week 2
Week 13	*Mailing May*	Unit 4, Week 3
Week 14	*Brave Irene*	Unit 4, Week 4
Week 15	*Brave Harriet*	Unit 5, Week 1
Week 16	*Wilma Unlimited*	Unit 5, Week 2
Week 17	*Sonia Sotomayor: A Judge Grows in the Bronx*	Unit 5, Week 3
Week 18	*Morning Meals Around the World*	Unit 6, Week 1
Week 19	*Homes*	Unit 6, Week 2

(continues)

(continued)

Making Meaning Vocabulary Teaching Guide	Read-aloud Text(s)	Making Meaning Teacher's Manual
Week 20	"Origami: The Art of Japanese Paper Folding"	Unit 6, Week 3
Week 21	*Morning Meals Around the World*; "Lincoln School Lunch Calendar for the week of May 21–25"; "How to Make a Paper Airplane"	Unit 6, Week 4
Week 22	*Flashy Fantastic Rain Forest Frogs*	Unit 7, Week 1
Week 23	*Explore the Desert*	Unit 7, Week 2
Week 24	*Polar Bears*	Unit 7, Week 3
Week 25	"Banning Tag"; "Smile—You've Got Homework!"; "Homework—Who Needs It?"	Unit 8, Week 1
Week 26	*Lifetimes*	Unit 8, Week 2
Week 27	*Fables*	Unit 8, Week 3
Week 28	*Pushing Up the Sky: Seven Native American Plays for Children*: "Possum's Tail"	Unit 8, Week 4
Week 29	*Keepers*	Unit 8, Week 5
Week 30	(No read-aloud)	Unit 9, Week 1

This table shows each word taught in grade 3 in alphabetical order, its definition, the week in which the word is introduced, and the number of its corresponding word card. An asterisk denotes a high-utility academic word listed in Averil Coxhead's "A New Academic Word List" (Coxhead 2000).

Word	Definition	Week	Card
abandon*	*Abandon* means "leave and not return."	17	98
achieve	*Achieve* means "do something successfully, especially something that requires a lot of effort."	20	118
adapt*	*Adapt* means "change to fit new situations or conditions." People adapt to new situations or conditions by changing their behavior or ideas.	23	133
adjust*	*Adjust* means "move or change something slightly to improve it or make it fit more comfortably."	15	90
adventuresome	If you are feeling adventuresome, you are feeling bold and ready for an adventure.	13	78
advise	*Advise* means "tell someone what you think he or she should do."	14	81
aggressive	*Aggressive* means "threatening or ready and eager to fight or attack others." Aggressive animals or people are frightening because they can be mean, dangerous, or violent.	26	152
appetizing	*Appetizing* means "tasty or good to eat."	18	105
aroma	An *aroma* is a "pleasant smell."	29	173
astounding	*Astounding* means "amazing or very surprising."	16	96
avoid	*Avoid* means "keep away from."	22	130
ban	*Ban* means "forbid something or prevent someone from doing something."	25	145
barricade	*Barricade* means "block the way by putting up barriers or obstacles."	10	59
belongings	*Belongings* are "the things someone owns, or the things that belong to someone."	11	61
bewildered	*Bewildered* means "confused or puzzled." When you are bewildered, you are not sure what to do or think.	4	24
blow your top	"Blow your top" means "get very angry."	12	72
boast	*Boast* means "brag." When people boast, they talk about themselves or something they have with too much pride or pleasure.	28	165
brainstorm	A *brainstorm* is a "sudden idea."	28	168
bustle	*Bustle* means "rush or hurry in an excited, noisy, or busy way."	2	7
caretaker	A *caretaker* is a "person whose job is to take care of a property (building or land) for the owner."	29	172

(continues)

Word	Definition	Week	Card
celebration	A *celebration* is a "happy event held to honor a special occasion."	5	29
challenge*	A *challenge* is "something that is hard to do or requires a lot of work or effort."	20	119
cherish	*Cherish* means "care for something deeply." If you cherish something, you treat it with great care because it is very important to you.	14	84
clatter	When things clatter, they bang together or rattle noisily.	5	27
clench	*Clench* means "hold or squeeze something tightly."	29	170
cling	*Cling* means "hold onto someone or something very tightly."	11	63
clutch	*Clutch* means "grab or hold onto something tightly."	4	20
cluttered	If a place is cluttered, it is messy. There are things scattered here, there, and everywhere.	9	51
coax	*Coax* means "persuade someone to do something by talking to the person gently and kindly."	14	79
collaborate	*Collaborate* means "work with others to make or do something."	26	151
comfy	*Comfy* means "comfortable."	17	100
command	*Command* means "order someone to do something."	7	42
commence*	*Commence* means "begin or start."	13	74
considerate	*Considerate* means "thoughtful of the feelings and needs of others."	26	156
contentment	*Contentment* is a "feeling of satisfaction and happiness." People feel contentment when they are doing something they enjoy.	27	162
convenient	If something is convenient, it is useful because it makes our lives easier or more comfortable.	19	113
cross	*Cross* means "annoyed and angry." *Cross* also means "go from one side of something to another."	8	46
customary	*Customary* means "usual or normal or happening regularly."	18	103
dazzle	*Dazzle* means "amaze or impress."	7	40
deadly	*Deadly* means "dangerous and likely to cause death."	22	131
debris	*Debris* is the "scattered pieces of something that has been thrown away, broken, or destroyed."	2	9
decline*	*Decline* means "get smaller or worse."	24	144
delirious	*Delirious* means "very happy and excited."	14	82
depend	*Depend* means "rely on or need someone or something for help or support."	23	134
detect*	*Detect* means "discover or notice something that is not easy to see, hear, or feel."	19	114
determination	*Determination* is "deciding you will do something and then doing it, even if it is difficult."	20	120

(continues)

Word	Definition	Week	Card
devastate	*Devastate* means "destroy or badly damage."	2	10
differ	*Differ* means "is different."	18	107
diligent	*Diligent* means "hard-working." When you are diligent, you work steadily or carefully on something because it is important to you.	27	157
disaster	A *disaster* is an "event such as a fire, flood, or storm that causes a lot of damage or suffering."	5	28
disorganized	If something is disorganized, it is not planned or arranged (put together) in a neat or orderly way. It is messy or confusing.	28	164
display*	*Display* means "show something or put something where people can easily see it."	29	171
disrupt	*Disrupt* means "disturb or interrupt something that is happening."	23	136
distress	*Distress* is a "feeling of deep sadness, worry, or pain."	26	154
diverse*	*Diverse* means "different from one another."	22	129
dodge	*Dodge* means "move quickly to avoid someone or something."	4	21
doubtful	*Doubtful* means "uncertain or unsure." When you are doubtful, you are full of doubt.	7	37
durable	If something is durable, it is tough. It can last a long time even if it is used a lot.	19	110
ease	*Ease* means "move slowly and carefully."	29	169
energize	*Energize* means "give energy or strength."	18	104
evacuate	*Evacuate* means "leave a place and go somewhere safer."	26	153
exhilarated	*Exhilarated* means "very happy and excited."	16	95
faint	*Faint* means "not clear or strong." If something is faint, it is difficult to hear, see, or smell. *Faint* also means "become dizzy and lose consciousness."	11	62
fantasize	*Fantasize* means "think about or imagine something that is pleasant or exciting but unlikely to happen in real life."	10	58
fantastic	*Fantastic* means "strange, unusual, or unbelievable."	22	128
fierce/fiercest	*Fierce* means "dangerous or violent." *Fiercest* means "most dangerous or most violent."	6	34
flabbergasted	*Flabbergasted* means "very surprised, or shocked or astonished."	13	75
flashy	*Flashy* means "very big, bright, or expensive." Something that is flashy catches your attention.	22	127
flick	*Flick* means "move, or make something move, with a quick, sudden motion."	3	14
flimsy	*Flimsy* means "thin and weak." If something is flimsy, it is not sturdy or strong.	15	85

(continues)

Word	Definition	Week	Card
floppy	*Floppy* means "soft and hanging down loosely."	5	25
flutter	*Flutter* means "wave or flap rapidly."	4	19
forbid	*Forbid* means "order someone not to do something."	23	138
fortunate	*Fortunate* means "lucky."	6	32
frank	When you are frank, you say what you think, openly and honestly.	27	158
fret	*Fret* means "worry or get upset about something."	14	83
fury	*Fury* means "great anger."	4	23
generally	*Generally* means "usually or almost always."	24	143
ghastly	*Ghastly* means "horrible."	7	39
graceful	*Graceful* means "moving in a smooth and beautiful way."	20	115
gruff	*Gruff* means "unpleasant or rude." If someone is gruff, he or she may seem unfriendly or mean.	15	87
handy	*Handy* means "useful or easy to use."	9	52
have a change of heart	If you have a change of heart, you change your opinion or the way you feel about something.	9	54
have eyes in the back of your head	If you have eyes in the back of your head, you seem to be aware of everything that is happening around you—even things you cannot see.	9	50
hazardous	*Hazardous* means "dangerous."	19	112
headstrong	*Headstrong* means "determined to do what you want no matter what anyone says."	27	160
heartbreaking	*Heartbreaking* means "very sad or upsetting."	4	22
horizontal	If something is horizontal, it is positioned from side to side rather than up and down.	21	125
immature	*Immature* means "childish or silly." An immature person acts like someone much younger.	10	56
immense	*Immense* means "huge or very large."	6	33
impermissible	*Impermissible* means "not allowed or permitted." If something is impermissible, you may not do it.	13	77
improvise	*Improvise* means "make up and perform something without any preparation." *Improvise* can also mean "make or do something using whatever materials are available."	28	167
industrious	*Industrious* means "hardworking."	17	99
intense*	*Intense* means "very great or strong."	16	94
joyful	*Joyful* means "full of joy or very happy."	11	65
likely	When something is likely, it probably will happen or is probably true.	1	5

(continues)

Word	Definition	Week	Card
lively	*Lively* means "active." Someone who is lively is energetic and full of life.	16	91
long	*Long* means "want something very much." *Long* also means "more than the average length, or not short."	15	86
lounge	*Lounge* means "sit or lie in a lazy or relaxed way."	2	12
magnificent	If something is magnificent, you admire it because of its great beauty or size.	6	35
mature*	*Mature* means "grown up or adult." A mature person is sensible and reasonable. He or she is not being immature or childish.	10	57
memorable	*Memorable* means "worth remembering." Something that is memorable is not easy to forget.	16	92
motion	*Motion* means "tell someone something through a movement of the hand, head, or other part of the body."	12	70
nifty	*Nifty* means "very good, clever, or useful."	7	38
obstinate	*Obstinate* means "stubborn." If you are obstinate, you are unwilling to change your mind about something.	10	55
opportunity	An *opportunity* is a "chance to do something."	24	142
original	*Original* means "completely new and different." If something is original, it is not like anything else.	20	117
overwhelmed	If you are overwhelmed by a feeling, you feel it very strongly—so strongly that you forget everything else.	27	161
particularly	*Particularly* means "especially or mainly."	8	43
permissible	*Permissible* means "allowed or permitted." If something is permissible, you can do it.	13	76
permit	*Permit* means "allow something to happen or let someone do something."	25	146
persist*	*Persist* means "keep doing something, even though it is difficult." If you persist, you refuse to give up.	15	88
plain	*Plain* means "without anything added or without decoration." If something is plain, it is simple, not fancy. *Plain* also means a "large area of flat land."	18	106
plop	*Plop* means "sit down heavily or put something down heavily."	3	18
prefer	*Prefer* means "like better." If you prefer something, you like it better than something else.	21	123
prowl	*Prowl* means "move quietly or secretly, trying not to be seen or heard."	12	71
quiver	*Quiver* means "tremble or shake."	7	41
rap	*Rap* means "tap or hit something sharply (forcefully) and quickly." *Rap* is also a "type of music in which words are spoken in time to music with a steady beat."	1	3

(continues)

Word	Definition	Week	Card
realize	*Realize* means "become aware of something or understand something that you did not understand before."	8	48
recall	*Recall* means "remember."	5	26
reconsider	*Reconsider* means "think again about a decision." Sometimes when you reconsider a decision, you change your mind.	10	60
refreshing	If something is refreshing, it makes you feel fresh (lively or not tired) and strong again.	18	108
reluctant*	If you are reluctant to do something, you do not want to do it.	9	49
require*	*Require* means "need."	21	121
retrieve	*Retrieve* means "bring or get something back."	5	30
reunite	*Reunite* means "come together again after being separated."	8	45
roam	*Roam* means "wander or move about without any particular purpose or place to go."	11	64
ruckus	*Ruckus* means "noisy confusion or excitement." Something unexpected or frightening can cause a ruckus.	2	11
savory	*Savory* means "pleasant to smell or taste."	8	47
scan	*Scan* means "examine something, or look at something carefully and closely." *Scan* also means "read something quickly, without looking closely for details."	23	135
secure*	*Secure* means "safe and protected."	19	109
self-confident	*Self-confident* means "sure of yourself." If you are self-confident, you are confident or sure you can do something.	27	159
serve	*Serve* means "give someone food or drink."	21	122
shuffle	*Shuffle* means "slide the feet along the ground or floor while walking." When people shuffle, they barely lift their feet. *Shuffle* also means "mix playing cards to change their order."	12	67
silky	*Silky* means "soft and smooth like silk."	28	166
skill	*Skill* is the "ability to do something well." A skill comes from training and practice.	24	140
skillful	*Skillful* means "good at doing something."	24	141
slog	*Slog* means "walk slowly and heavily, as if you are walking through deep snow or mud."	13	73
slump	*Slump* means "fall or sit down suddenly and heavily."	29	174
snap	*Snap* means "speak sharply or angrily."	1	4
snug	*Snug* means "comfortable, warm, and cozy."	80	14
sorrowful	*Sorrowful* means "full of sorrow or very sad."	11	66

(continues)

(continued)

Word	Definition	Week	Card
spectacular	*Spectacular* means "amazing to look at."	20	116
speechless	*Speechless* means "unable to speak because you are shocked, surprised, or very angry."	8	44
speedy	*Speedy* means "fast."	3	15
squirm	*Squirm* means "wiggle, or twist your body from side to side, usually because you are bored or uncomfortable."	1	2
strain	*Strain* means "pull or push hard."	15	89
stressful	*Stressful* means "causing worry or tension."	25	150
struggle	*Struggle* means "try very hard to do something."	24	139
successful	If you are successful, you do what you set out to do or do something well.	17	101
swarm	A *swarm* is a "large group of people or insects that gather or move together."	12	68
swerve	*Swerve* means "change directions quickly, usually to avoid something."	3	13
task*	A *task* is a "job, chore, or other particular thing you have to do."	25	148
texture	*Texture* is "how a material feels—for example, rough or smooth."	19	111
threatened	If something is threatened, it is in danger or likely to be harmed or destroyed.	22	132
throw yourself into something	"Throw yourself into something" means "do something with a lot of energy and enthusiasm."	16	93
tip	A *tip* is a "piece of advice or useful information."	21	126
trample	*Trample* means "damage or crush by walking or stepping on something heavily."	23	137
unaggressive	*Unaggressive* means "not aggressive, or not threatening or ready and eager to fight or attack others."	26	155
unexpected	*Unexpected* means "not expected." If something is unexpected it is surprising. You did not expect, or think, that it would happen.	17	97
unfortunate	*Unfortunate* means "unlucky."	6	31
ungrateful	*Ungrateful* means "not thankful or not grateful." If you are ungrateful, you do not thank someone who has done something for you or show your appreciation.	6	36
unlikely	*Unlikely* means "not likely." When something is unlikely, it probably will not happen or is probably not true.	1	6
unsuccessful	*Unsuccessful* means "not successful." If you are unsuccessful, you do not accomplish what you set out to do.	17	102
unwind	*Unwind* means "relax."	25	149
urgent	*Urgent* means "very important." If something is urgent, it needs to be taken care of immediately.	12	69

(continues)

(continued)

Word	Definition	Week	Card
utter	*Utter* means "say something or make some sort of sound."	3	16
valuable	*Valuable* means "very important or useful in some way."	25	147
vertical	If something is vertical, it is positioned up and down rather than from side to side.	21	124
volunteer	*Volunteer* means "offer to do something or help someone by choice." When you volunteer, you do something because you want to do it. You do not expect pay or a reward.	2	8
well-organized	If something is well-organized, it is planned or arranged (put together) in a neat or orderly way.	28	163
whiz	*Whiz* means "move very fast." Some things that whiz make a buzzing or hissing sound.	1	1
whoop	*Whoop* means "shout from excitement."	3	17
whoosh	*Whoosh* means "move very fast." When something whooshes, it makes a rushing or hissing sound.	9	53

INDEPENDENT WORD-LEARNING STRATEGIES

The tables below show the weeks in which each independent word-learning strategy is introduced or reviewed, and which words are used to introduce or review the strategy. (Words formally taught in the vocabulary lessons are in bold.) Whenever a strategy is reviewed in a More Strategy Practice (MSP) activity, the activity is listed in the table as well.

Recognizing Synonyms

Week	Word(s)
2	**bustle**, hurry, rush (Day 1, Step 1) **devastate**, destroy (Day 3, Step 1) MSP: Start a Synonym Chart
3	**speedy**, fast (Day 1, Step 5)
4	**fury**, anger (Day 3, Step 3) **bewildered**, confused, puzzled (Day 3, Step 5)
5	**recall**, remember (Day 1, Step 5)
7	**ghastly**, horrible (Day 1, Step 6) **dazzle**, amaze, impress (Day 3, Step 1)
8	**particularly**, especially, mainly (Day 1, Step 1)
9	**handy**, useful (Day 3, Step 1)
10	**obstinate**, stubborn (Day 1, Step 1) MSP: Play "Synonym Match"
11	**cling**, **clutch** (Day 1, Step 5)
13	**commence**, begin, start (Day 1, Step 3)
14	**fret**, worry (Day 3, Step 3)
17	**industrious**, hardworking (Day 1, Step 5)
18	**customary**, usual, normal (Day 1, Step 1)
19	**hazardous**, dangerous (Day 3, Step 1)
21	**require**, need (Day 1, Step 1)
23	**depend**, rely, need (Day 1, Step 4)
24	**opportunity**, chance (Day 3, Step 1)
25	**unwind**, relax (Day 3, Step 3)
26	**collaborate**, cooperate (Day 1, Step 1) **considerate**, thoughtful, kind (Day 3, Step 5)
27	**frank**, truthful, honest (Day 1, Step 3) **headstrong**, obstinate, stubborn (Day 3, Step 1)
28	**boast**, brag (Day 1, Step 5)

Recognizing Antonyms

Week	Word(s)
1	**likely**, **unlikely** (Day 3, Step 5) MSP: Start an Antonym Chart
5	**floppy**, stiff (Day 1, Step 1)
6	**unfortunate, fortunate** (Day 1, Step 2)
10	**immature, mature** (Day 1, Step 4)
11	**joyful**, **sorrowful** (Day 3, Step 6)
13	**permissible**, **impermissible** (Day 3, Step 2)
17	**successful, unsuccessful** (Day 3, Step 4) MSP: Play "Antonym Match"
18	**appetizing**, unappetizing (Day 1, Step 6)
19	**flimsy, durable** (Day 1, Step 3)
21	**vertical, horizontal** (Day 3, Step 2)
25	**ban, permit** (Day 1, Step 2)
26	**aggressive, unaggressive** (Day 3, Step 3)
28	**well-organized, disorganized** (Day 1, Step 3)

Using the Prefix *un-* to Determine Word Meanings

Week	Word(s)
1	**unlikely** (Day 3, Step 5)
6	**unfortunate** (Day 1, Step 1) **ungrateful** (Day 3, Step 5)
17	**unexpected** (Day 1, Step 1)
18	unappetizing (Day 1, Step 6)
26	**unaggressive** (Day 3, Step 3)

Using the Prefix *re-* to Determine Word Meanings

Week	Word(s)
8	**reunite** (Day 1, Step 5) MSP: Explore Words with the Prefix *re-*
10	**reconsider** (Day 3, Step 5)
12	replanted MSP: Review the Prefix *re-* and Discuss the Word *Replanted*
18	**refreshing** (Day 3, Step 6) reenergize MSP: Review the Prefix *re-* and Discuss the Word *Reenergize*

Using the Suffix -*est* to Determine Word Meanings

Week	Word(s)
6	**fiercest** (Day 3, Step 1) MSP: Discuss Other Words with the Suffix -*est*
7	niftiest, ghastliest MSP: Review the Suffix -*est* and Discuss the Words *Niftiest* and *Ghastliest*
15	flimsiest (Day 1, Step 2) MSP: Discuss Other Words with the Suffix -*est*
16	liveliest (Day 1, Step 3) sickliest, fastest MSP: Explore the Words *Sickliest* and *Fastest* in *Wilma Unlimited*

Using the Suffix -*ful* to Determine Word Meanings

Week	Word(s)
7	**doubtful** (Day 1, Step 2) MSP: Discuss Other Words with the Suffix -*ful*
11	**joyful** (Day 3, Step 4)
17	**successful** (Day 3, Step 3)
20	**graceful** (Day 1, Step 1) MSP: Review the Suffix -*ful* and Discuss *Painful* and *Delightful*
24	**skillful** (Day 1, Step 5)
25	**stressful** (Day 3, Step 5)

Using Context to Determine Word Meanings

Week	Word(s)
2	**ruckus** (Day 3, Step 3)
4	**dodge** (Day 1, Step 6)
9	**cluttered** (Day 1, Step 6)
11	**faint** (Day 1, Step 3)
15	**persist** (Day 3, Step 1)
20	MSP: Play "Use the Clues"
29	**clench** (Day 1, Step 3)

Recognizing Idioms

Week	Word(s)
9	**have eyes in the back of your head** (Day 1, Step 4) **have a change of heart** (Day 3, Step 5) MSP: Discuss Idioms and Start an Idiom Chart
12	**blow your top** (Day 3, Step 5)
16	**throw yourself into something** (Day 1, Step 6)
28	**brainstorm** (Day 3, Step 6)

Recognizing Shades of Meaning

Week	Word(s)
3	**plop** (Day 3, Step 6)
4	**heartbreaking** (Day 3, Step 1) MSP: Discuss Shades of Meaning with *Sad* and *Heartbreaking*
6	**immense** (Day 1, Step 4)
9	**whoosh** MSP: Review *Whoosh* and Discuss Shades of Meaning
13	**slog** (Day 1, Step 1) **flabbergasted** (Day 1, Step 5) MSP: Discuss Shades of Meaning and the Words *Surprised* and *Flabbergasted*
14	**delirious** (Day 3, Step 2)
16	**exhilarated** (Day 3, Step 3) **astounding** (Day 3, Step 5)

Recognizing Words with Multiple Meanings

Week	Word(s)
1	**rap** (Day 1, Step 10) **snap** MSP: Discuss the Multiple Meanings of *Snap*
6	trail MSP: Explore Multiple Meanings of *Trail*
8	**cross** (Day 3, Step 3)
11	**faint** (Day 1, Step 4) MSP: Use a Dictionary to Discuss Words with Multiple Meanings
12	**shuffle** (Day 1, Step 3)
14	**delirious** MSP: Discuss Another Meaning of *Delirious*

(continues)

(continued)

Week	Word(s)
15	**long** (Day 1, Step 6) **adjust** MSP: Discuss Another Meaning of *Adjust*
18	**plain** (Day 3, Step 3)
21	**tip** MSP: Discuss Another Meaning of *Tip*
22	**fantastic** MSP: Discuss Another Meaning of *Fantastic*
23	**scan** (Day 1, Step 8)
24	**decline** MSP: Discuss Another Meaning of *Decline*
25	**unwind** MSP: Discuss Another Meaning of *Unwind*
28	**improvise** (Day 3, Step 5) **brainstorm** MSP: Discuss Another Meaning of *Brainstorm*
29	**ease** MSP: Discuss Another Meaning of *Ease*

Using a Print Dictionary to Determine Word Meanings

Week	Word(s)
5	**recall** (Day 1, Step 5) sniff, smoky, cheer, ripple MSP: Use a Print Dictionary
11	fine, collect, spread MSP: Use a Dictionary to Discuss Words with Multiple Meanings

Using an Online Dictionary to Determine Word Meanings

Week	Word(s)
14	bumble, helter-skelter, pounce, meddle, squall, trudge MSP: Use an Online Dictionary

Using a Glossary to Determine Word Meanings

Week	Word(s)
19	property, texture, appliance, electricity, detergent MSP: Discuss Using a Glossary

Appendix

D

ADDITIONAL ACTIVITIES

EXTENSION ACTIVITIES

Extension activities provide an opportunity to introduce the students to independent word-learning strategies not formally taught in the program, such as exploring how authors use language in interesting ways. The table below shows the weeks in which Extension activities appear and the names of the activities.

Week	Activities
1	Explore Onomatopoeia
2	Explore Vivid Verbs in *Two Bobbies*
3	Explore Movement Words in "Seal" Explore Onomatopoeia
4	Explore Homophones with *Tail* and *Tale* Explore Sensory Details in *The Spooky Tail of Prewitt Peacock*
5	Explore the Suffix *-ion* Discuss the Compound Word *Hatboxes*
8	Introduce and Discuss the Suffix *-less* Discuss the Compound Words *Roadside* and *Watermelon*
10	Introduce and Discuss the Prefix *im-*
11	Explore Similes in *The Girl Who Loved Wild Horses*
12	Discuss the Suffix *-ly* Explore Spanish Words in *A Day's Work* Discuss the Suffix *-er* and the Word *Prowler*
13	Explore the Suffix *-some* Explore the Prefix *im-*
14	Discuss the Suffix *-er* and the Word *Adviser* Discuss the Related Words *Snug* and *Snuggle* Explore Vivid Verbs in *Brave Irene*
15	Explore Related Words: *Persist* and *Persistence*
17	Explore Related Words: *Comfy*, *Comfortable*, and *Comfort* Explore Similes in *Sonia Sotomayor: A Judge Grows in the Bronx*
18	Discuss *Plain* and *Plane* and Other Homophones
19	Explore Related Words: *Detect*, *Detector*, and *Detective* Explore Domain-specific Words: *Wire*
22	Explore Domain-specific Words: *Rain Forests* Discuss the Compound Word *Painkiller*
23	Explore Domain-specific Words: *Evaporate*
26	Explore Related Words: *Considerate* and *Consider*

(continues)

(continued)

Week	Activities
27	Discuss the Suffix -*ly* Discuss the Compound Word *Headstrong*
28	Explore the Prefix *dis-* Explore the Suffix -*y*
29	Discuss the Compound Word *Caretaker* Explore Related Words: *Aroma* and *Aromatic*

MORE ELL SUPPORT ACTIVITIES

More ELL Support activities provide English Language Learners with additional opportunities to build vocabulary and oral language skills. The table below shows the weeks in which More ELL Support activities appear and the names of the activities.

Week	Activities
3	Discuss Other Speedy Animals
5	Discuss a Family Member or Special Older Person
7	Further Explore the Suffix -*est*
13	Discuss Where the Students Would Like to Be "Mailed To"
18	Draw a Picture of a Plain Object and Not Plain Object
22	Discuss a Pair of Illustrations in *Flashy Fantastic Rain Forest Frogs*
23	Scan, Write About, and Draw an Object
25	Draw a Picture of Unwinding
26	Discuss Being Considerate
27	Discuss Being Headstrong

Appendix E

SPANISH COGNATE PRONUNCIATIONS

Week	Spanish Word	Pronunciation	English Word
2	voluntario/a	voh-loon-TAH-reeoh/reeah	volunteer
2	devastar	deh-vahs-TAHR	devastate
4	furia	FOO-reeah	fury
5	desastre	deh-SAHS-treh	disaster
5	celebración	ceh-leh-brah-seeOHN	celebration
6	desafortunado/a	deh-sah-for-too-NAH-doh/dah	unfortunate
6	afortunado/a	ah-for-too-NAH-doh/dah	fortunate
6	inmenso/a	een-MEHN-soh/sah	immense
8	particularmente	pahr-tee-coo-LAHR-mehn-teh	particularly
8	sabroso/a	sah-BROH-soh/sah	savory
10	obstinado/a	ohbs-tee-NAH-doh/dah	obstinate
10	inmaduro/a	een-mah-DOO-roh/rah	immature
10	maduro/a	mah-DOO-roh/rah	mature
10	barricada	bah-ree-CAH-dah	barricade
10	reconsiderar	reh-cohn-see-deh-RAHR	reconsider
13	comenzar	coh-mehn-SAHR	commence
15	persistir	pehr-sees-TEER	persist
15	ajustar	ah-hoos-TAHR	adjust
16	memorable	meh-moh-RAH-bleh	memorable
16	intenso/a	een-TEHN-soh/sah	intense
17	abandonar	ah-bahn-doh-NAHR	abandon
18	apetitoso/a	ah-peh-tee-TOH-soh/sah	appetizing
18	diferir	dee-feh-REER	differ
19	seguro/a	seh-GOO-roh/rah	secure
19	durable	doo-RAH-bleh	durable
19	textura	tehks-TOO-rah	texture
19	detectar	deh-tehk-TAHR	detect
20	espectacular	ehs-pehk-tah-coo-LAHR	spectacular
20	original	oh-ree-hee-NAHL	original
20	determinación	deh-tehr-mee-nah-seeOHN	determination

(continues)

(continued)

Week	Spanish Word	Pronunciation	English Word
21	requerir	reh-keh-REER	require
21	servir	sehr-VEER	serve
21	preferir	preh-feh-REER	prefer
21	vertical	vehr-tee-CAHL	vertical
21	horizontal	oh-ree-sohn-TAHL	horizontal
22	fantástico/a	fahn-TAHS-tee-coh/cah	fantastic
22	diverso/a	dee-VEHR-soh/sah	diverse
23	adaptar	ah-dahp-TAHR	adapt
23	depender	deh-pehn-DEHR	depend
24	generalmente	heh-neh-RAHL-mehn-teh	generally
25	permitir	pehr-mee-TEER	permit
26	colaborar	coh-lah-boh-RAHR	collaborate
26	agresivo/a	ah-greh-SEE-voh/vah	aggressive
26	evacuar	eh-vah-cooAHR	evacuate
26	considerado/a	con-see-deh-RAH-doh/dah	considerate
27	franco/a	FRAHN-coh/cah	frank
27	contento/a	cohn-TEHN-toh/tah	contentment
28	desorganizado/a	dehs-ohr-gah-nee-SAH-doh/dah	disorganized
28	improvisar	eem-proh-vee-SAHR	improvise
29	aroma	ah-ROH-mah	aroma

VOCABULARY WORDS K-6

GRADE K

active
allow
amusing
assist
assortment
bright
care for
collide
comfort
comfortable
communicate
companion
complete
concerned
confident
container
courageous
cozy
creature
creep
crowded
cupboard
decide
delicious
depart
describe
determined
diet
difficult
disappointed
drowsy
eager
edge
energetic
enjoy
enormous
evening

excited
exhausted
explore
face
fact
fits
fluffy
frightened
frustrated
furious
generous
glance
gooey
greet
grin
haul
healthy
icy
imitate
invite
kind
land
lonely
machine
mend
mighty
need
nuisance
observe
overhead
passenger
patient
pedestrian
peer
persistent
playful
pleasant
pleased

pointy
pounce
practice
proud
release
repair
rocky
rough
scoop
scoot
scramble
signal
similar
snatch
snooze
soar
soggy
sphere
straight
stuck
survive
swiftly
switch
tame
tangled
tasty
tip
train
transportation
travel
uncomfortable
uncrowded
unhealthy
unkind
unpleasant
upset
useful
various

visible
wade
warn
weak
welcome
whirl
wild

GRADE 1

admire
adult
adventure
affectionate
amazing
appetite
arrange
arrive
astonished
audible
bad-tempered
beam
bob
bold
chomp
collapse
commotion
contents
cooperate
crabby
crush
curious
dart
delighted
destination
dine
disappear
discover
disgusting

dump
earsplitting
essential
evidence
exclaim
extraordinary
faint
feast
ferocious
firm
flash
fond
frigid
future
gather
gigantic
glide
glow
gulp
habitat
hero
hope
hover
howl
humorous
impolite
inaudible
independent
inspect
journey
lunge
match
meadow
memory
migrate
miserable
moan
munch

(continues)

(continued)

mutter
neighborhood
neighborly
nervous
odd
odor
ordinary
pack
peaceful
persevere
pile
popular
possession
pout
powerful
predator
prey
protect
quarrel
rapidly
relax
remain
rescue
resent
respect
ridiculous
rumble
rush
scrumptious
shallow
snuggle
sob
spot
squint
stomp
store
study
surroundings
thrilling
tidy
timid
track
tremble

trust
tug
twirl
underground
untidy
vegetation
wander
wobble
wonder
wriggle

GRADE 2

accompany
annoy
appreciate
approach
approve
attach
attract
behave
beneficial
blob
bulge
chaos
characteristic
collect
compassionate
complex
congratulate
conserve
consume
content
convince
create
damp
dash
decrease
delightful
disapprove
discover
disguise
disobedient
downcast

dull
duplicate
eavesdrop
eavesdropper
ecstatic
embarrass
encourage
expand
expert
fabulous
fade
familiar
fearful
fearless
fetch
flap
flexible
flop
fragile
fragrant
fresh
genius
glare
gleam
gobble
gratitude
grip
grumble
guide
hospitality
host
huddle
hurl
insist
miniature
misbehave
murmur
mushy
necessary
notorious
numerous
obedient
occasionally

optional
overalls
overjoyed
pester
picky
plenty
precaution
predict
prepare
provide
racket
rarely
recently
recreation
regularly
routine
rude
scrunch
shelter
shimmer
shriek
sip
slurp
sniffle
solid
steer clear
stream
strenuous
stuff
stunned
sturdy
swirl
teamwork
terrible
terrific
tourist
treat
tumble
unique
unusual
unwelcome
usual
valuable

vanish
variety
whimper

GRADE 3

abandon
achieve
adapt
adjust
adventuresome
advise
aggressive
appetizing
aroma
astounding
avoid
ban
barricade
belongings
bewildered
blow your top
boast
brainstorm
bustle
caretaker
celebration
challenge
cherish
clatter
clench
cling
clutch
cluttered
coax
collaborate
comfy
command
commence
considerate
contentment
convenient
cross
customary

(continues)

(continued)

dazzle
deadly
debris
decline
delirious
depend
detect
determination
devastate
differ
diligent
disaster
disorganized
display
disrupt
distress
diverse
dodge
doubtful
durable
ease
energize
evacuate
exhilarated
faint
fantasize
fantastic
fierce/fiercest
flabbergasted
flashy
flick
flimsy
floppy
flutter
forbid
fortunate
frank
fret
fury
generally
ghastly
graceful
gruff

handy
have a change of
    heart
have eyes in the back
    of your head
hazardous
headstrong
heartbreaking
horizontal
immature
immense
impermissible
improvise
industrious
intense
joyful
likely
lively
long
lounge
magnificent
mature
memorable
motion
nifty
obstinate
opportunity
original
overwhelmed
particularly
permissible
permit
persist
plain
plop
prefer
prowl
quiver
rap
realize
recall
reconsider
refreshing

reluctant
require
retrieve
reunite
roam
ruckus
savory
scan
secure
self-confident
serve
shuffle
silky
skill
skillful
slog
slump
snap
snug
sorrowful
spectacular
speechless
speedy
squirm
strain
stressful
struggle
successful
swarm
swerve
task
texture
threatened
throw yourself into
    something
tip
trample
unaggressive
unexpected
unfortunate
ungrateful
unlikely
unsuccessful

unwind
urgent
utter
valuable
vertical
volunteer
well-organized
whiz
whoop
whoosh

GRADE 4

adequate
adore
alternative
ambition
amiable
analyze
apprehensive
bellow
bizarre
bliss
blotch
blurt out
boost
ceremony
circulate
circumstances
compromise
conceal
conditions
consistent
consistently
crave
creak
critical
crouch
custom
dazed
deceive
defy
dejected
dense

desire
desperate
dissimilar
dubious
edible
eerie
effective
elated
eligible
endure
engage
enraged
ensure
enthusiastic
envision
equitable
exclusive
experience
feat
flee
focus
formal
fume
function
get-up-and-go
gleeful
glower
glum
greedy
harass
hardship
hazard
hinder
humane
humble
humdrum
ideal
imposing
impressive
imprudent
in the blink of an eye
inadequate
inclusive

(continues)

inconsistent

indignantly

inedible

ineffective

ineligible

inequitable

informal

inhumane

initial

inspire

integrate

intimidate

intricate

jittery

jubilant

keen

labor

landscape

launch

lend a hand

lethal

loathe

luscious

manually

merit

misfortune

misjudge

mislead

mistreat

mysterious

neglect

nosing around

note

obstacle

offer

optimistic

pelt

perilous

permanent

pessimistic

plead

plunge

precarious

precise

prior to

process

proficient

prudent

pursue

raises eyebrows

recede

reduce

refuge

rejoice

reminisce

reputation

resemble

revere

rickety

rove

rowdier

rowdy

rubble

rugged

rummage

safeguard

sag

sandwiched

scrutinize

secure

seek

segregate

sensitive

serene

severe

sidesplitting

slight

speculate

stalk

survey

sustain

temporary

thoroughly

tilt

topple

transform

trend

trim

uniform

unwise

valiant

vigilant

wise

yearn

GRADE 5

academic

advantage

argue

battered

befuddled

billow

blow off steam

blunt

breathtaking

budge

bundle

calamity

cantankerous

clamber

clamor

clank

clash

cluster

commit

compel

comply

conspicuous

consume/consumer

contact

contemplate

contented

convert

cuisine

currently

dab

daring

defenseless

delectable

deliberately

dependent

desert/deserter

desirable

deteriorate

device

devour

dignified

dilapidated

dim

disadvantage

discontinue

discourteous

disposition

dissatisfied

drastic

dwelling

efficient

emerge

engrossed

envious

establish

ethical

exert

extend

fanciful

get on board

grimace

grotesque

hair-raising

harbor

heartless

heave

helter-skelter

heroine

hospitable

hunch

hunger

impact

indicate

inefficient

influence

inform

injustice

insignificant

interact

international

intrigue

knowledgeable

loll

lose your nerve

lurch

lurk

lush

luxurious

master

meager

memento

mobile

moist

momentous

moocher

motionless

mystify

negative

nourish

on pins and needles

pandemonium

peculiar

peer

picturesque

plummet

pollute

positive

prejudice

preposterous

preteen

priority

procedure

protest

quality

reassure

regulate

reliable

resilient

resist

(continues)

resolve

restore

restriction

reuse

reverie

rustle

scarce

scour

selfless

sequence

significant

sociable

solitary

soothe

spectacle

squander

stamina

stroll

stun

suit

supporter

supreme

surge

tattered

thoughtful

thoughtless

throng

thrust

thunderous

towering

tranquil

trickle

typical

uneasy

unethical

values

vary

vast

vexed

vivid

wide-eyed

widespread

wobbly

GRADE 6

abruptly

access

accessible

acknowledge

acquire

acute

adamant

adhere

adjacent

adversity

altruistic

appeal

appropriate

arduous

aspire

assert

awkward

bark

beckon

bind

catastrophe

clump

commercial

compatible

competent

composed

conceivable

condone

confide

congested

consensus

consider

cordial

counsel

cower

cruise

despair

dismal

distinctive

document

dramatic

elegant

encounter

enigma

erroneously

eventful

exasperated

excel

exceptional

excessive

expose

external

extract

extreme

flail

forethought

forlorn

frail

frantic

gargantuan

get down to business

gregarious

grit

guidance

heartwarming

hideous

hostile

hullabaloo

hurtle

hypocrite

impermanent

in the doghouse

inch

incident

incompetent

inconceivable

inconsolable

inconspicuous

incredulous

initiative

intensify

intently

internal

intrude

jostle

just

leisure

linger

livelihood

magnanimous

majestic

meticulous

mimic

mistrustful

modify

monitor

mount

muddled

nimble

nonhuman

nonviolent

obligation

ooze

overcome

overworked

particular

passionate

pastime

plot

pluck

potential

precede

presentable

press

prickly

prohibited

promote

rate

ravenous

reasonable

reflect

resigned

salvage

scamper

scavenge

scurry

self-sufficient

shatter

sheepish

shift

skim

sleek

sling

spew

step up to the plate

stew

stoop

storm

subterranean

summon

sumptuous

supervision

suppress

surreptitiously

teeter

tenacious

tongue-tied

trace

trek

tribulation

trigger

trudge

turmoil

ubiquitous

understanding

unjust

unpredictable

unreasonable

unsettled

view

vital

vulnerable

(continues)

BIBLIOGRAPHY

Anderson, Richard C., Elfrieda H. Hiebert, Judith A. Scott, and Ian A. G. Wilkinson. *Becoming a Nation of Readers: The Report of the Commission on Reading*. Washington, DC: The National Institute of Education, 1985.

Baumann, James F. and Edward J. Kame´enui, eds. *Vocabulary Instruction: Research to Practice*, 2nd ed. New York: The Guilford Press, 2012.

Baumann, James F., Edward J. Kame´enui, and Gwynne E. Ash. "Research on Vocabulary Instruction: Voltaire Redux." In *Handbook of Research on Teaching the English Language Arts*, 2nd ed., edited by J. Flood, D. Lapp, J. R. Squire, and J. M. Jensen. Mahwah, NJ: Lawrence Erlbaum Associates, 2003.

Beck, Isabel L., Margaret McKeown, and Linda Kucan. *Bringing Words to Life: Robust Vocabulary Instruction*, 2nd ed. New York: The Guilford Press, 2013.

Brock, Cynthia H., Virginia J. Goatley, Taffy E. Raphael, Elisabeth Trost-Shahata, and Catherine M. Weber. *Engaging Students in Disciplinary Literacy, K–6*. New York: Teachers College Press, 2014.

Coxhead, Averil. "A New Academic Word List." *TESOL Quarterly*, 34, 2 (2000).

Graves, Michael F. *The Vocabulary Book: Learning and Instruction*. New York: Teachers College Press, 2006.

Hiebert, Elfrieda H. "In Pursuit of an Effective, Efficient Vocabulary Curriculum for the Elementary Grades." In *The Teaching and Learning of Vocabulary: Bringing Scientific Research to Practice*, edited by E. H. Hiebert and M. Kamil. Mahwah, NJ: Lawrence Erlbaum Associates, 2005.

Johnson, Dale D. *Vocabulary in the Elementary and Middle School*. Needham Heights, MA: Allyn and Bacon, 2001.

Krashen, S. D. *Explorations in Language Acquisition and Use*. Portsmouth, NH: Heinemann, 2003.

Krashen, S. D., and T. D. Terrell. *The Natural Approach: Language Acquisition in the Classroom*. Englewood Cliffs, NJ: Prentice Hall, 1992.

Morrow, Lesley Mandel and Linda B. Gambrell. *Best Practices in Literacy Instruction*, 4th ed. New York: The Guilford Press, 2011.

Neuman, Susan B. and Tanya S. Wright. *All About Words: Increasing Vocabulary in the Common Core Classroom, Pre K–2*. Common Core State Standards in Literacy. New York: Teachers College Press, 2013.

Stahl, Steven A. *Vocabulary Development*. From Reading Research to Practice. Newton Upper Falls, MA: Brookline Books, 1999.